DRY STONE WALLING

a practical handbook

Compiled by Alan Brooks, revised by Elizabeth Agate.

Illustrated by Roy Allitt.

ISBN 0 9501643 5 6

First Published March 1977

Reprinted 1978, 1983, 1986 (twice), 1992, June 1994
Revised 1989
Printed by The Eastern Press Ltd., Reading, on recycled paper.

Acknowledgements

BTCV acknowledges with thanks the help it has received in producing this publication from the following individuals and organisations:

S M Algar
E M P Audland
Eric Boyes
Frank Brightman
Margaret A Brooks
P M Bunt
N C Butchart
Paul Clayden
Peter Davies
B N K Davies
Dry Stone Walling Association
I Ellis-Williams
Helen Fooks
Charles S Jardine
Richard Jennings
J M Lander
J R Laundon
F Main
W G Martin
W McArevey
Ivor Morten

Mrs Murray-Usher
National Proficiency Tests Council
A R Perry
W A J Prevost
Archie Radmore
Mrs Rainsford-Hannay, for permission to use extracts from her late husband's book, 'Dry Stone Walling'
R W Rainsford-Hannay
Jeff Redgrave
John Ellis Roberts
Tom Roberts
Francis Rose
Ann Louise Rule (now Pearce)
S F Sanderson of the Institute of Folk Life Studies, University of Leeds
Bill Shaw
Alan Stubbs
F A Turk
E M Yates

The other craftsmen and people with an interest in dry stone walling who were consulted:

Andrew Brown for general work on this handbook

The staff and volunteers of the Trust who have contributed their advice and experience.

Contents

Introduction   5

1 Walls in the Landscape
Characteristic Regional Walls   6
Walls in History   22
Wall Dating   26

2 Dry Stone Walls and Conservation
The Loss of Walls and Banks   29
The Farmers' Viewpoint   29
The Wildlife Value of Walls   34
The Future of the Walling Craft   36

3 Walls and the Law
Wall Ownership   38
Boundary Wall Maintenance   39
Obligation to Fence   39
Tenant and Landlord   39
Rights of Use   39
Treasure Trove   40

4 Safety, Equipment and Organisation
Safety Precautions   41
Clothing   43
Tools and Accessories   44
Organising Group Work   50

5 Know Your Stone
Building for Durability   52
Characteristic Walling Stones   53
Sources of Stone and Amounts
   Required   55
Breaking and Shaping Stone   56

6 Building a Free-Standing Wall
General Features   61
The Use and Abuse of Concrete
   and Mortar   61
Walling Procedure   63
The Foundation   65

Use of Batter Frames   66
Courses   66
Throughs   72
Coping   73
Wall Heads   77
Changes of Direction   79
Walls on Slopes   80
Obstacles   83
Gapping and Rebuilding   84
Final Points   86

7 Retaining Walls and Stone Hedges
Retaining Walls   88
Stone Hedges   91
Protection, Maintenance and Repair   94

**8 Wall 'Furniture' and Special
    Applications**
Smoots and Cripple Holes   96
Stiles   97
Gates   100
Walls with Fences   103
Other Applications   105

Appendix A: Conservation and the
   Volunteer Worker   107

Appendix B: Studies and Surveys   108

Appendix C: Associations, Competitions
   and Courses   110

Appendix D: Relevant Organisations   112

Bibliography   115

Glossary   118

Index   120

Introduction

This handbook describes how to construct, maintain and repair dry (unmortared) stone walls and stone-faced earth banks. It is intended to be used by conservation volunteers and all others interested in maintaining our landscape heritage through manual work, fostering an ancient craft and protecting a valuable wildlife habitat.

Dry stone walls dominate the traditional British stock and boundary fence types wherever the soil is thin and poor, exploitable woodland scarce and surface rocks, outcroppings or accessible quarry faces abundant. In the South West and some other areas where the soil is more fertile or where fewer field stones require clearance, stone walls give way to stone- or turf-faced banks, often with ditches at their sides and live hedges growing along their tops. Other combination barriers which occasionally are found include earth banks filled with stones, stone walls backed by hedges and walls with built-in post-and-wire fences. These local adaptations often successfully overcome the weaknesses inherent in the use of any one material alone. A hedge or fence adds height to a low wall and protects a weak coping, while the wall shields the hedge from grazing and covers a gappy base or high bottom fence line.

Like hedgerows, many stone walls and banks have fallen foul of recent changes in land use and farming methods. Dereliction and decay rather than outright removal are the chief results, especially where traffic vibration, vandalism or accidental damage caused by off-track walkers increases the need for maintenance. Wages and the cost of furnishing extra stones are now so high that even landowners who see the value of walls may not have the time or money to repair them. The number of professional dry wallers has always been low, at least since the completion of the Parliamentary Enclosures a century and a half ago, but now fewer and fewer farmers and labourers are capable of maintaining their own walls in reasonable condition when needed. The Dry Stone Walling Association and the other organisations listed on page 112 are helping to counter this trend. Although it is undoubtedly best to learn walling direct from a skilled craftsman, this handbook should help anyone, working alone or in an organised party, to build or rebuild a dry wall anywhere in the country in a style appropriate to the area.

Walls and banks, like other traditional fences, have a story to tell. They speak of local geology, geography and history. Occasionally they reveal vividly who it was that built them and for what purpose: sometimes the makers' names are inscribed on a foundation stone or tucked into the base in a bottle; in Cornwall evidence has been found of animals sacrificed in the heart of an ancient earth bank. While no such discoveries may await you as you begin to dismantle an old wall for rebuilding, you may still learn much by examining the wall's size and shape, type of stone, alignment, relation to walls around it and unusual features such as water smoots, cripple holes or bee boles. And as you start to replace the intricate puzzle which becomes the wall, remember that when it is next repaired by some future craftsman, who may be just as keen to learn when and by whom the wall was last rebuilt, generations or even a century or two may have passed. If you have worked with care, that is.

Throughout the text, points which it is desired to stress and lists of items of equipment etc are set out in a,b,c order. Sequential operations and procedures are given in 1,2,3 order. Words used in a technical sense, eg 'batter', 'scarcement', 'whinstone', are defined in the Glossary. References to written source material are incorporated in the text and give the author first, followed by publishing date and page number. Full listings of these and other useful works are given in the Bibliography.

Measurements are given first in metric units, followed in brackets by the imperial equivalent approximated to the accuracy required. Occasionally a dimension, and more often a product specification, is given in one unit only, according to current manufacturers' listings. It is worth remembering that the traditional unit of wall length is the rood, although the yard (910mm) or chain (20m, 22 yards) is used by some wallers. The rood is unstandardised: 6 yards in the granite districts of Scotland, 7 yards in limestone districts and through most of Yorkshire. Whatever the exact distance, it was considered to be a reasonable length for a craftsman dry waller to build in a day, assuming the foundation trench was cut, the stones ready to hand and the wall not unusually high. Now that the work day has shortened, few wallers would care to attempt this rate except in repair work where the foundation and lower courses are still secure.

1 Walls in the Landscape

Characteristic Regional Walls

Dry stone walls give intimate expression to the bedrock or glacial drift material which lies beneath them. Originally built with what came to hand during field clearance, for long they remained far too humble to warrant the transport of stones over any great distance. The Enclosure Era, it is true, blurred the lines slightly, for example on the borders of the Craven district of Yorkshire where labourers sometimes carried sandstone 'throughs' for several miles across country to add to the limestone walls. And in the Cotswolds much walling stone was produced as a by-product of building-stone quarries which might be located some miles away. But on the whole, even during the most intensive period of new walling, most quarries were immediately beside or at most a few score yards from the lines of the walls. Stones were carted, carried or sledged downhill to the work site. Then when the wall had been built to the quarry's level the quarry was abandoned and a new one started farther uphill.

Since the last war some roadside walls, usually those built by county councils as part of road widening or straightening schemes, have lost their distinctive local identity. In the Lake District and Cornwall, particularly, much new work is in cut slate supplied by a few big quarries. Although relatively cheap and convenient to produce, walls built of the new material look quite foreign next to those using other types of stone or even those in local slate of a different colour. Elsewhere, notably in the Cotswolds and Yorkshire, the policy seems to be, when possible, to blend new work with old so that the two can hardly be distinguished once the harsher angles have weathered. Even here there are small discrepancies, since the modern quarries are usually different from the original ones. The closest possible match with older surrounding walls may be achieved where derelict walls and buildings are demolished and their stones reused, although where cut slabs or blocks are added to a rubble wall, or where the stones used are from another neighbourhood, the finished product may be curiously patchy and inappropriate.

Despite these qualifications, dry stone walls provide an excellent introduction to local geology. At the same time, geology reveals why the walls are there in the first place and why they take on rather different forms in different areas.

It is this connection which is stressed in the survey which follows.

The simplified geological column below should help to put into perspective the approximate ages of the various types of walling stone mentioned in this handbook.

Era	Period or System	Start of Period (millions of years ago)
Cenozoic	Quarternary	2
	Tertiary	63
Mesozoic	Cretaceous	135
	Jurassic	180
	Triassic	230
Palaeozoic	Permian	280
	Carboniferous	345
	Devonian	405
	Silurian	425
	Ordovician	500
	Cambrian	600
Precambrian		

Virtually all stone used in this country for dry walling dates from the Jurassic Period or earlier, although Cretaceous materials such as flints are found in mortared walls in southern England, where more suitable stone is generally lacking. The most important types of stone for dry walling include Jurassic and Carboniferous limestones, Triassic, Permian, Carboniferous and Devonian sandstones, Silurian, Ordovician and Cambrian slates and shales, Precambrian metamorphic rocks, and volcanic and granitic and other intrusive rocks of various ages.

One can get a rough idea of where walls are likely to be found in Britain by looking at a geological map such as one of those published by the Ordnance Survey. It is important, though, when doing this to keep in mind the complicating effects of glaciation throughout large parts of these islands. In some areas (much of Ireland in particular) glacial drift has covered up the useful walling stone. In other locales, poor native stone deposits have been augmented by glacially transported boulders so that walls have been built where, on the map at least, none would be expected.

The design of a typical dry stone wall is shown schematically in the following diagram. This should help to clarify the regional and local variations which are discussed in the following pages. The diagram's parts are named in accordance with widespread north-of-England usage.

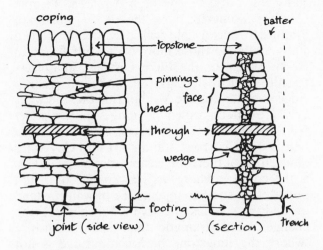

PARTS OF A DRY STONE WALL

coping, topstone, pinnings, face, head, through, wedge, batter, footing, joint (side view), (section), trench

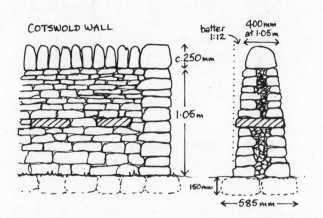

COTSWOLD WALL

batter 1:12, 400mm at 1·05m, c.250mm, 1·05m, 150mm, 585mm

which are several courses high) and 'jack bits' (little face stones) may be used when required.

In terminology just as in design there are geographical differences, which, once one is aware of them, give added personality to walls in the field.

SOUTHERN AND CENTRAL ENGLAND

If one thinks of walling in southern or central England, it is the landscape of the Cotswolds which immediately springs to mind. Stone villages, thin stony soils and warm russet-brown or yellowy dry stone walls which, according to J B Priestley, know 'the trick of keeping the lost sunlight of centuries glimmering upon them' (Trueman, 1949, p15). The stone is Jurassic limestone. The thicker oolitic beds supply freestone for building purposes while the shelly limestones, which break irregularly, provide ragstone for the walls. Most Cotswold walling stone is quarried from a layer about a foot below the subsoil, under which lies the more regularly jointed building stone. In the old days, large areas of quarry land would be scalped of their overburden to expose the wall stone layer, which would be allowed to weather and break up naturally over the winter frosts. Sometimes, as at the top of Bredon Hill, the walling stone is fairly hard and rings when hit, but elsewhere it is soft or grades into sandstone and sounds dead when tapped. The harder the stone the better it lasts, and experienced Cotswold wallers can tell at a glance where their supply has been quarried and what its qualities are. But most of the quarries are closed now, even where they contain much good stone, so these days it is seldom possible to specify the type wanted.

Most Cotswold stockproof walls are built to the design and dimensions shown.

As in most areas where the craft is still active, Cotswold wallers have distinctive local terms for the parts of the wall. Besides the ordinary face or wall stones, 'jumpers' (thick face stones

In addition to the fillings, wedges or 'pinners' are placed against the inside joints of the face stones so that they are secure and slightly higher at the centre than at the face of the wall. Where they are available, 'bonders' (throughstones) are deployed along a course about half way up the wall to bridge the two faces and hold them together. Although not to be recommended, a layer of concrete or mortared stones sometimes is used in place of throughs: an example may be seen just south of Tetbury, Gloucestershire, on the A433. At the top of Cotswold walls, 'combers' are used to form the coping.

Cotswold walling technique has several notable features. As mentioned, great emphasis is placed on wedging the wall stones so that each course tends to shed rainwater and is protected from disruption by frosts. This is also a practice in other parts of the country where the stones are flat enough to allow it. But another characteristic, the placing of wall stones with their long edges alone the wall, is frowned on elsewhere because it produces a weaker finished product (point b, p65). While the Cotswold method ensures a handsome, regular wall face, it results in poor bonding between the stones. Perhaps this is why one often sees Cotswold walls which are flaking away course by course. The individual stones are small, relatively light and quite regular, which increases the problem. This is one reason why the combers are generally mortared – they are seldom big and heavy enough to bridge the wall top and anchor the courses below. The preferred coping is upright, with roughly trimmed semi-circular combers as shown in the preceding diagram. Often a trick or two must be used to achieve this effect (p77), but seldom is such an interesting solution found as that employed near Seend, between Melksham and Devizes, where some of the roadside walls use small stones mortared into an arch as shown by the following diagram.

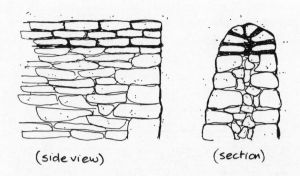

(side view)　　　　　(section)

A more widespread innovation in this region is the mortared jump – a short section of concrete coping situated for the convenience of the local Hunt.

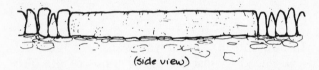

(side view)

Cotswold stone is easily trimmed and shaped and craftsmen take great pride in producing evenly battered walls of well-graded courses. They first make a mental estimate of the thicknesses of the stone supplied and set the guidelines accordingly. Most of the stones are from 50–100mm (2–4″) thick, so if, for example, a waller has a lot of 100mm (4″) and 75mm (3″) stones, he first sets the guidelines approximately 175mm (7″) above the foundations. After this he raises the lines 3–4″ at a time, depending on how he can best grade the remaining thinner stones. Cotswold wallers use their hammers almost continuously, not to dress the stones' faces but to give them a better fit, knock off awkward projections and achieve the required batter on each face:

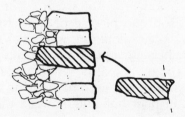

Old Cotswold stone sometimes becomes crumbly and easily disintegrated. For this reason, expert wallers in this area try to place the old faces outward on reused stone, when this is consistent with other requirements, so that they need chip away as little as possible. In parts of the country where the stone is more durable there is little reason to do this.

The Cotswolds form only one part of the Jurassic limestone belt which runs right across southern and central England from the Isle of Purbeck north–northeast to the Cleveland Hills. Each district shows the influence of local variations in its stone. Purbeck walls are a brilliant white

coarse rubble. Somewhat farther north large slabs are found in one or two places: Temple Combe, Somerset, on the A357 north of Stalbridge, has a field wall of vertically placed slabs similar to those more commonly found in North Wales or the Lake District. In Leicestershire the Middle Lias ironstone forms a sharp ridge overlooking the Vale of Belvoir: the walls here are a deep brown or orange, quite distinct from those of the oolite tracts. Everywhere the belt is quite narrow, trailing off into clay vales along the southern or eastern dip slopes. This is the country where, as Hawkes (1951, p105) puts it, 'the sudden appearance of walls instead of hedges catches the eye'. Nowhere is the change more dramatic than in Lincolnshire 'where the limestone of Lincoln Edge is not more than a few miles wide and the transformation from hedges to the geometrical austerity of dry-walling, from the black and white, red and buff of timber and brick to the melting greys of limestone buildings, is extraordinarily abrupt'.

There are other walls in south and central England, although some, such as those of flint and brick in Oxfordshire and East Anglia or of Kentish ragstone in the belt from Maidstone to Hindhead, depend on mortar for their solidity and so are passed over here. The cob walls of Devon, Dorset and west Hampshire deserve a mention: like cob houses they require a crown of thatch or flat coping stones to throw off the rain, otherwise they soon dissolve. In northwest Leicestershire, the hills of Charnwood Forest, rising unexpectedly from the Midlands plain and representing an island of Precambrian granitic, volcanic and slaty rocks, possess rough and intractable boulder walls which seem more in keeping with the mountainous West than with the fertile and gentle country round about. Here as well as in the Cotswolds and Northamptonshire the walls are often backed by unditched thorn hedges, a combination which according to Beddall (1950, p19) provides the most shelter for the least taking of land or precious topsoil.

The rocks of the Mendips, while not nearly as ancient as those of Charnwood Forest, form an equally interesting inlier among the more recent deposits of this region. The Mendips consist largely of a plateau of Carboniferous Limestone, the oldest widely occurring limestone in Britain, out of which protrude a few higher hills of still older (Devonian) and more resistant Old Red Sandstone. Limestone dominates the walls, although sections built of sandstone or breccia occur where these rocks form the uppermost strata. The breccia is known locally as 'puddingstone', a term which in this area is also loosely applied to any round stone in order to distinguish it from the more angular 'ploughshare' stones. Many of the fields are large, with the north–south walls often higher than those orientated east–west.

At first glance the walls look very much like those of the Craven district of Yorkshire (p10); on close inspection their stones appear even rougher and more irregular and they can be seen to lack such finishing touches as throughs and topstones.

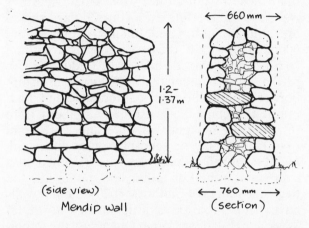

(side view)
Mendip wall

← 660 mm →

1.2–1.37 m

← 760 mm →
(section)

'Bonders' are used instead of throughs but to much the same purpose. These stones, extending part way through the wall or almost reaching the other side, are especially important because Mendip wallers tend to place many of the face stones with their long edges running along rather than into the wall. When short stones are used with their long edges into the wall they are known as 'key stones'. 'Infill' (fillings) are used to pack the centre as in other dry walling styles, and, as in many locales, the use of pinnings on the outside of the wall is frowned on. Mendip walls are built with rather little batter – only about 50mm (2″) for a 1.2–1.37m (4–4′6″) high wall.

In general, walls throughout southern and central England lack the variety of openings and associated 'furniture' which are such a feature of Pennine, Lakeland and Scottish walls. Mendip walls sometimes do contain 'pop holes' for catching rabbits or badgers – a reminder of the days when trapping was an important supplement to farmers' incomes. Many pop holes are built to the zig-zag pattern shown below. The

pop hole

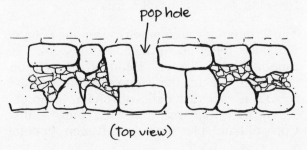

(top view)

idea is to prevent a rabbit chased by a fox from bolting through the passage where it could be snapped up by the fox's mate who may be waiting on the far side. The zig-zag forces the rabbit to halt inside the wall, giving it time to notice the fox before making a fatal mistake.

Foxes are suspicious of holes in walls and cannot be snared by luring them through. So Mendip wallers sometimes built a short section of wall with a more gradual batter where the wall intersected the line of an existing run. Since foxes prefer to climb walls by the easiest route, a snare could be positioned at the foot of this section to trap them.

THE PENNINES

The Pennines represent the single greatest expanse of walled country in England. Rising from the Midlands plain on the Staffordshire–Derbyshire border, the moors run northward for some 220km (140 miles) to the Tyne Gap. Immediately beyond, the Cheviots continue the uplands to the Border Country, while to the west the Howgill Fells create a link with the Lake District. The bedrock geology of this area is fairly simple but contains striking contrasts. In the Craven district of northwest Yorkshire and in the central Peak District of Derbyshire, Carboniferous Limestone forms the surface cover. Here, over the ages, water and ice have carved a landscape of glaring white crags and scars where underground watercourses abound but there are few surface streams and pools. Farther south and east, through most of South and West Yorkshire and Derbyshire, the relatively acid and impervious shales and sandstones of the Millstone Grit and Coal Measures cap the geological series. Here, and over wide areas throughout the Pennines where glacial deposits obscure the solid geology, drainage is poor and surface waterlogging has encouraged the formation of sombre heather moors or blanket peat bogs.

The limestone pavements of the Craven district are of particular interest. Their glacial and post-glacial development is too complex to outline here, but their geological and botanical importance is noteworthy. The Iron Age wall shown on page 23 probably took its stone from one of the pavements, which throughout history have formed tempting sources of ready supply. Victorian and recent times have seen the pavements robbed not only for walling and building purposes but for ornamental and rockery stone as well. But, as explained in a leaflet by the Nature Conservancy Council (undated), these relict land surfaces are of far more value when left intact than they are when wrenched apart for their constituent boulders.

The walls of the Pennines reflect the geological contrasts in their colouration: clean grey–white in the limestone districts, dappled at their border with other formations and sooty grey or dark brown elsewhere. As Raistrick (1966, p23) notes, this alone is enough to tell you when you have crossed the Craven Fault near Stockdale or along the Settle–Malham road and to reveal the alternating grits and limestones in the Yoredale series as the walls change from dark to light to dark again as they mount the upper slopes of Wensleydale.

The design of the walls is equally revealing. In the Craven district, throughstones are often unavailable and even the fairly recent walls (or recent repairs of old walls) are wide-based and seemingly haphazard. Fortunately, the blocky limestone binds firmly together despite the lack of throughs and settles into a more durable wall than do many more regular types of stone.

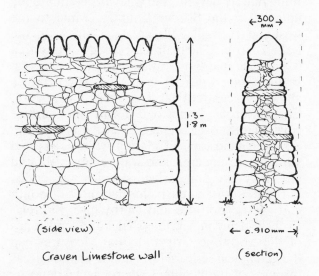

(side view)

Craven Limestone wall.

(section)

Even in this area throughs are used where possible. Raistrick (1966, p23) says that in parts of Wharfedale and much of Ribblesdale, wallers split large slabs from glacial erratics of Silurian slate for this purpose. As mentioned previously, gritstone throughs are sometimes carried some distance into the limestone areas. And where walls cross various strata of the Yoredale Series the more strongly bedded rocks are quarried for throughstones which are used all along the walls including their limestone sections. The diagram shows the start of two rows of throughs: one or two rows are normal depending on the wall's height. Rainsford–Hannay (1972, p73) says, however, that around Derbyshire High Peak both limestone and gritstone walls have three rows of throughs. Perhaps this is because of their height, since Enclosure Awards often specify this design where the wall is 1.5m (5′) high

or more from the ground level to below the topstones. Examples of three-through walls may also be found north of Skipton and elsewhere in North Yorkshire as well as in Cumbria. And in the Northern Pennines, on the north side of the A66 in Stainmore Pass, a few very tall limestone walls contain four rows of throughs.

On the Millstone Grit and Coal Measures, throughs are plentiful and the walls typically take the form shown on page 62. Gritstone walls are of rough blocks or flags and have less batter than those of limestone, while Coal Measures walls usually use fine even-coursed flags and so are still straighter and thinner – only about 600mm (2′) wide at the base, tapering to 450mm (1′6″) for a 1.5m (5′) high wall. Beddall (1950, p19) mentions that on the Yorkshire–Lancashire border around the vales of Rochdale and Todmorden, rectangular gritstone flags about 1.8m (6′) high by 600mm (2′) wide and 75–100mm (3–4″) thick may be seen placed on end, sunk about a foot into the ground and fastened with iron plates bolted on either side, rather like the flagstone fences of Caithness (p20). Similar walls have been reported a little farther north, at Wycoller Hall near Colne, and across the Pennines in Halifax.

In the northern Pennines the rocks are mostly of Carboniferous age, as in the Craven and Peak districts, but here the strata are more mixed than farther south and the walls are more often of varied sandstones and shales than of limestone. Of quite different origin are the walls of the Whin Sill, a dark blue–grey dolerite which was injected into the Carboniferous beds at a later date. The most famous of these walls, of course, is Hadrian's, which takes advantage of the craggy scarp formed by the Whin Sill along most of its north side. Parts of the Roman structure may be seen among the rough rubble of the farm walls which run back from its line. Also distinct from the main mass of sedimentary rock of this region are the Cheviots: a granitic core surrounded by a dissected dome of lavas of Devonian age, from above which the Carboniferous rocks have eroded. Trueman (1949, p182) reports that 'although some of the rocks have been used for rough walling, surprisingly few local rocks have been used in building, the isolated shepherds' dwellings being built from free-stones carried into the area'.

The terminology in common use among Pennine wallers is followed throughout this book (see especially the chapter, 'Building a Free-Standing Wall'), so that there is no need to mention it here. A few characteristics of Pennine technique are worth summarising at this point. Unlike Cotswold and also Scottish craftsmen, Pennine wallers seldom use batter frames, in keeping with their general avoidance of excess paraphernalia, although they admit that frames and guidelines are helpful when building long sections of new wall. Similarly, they tend not to use hammers, although they may carry a lump or mason's hammer in case of need. This is especially true of wallers in Carboniferous Limestone areas where the stone is too massively jointed to shape easily. Mendip wallers, it is interesting to note, feel the same way about hammers. Pinnings are avoided, also as in the Mendips, or, if absolutely necessary, are placed for each course as it is built up rather than after completing the wall. There is no compulsion to disguise holes in the wall's face as long as the fillings inside are unable to slip out. One well-built gritstone wall on Ilkley Moor (Ordnance Survey grid reference: SE 095467) has upper courses which look almost lacey but which are, nevertheless, well anchored by two rows of throughs and a coverband under the topstones. Rainsford–Hannay (1972, p51) mentions one or two similar walls in Derbyshire, purposely built to let the snow through and keep it from piling up in deep drifts and to dissuade sheep from climbing the apparently precarious structure. The latter reason is also given for the design of Galloway single dykes (p18) and some Irish walls (p21) and it would be interesting to know if ideas had been exchanged between these regions.

Pennine wallers prefer upright copings of even-sized topstones, although rubble copes are often used on subdivision walls and others of secondary importance. Topstones on late 19th century roadside walls in gritstone and Coal Measures areas are often trimmed to semi-circles but limestone walls are invariably topped by chunky blocks. Tilted copings using rough rectangular blocks, taller than they are wide, are found mainly on hillside walls, while the locked top (p75) is known and appreciated but seldom used. It is always worth keeping an eye out for unusual copings, since even where one type predominates there may be local exceptions. Raistrick (1966, p19), for instance, says that walls in Weardale, County Durham, have a layer of turf rather than stone tops, another possible link with Irish and Scottish traditions.

Walls throughout northern England and Scotland are frequently supplied with a variety of openings, discussed further in the chapter, 'Wall Furniture and Special Applications'. Margaret Brooks (1973) considers these in some detail for the West Riding of Yorkshire. Here there are two main types of holes aside from gates and stiles: small 'water' or 'rabbit smoots' and larger 'cripple holes'. Smoots allow water to flow through walls which are built in hollows or along the contours of a hillside. At the same time they allow rabbits to cross the wall, which is why two terms are used depending largely on whether or not holes are obviously required from drainage. One reason why smoots may be built for rabbits is to keep them from burrowing under the wall by giving them easy passage through it. A more likely motive is suggested by the fact that rabbits may easily be driven through such holes into nets, snares or pit-traps. One theory has it that these holes had to be built in some cases to allow rabbits free access to properties which held pre-Enclosure game rights (Brooks, 1973, pp103–4) and there are wallers and farmers still living who supplemented their meagre incomes in the 1920's by trapping rabbits along the walls.

Cripple holes, also known as 'hogg holes', 'thawls', 'thirl holes', 'smout holes', 'sheep runs', 'sheep creeps', 'sheep smooses' and 'lunky holes', are built large enough to let sheep through but are too small for cattle. They allow the wall to have great flexibility of usage if built with forethought, since they can be used to drive sheep through fields which contain cattle without opening any gates. At other times they can be blocked off with flagstones, walled up or covered with wooden doors or sheet metal to make them impassable. For moving a big flock more quickly, two cripple holes are sometimes built side by side (Brooks, 1973, pp105–6). The following drawing (adapted from Wood, 1973, plate 27) shows an unusual hole in a wall in Grassington, North Yorkshire. The wedge-shaped opening is built so that lintel stones can be placed securely across to form an ordinary cripple hole. But the stones above are added loosely so that they and the lintels can be removed when necessary to form a full-height 'cattle creep'.

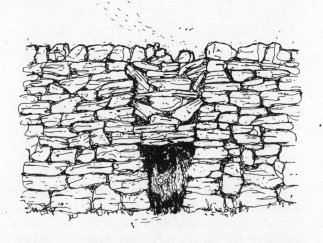

Another interesting use for cripple holes is found on the Isle of Noss, Shetland. Here the holes are designed to let sheep through to graze the cliffs, while the purpose of the dyke itself is to prevent the Shetland ponies from falling off into the sea.

Unusual openings are sometimes found for which no easy explanation is possible. Margaret Brooks (1973, pp106–9) describes the 'mystery holes' which occur in scores along several of the walls at Worlds End near Keighley. These are identical to smoots but are located midway up the wall. Among the ideas offered by wallers and countrymen for these holes is that they were built to shoot through, to relieve the walls of wind or water pressure in times of storm or flood, to allow rabbits to run through on top of 600mm (2′) drifts of snow, to allow snow-bound sheep to breath through the wall or to provide a place to lodge blocks of salt or the farmer's lunch or wooden beams for a low structure. None of these explanations, serious or not, seems satisfactory for the number of holes concerned.

THE LAKE DISTRICT

The Lake District, a compact area only about 48km (30 miles) across, contains a surprising number of different rock types and corresponding styles of walling. Starting with the oldest formations in the district, the Skiddaw Slates of the northern peaks, one finds walls of dark or occasionally greenish fissile slates and flags. These also occur in a small area in the Black Combe range west of Broughton, near the coast. The sketch shows a wall with one row of throughs but two rows may be used depending on the height.

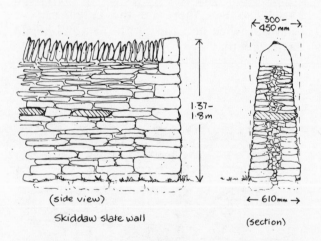

Skiddaw slate wall

Between Keswick and Ambleside, in a broad zone which includes the most rugged part of the district, the Borrowdale Volcanics contribute a varied group, mostly relatively erosion-resistant massive lavas and tuffs. The granites and granophyres of Ennerdale, Eskdale and several other localities produce walls similar to these

but coloured a warm mottled pink. The volcanic walls are similar in design to those of slate but are generally coarser and more massive, in keeping with the nature of the stone. Although there are few opportunities for innovation with such coarse material, this area does hold surprises. At Little Langdale there are several roadside walls incorporating milestones at their heads or gate ends. The one shown below (OS grid ref: NY325032) has a short section of ash hedge laid along the top.

At Stephenson Ground in the upper Lickle Valley (OS grid ref: SD235932) two or three water smoots show an ingenious use of hexagonal columns of rhyolite to prevent sheep passing through the opening.

This area is also full of historically fascinating examples, such as the clearance walls discussed on page 25 and the 'cyclopean' walls of huge boulders found in several locations. The most impressive of these, about 2.7m (9′) high on the downhill side with enormous footings, runs beside the road near Far Kiln Bank above the Duddon Valley (OS grid ref: SD214935).

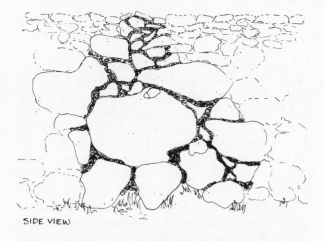

SIDE VIEW

The Southern part of Lakeland is made up of Silurian slates, which includes shales and flags as well as true slates. These resemble the Skiddaw Slates in their well-marked cleavage which produces slabs for walling. A typical example with a slate stile is shown on page 97. When quarry waste is used the result can be disappointing, as the following sketch (after Rollinson, 1972, p27) shows. This wall is beside the Garburn Road, Troutbeck, but similar examples in complete decay may be found farther south on Broughton Moor (OS grid ref: SD254931).

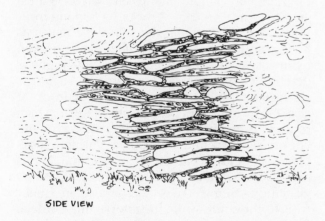

SIDE VIEW

Where the Coniston and Brathay Flags occur at the boundary of the Silurian slates and Borrowdale Volcanics, roughly quarried slates are sometimes used upright to make stone fences.

SIDE VIEW

These are to be found around Coniston, Hawkshead and Ambleside, but the example

shown is at Jackson Ground (OS grid ref: SD233928) very near the rhyolite smoots mentioned above.

This example has an associated hedge which, while now overgrown, was once presumably trimmed to form a combination barrier. The upright flags are best suited for use with some additional fencing, since once dug in they are only 400–600mm (1′6″–2′) high. Where no hedge exists, a post-and-wire or post-and-netting fence is often erected just behind the flags to give the required height. The detail below shows how the flags are roughly shaped to interlock at their edges. No metal is used, in contrast to the fences of North Wales, Caithness and Yorkshire/ Lancashire mentioned elsewhere in this chapter.

Slate fences require more upkeep than the usual dry stone wall and often assume a drunken appearance through neglect. They are not necessarily old, however: a few sections near the Duddon Valley (OS grid ref: SD214941) were freshly placed when seen in 1975.

Around the edges of the Cumbrian dome other newer rocks occur which connect Lake District walls with those of the Pennines and the Carlisle area. Carboniferous Limestone around Furness, in the area south of Kendal and in parts of north and west Cumberland is used to build silvery– grey walls quite similar to those found farther east in Yorkshire. New Red Sandstones occur on the coast around St Bees and in the long tongue of the Eden Valley, where the walls are rusty red and often of shaped and well-bedded blocks, while between here and the limestone area is a narrow belt of Coal Measures gritstone walls. Near the coast, where salt winds stunt the growth of hedgerows, rounded seashore pebbles have been packed together with the interstices filled with soil to form banks such as the one shown in the following diagram (after Rollinson, 1972, p16).

Rollinson (p17) goes on to say that 'after a year or so they become so completely grassed over that it is often difficult to detect the layers of stones which form the heart of the wall'.

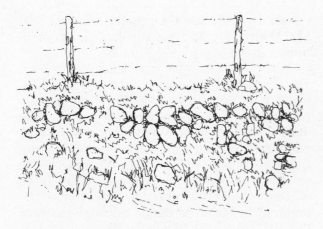

Examples occur on the Furness and West Cumberland seaboard, notably on Walney Island where the late 18th–early 19th century enclosures are bounded by these banks.

Lakeside walling technique differs little from that found in the Pennines except as required by the different material. Copings are usually rubble or tilted, as is easiest on steep slopes. Surprisingly, many of the hillside walls have topstones tilted downhill and this often leads to long lengths falling into disarray. Nevertheless the area is justly famous for its Enclosure Era walls and for the steep slopes which they negotiate without altering direction.

WALES

Many parts of Wales once supported the walling craft but it has tended to become more and more restricted in recent years. On the Gower Peninsula, for instance, there are numerous walls of both sandstone and limestone. Whoever built the Gower wall shown below was a real expert, because it successfully breaks all the rules of batter and is deliberately constructed with an overhang on one face.

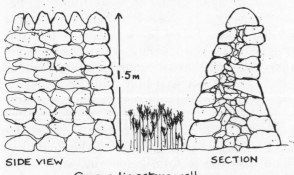

SIDE VIEW   SECTION

Gower limestone wall

The wall is of Carboniferous Limestone and the lower part tapers normally like the typical rough walls to which it is joined. It is rounded at the back, where the fields are in permanent arable use, while the concave front presents a formidable barrier to the sheep which graze between it and the sea cliff.

Moving north, the Welsh coalfields present a scene more like that of the southern Pennines than of the rest of Wales, with grits and flags predominating. The wide expanse of central Wales, with its rounded hills of various mudstones, shales and slates, tends more to hedgerows and wire fences than to walls although quite often a wall separates the rough grazing of the highest land from the better fields below. Roadside walls in this area are sometimes so fissile that they lack topstones and tend to flake off layer by layer due to vibration from traffic. In Dyfed, and occasionally elsewhere as in the Lleyn Peninsula, stone-faced banks rather than free-standing walls predominate, often with a hedge growing on top. Usually the stones are set vertically but sometimes they are placed herringbone fashion. Wood (1973, p211) singles out as particularly noteworthy the seawall at Parrog, east of Fishguard, and the churchyard wall at Mwnt (Traeth-y-Mwnt), near Cardigan.

Gwynedd, which contains most of the oldest rocks in the province, more than makes up for the relatively simple picture elsewhere. Slates, granite and volcanic rocks, Carboniferous Limestone and Precambrian schists and gneisses lie in a series of roughly parallel bands broken by intrusive dykes and sills. The topography is determined by many factors. Most of Anglesey, for instance, belies its diversity of bedrock: it is a fairly uniform, rather low plateau which represents an old platform cut by the waves and later raised. Around Snowdonia, volcanic rocks play a significant part in the strong relief: this area is a syncline of resistant rocks sculpted by glaciation. Similar rocks occur also in Cader Idris to the south while the intervening Harlech Dome consists of more highly eroded Cambrian grits and slates.

Volcanic rocks dominate the walled farmsteads of the western foothills of Snowdonia and parts of the passes of Llanberis, Nant Ffrancon and their surroundings. The stone is tough and coarse, the walls rough and grey. Where the belt of Cambrian slate has been quarried, notably at Nantlle, Waunfawr, Llanberis and Bethesda, vast amounts of quarry waste have provided a completely different material. Here the dark grey walls are made up of regular blocks which are frequently split and dressed. Along the roadsides in this vicinity every sort of combination may be seen: rough volcanic copings on slate walls, slate copings on slate walls, slate copings on rubble walls and uncoped walls and slate fences. The view below is between Bethesda and Capel Curig (OS grid ref: SH643626).

14

Slate is used extensively in fences which are normally wired together after being dug into the ground about 600mm (2'). The spacing between slates varies from a few inches up to several yards; for close spacings the wire may be looped around the slate or put through holes

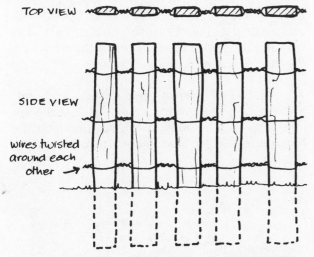

TOP VIEW

SIDE VIEW

wires twisted around each other →

drilled in it, while for greater spacings drilling is usual and the wire may be strained as in a normal post-and-wire fence.

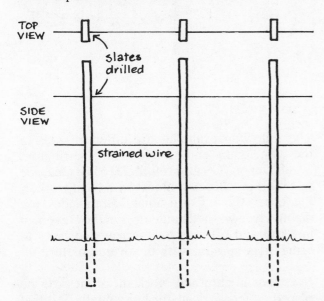

TOP VIEW

slates drilled

SIDE VIEW

strained wire

Some of the most impressive walls are found around the slate quarries themselves, where everything from roadside retaining walls to roofs is made of the native material. At Blaenau Ffestiniog, long inclined planes rise half way up the mountainsides while the spoil heaps seem always about to crush the town at their feet. The walls associated with these workings were made by the quarrymen themselves, and their success depends on a knowledge of how to shape slate (pp58–9). Also at Blaenau Ffestiniog (OS grid ref: SH693459) are a few 'headstone' fences, built like the flag fences of the Lakes but taller and thinner and without any effort at interlocking although there is some overlap.

THE SOUTH WEST

According to Rule (1974, p23), all linear enclosing mounds which are not regular masonry are termed 'hedges' in mid- and west-Cornwall. Through much of this area the hedges are earth banks faced with stone or turf, but on the high downs and moors, especially in the far west, dry stone hedges are common. Crawford (1936, p162) says that these are often reinforced by earth of by 'a kind of daub that sets fairly hard'; in this area the distinction between dry and mortared walls and earth banks is sometimes blurred. On the moors and country around Camelford some dry stonework is found but most of the hedges are of earth capped with stone or brushwood. A type of hedge found rarely but occurring here and there in the Boscastle–Tintagel district consists of stonework of only a single stone's thickness. Dr Francis Turk of the Institute of Cornish Studies and the University of Exeter relates that similar walls are common on the Isles of Scilly and says that he was told, some quarter century ago, by islanders on the 'off' islands that such walls were built so that they could easily be pushed down when necessary to take boats across the fields to the sea.

It is the stone- or turf-faced bank which is most commonly called a hedge in other parts of the South West, and this forms the dominant type of fence whether or not it is crowned with a row of living shrubs. Turf hedges and ordinary hedgerows have been described in detail in another handbook in this series, *Hedging* (BTCV, 1975); the discussion here is limited to stone-faced and dry stone hedges. Design and construction techniques are detailed in the chapter, 'Retaining Walls and Stone Hedges'. The Hedgerow Survey record card on page 109 gives an idea of the variety of types of Cornish stone hedges. Elsewhere in the South West the stone hedges are generally similar except that they usually show less stone and are clothed and crowned in more luxuriant vegetation due to the more moderate climate away from the coast.

The 'standard' Cornwall County Council stone hedge is shown on page 91. This is the type specified in county road-widening schemes. It may be built in two forms, depending mainly on whether the stone used is slate or granite. Although the county has extended the use of quarried slate from north Cornish mines into the western granite areas, this is very unpopular with local craftsmen who prefer the traditional material however expensive. In farm work the source of stone is normally the land being cleared. Rule (1974, p26) says that the stone is mainly fragments cleared from the surface or within a plough's depth (about 150mm (6″)), and that 'pop' or decomposed granite is favoured because it has flat surfaces. Blue elvan, which is also found, is harder to handle because it is smooth and splinters into wedge-shaped pieces. Around Truro most of the stone used is spar, supplemented by waste stone from the tin and copper mines and by quarried granite. The latter is an expensive material which is usually laid in even courses of smooth blocks to produce a neat, masonry-like finish. Unfortunately these blocks bind poorly with each other and with the earth packing and tend to slump, especially when placed, as they often are, with their long edges along rather than into the bank.

The Cornwall County Council specifies that the last two rows of slate hedges should be built in the herringbone ('Jack and Jill' or 'Darby and Joan') pattern. This helps to use up the small pieces which are often cracked from the 'raisers' (face stones) during work as well as to provide a good rooting medium for the turf capping. Herringbone work is usually found wherever thin, splintery stone must be used which would otherwise be hard to manage. The hedge shown below, which is entirely herringbone, is from Veryan in Cornwall.

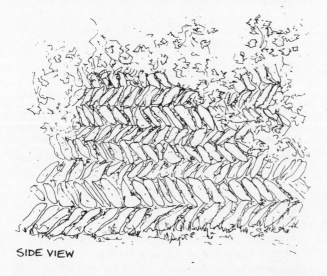

SIDE VIEW

We met one Devon hedger who described the herringbone pattern as distinctly Cornish, and refused to use it because he said it slipped. Most of his own work around Plymouth was in Devonian limestone, and perhaps he had not seen the herringbone hedges of Hartland Point on the north Devon coast or the slate-faced banks of Exmoor. This same craftsman was prepared to build what he called 'the professional way', using either trimmed horizontal courses or vertically placed stones, when demanded for appearance sake. But he preferred rough horizontal coursing using largely untrimmed material, which is supposed to be stronger as well as easier and faster to build. This point is emphasised by other Devon stone hedgers, who call their preferred style 'chip and block'. Although the stones are roughly graded from biggest at the bottom to smallest at the top, there is a mixture between small stones ('chips') and large stones ('blocks') within each course. Great emphasis is given to placing the stones tightly together and to wedging them from behind so that they sit well and bond with the earth packing. Cornish work often shows considerably more earth between the stones on the face of the wall.

The gate end shown below (OS grid ref: SX548520) is in the 'professional' style using up-and-down stones built in courses in which the horizontal rather than the vertical joints are broken.

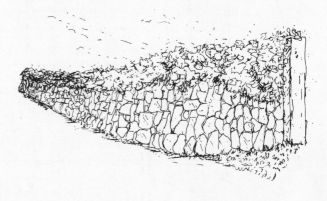

The following examples are different sides of the same gate end, found near Dartington, South Devon (OS grid ref: SX771634). One side was built in 'chip and block' by a local worker, the other by a Cornishman. Both sides use mainly river-washed boulders, but the Devonian has knocked off most of the rounded faces to bring them into line with the overall batter.

Note that in chip and block the stones can be placed either vertically or horizontally and that the joints are broken depending on the alignment of the stones.

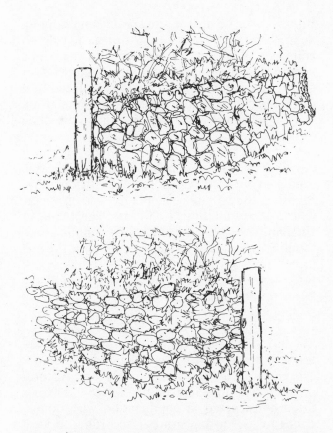

Devon craftsmen emphasise the need to build hedges with a concave batter, for reasons explained on page 92. They accuse Cornish hedgers of building with a straight taper, which, they say, contributes to poor settling. The Cornwall County Council specifications, however, allow for either a straight or concave batter and this seems to be a matter of individual preference.

In the South West, free-standing dry stone walls are mainly limited to the edges of the granite moorlands: Dartmoor, Bodmin Moor, the Land's End area and the Isles of Scilly especially. They are of rough horizontal courses, sometimes topped with vertical copings, sometimes topped with turf. In a few places granite walls give way to more geologically diverse structures, such as at Sticklepath on the north edge of Dartmoor where a major tear fault intersects the folded, metamorphosed and intruded aureole ringing the moor to yield a remarkable range of rock types, colours and textures in the local walls. Frequently free-standing walls and stone hedges bound different sides of the same field or even alternate within one stretch. Often it would seem that free-standing walls are rebuilt as stone hedges – we met a local farmer near High Tor on Bodmin Moor who said the art of free walling was completely lost in his area. Crawford (1936, pp163–4) implies that this sort of transformation may in some cases be the work of centuries. Describing how ancient clearance walls deteriorate, he reports that 'On stony ground the process of collapse is assisted by the formation of negative lynchets which undercut the foundations, causing subsidence. The wall then assumes a dilapidated aspect, is full of repair-patches, and becomes in part a retaining wall for the soil above'.

One sort of wall which is unlikely to ever need repair is that found in a few places on Dartmoor but most spectacularly near Zennor, west of St Ives (OS grid ref: SW457387). Some of the tiny fields here are enclosed with single rows of enormous granite boulders or 'grounders' rising up to 2.1m (7′) from the grass. These are relics of ancient enclosure and may be 2,000 years old or more (Brooks, 1973, volume 2).

Although such walls seem primitive, the clever granite cattle grid shown on page 100 is from the same field system.

SCOTLAND AND THE ISLE OF MAN

Although the bedrock geology of Scotland is bewilderingly complex, its 'drystane dykes' may be grouped for the most part into two major types. These are the Galloway dyke, which apparently originated in southwestern Scotland but is now the typical form from Kircudbrightshire east to Forfar and right up the west coast, and the Aberdeenshire dyke, which is typical of the cattle-breeding areas of the northeast.

The Galloway dyke is designed to fence sheep. The 'standard' form, publicised by Rainsford–Hannay (1972, p35) and the Stewartry Drystane Dyking Committee, is based on Kircudbrightshire enclosure specifications. It features one or two rows of throughstones plus a 'coverband' below the coping. These courses project about 50mm (2″) from the wall face and, along with the high coping, dissuade sheep from attempting to jump the wall. (See diagrams on following page.)

This type of wall is known in Scotland as a 'double dyke' because it has two faces packed between with 'hearting' (fillings) in the manner of most dry walls. It can use almost any type of stone, but whinstone double dykes are perhaps most common throughout central Scotland while sandstone dykes are found in certain districts in southern Scotland and the west coast.

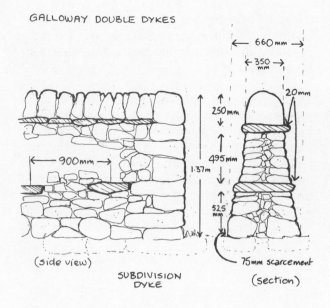

(side view) SUBDIVISION DYKE (section)

900mm 1·37m 660mm 350mm 20mm 250mm 495mm 525mm

75mm scarcement

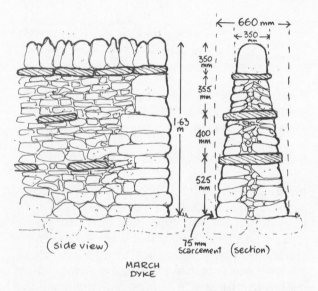

(side view) MARCH DYKE 75mm scarcement (section)

1·63m 660mm 350mm 350mm 355mm 400mm 525mm

Whinstone is rough and makes a varied and irregular dyke such as that shown above, containing ordinary 'doubling' stones, 'blonks' (big face stones), 'nickers' (wedge-shaped stones which help bring the course up to level) and pinnings between holes in the face. Sandstone dykes are often cut and trimmed and built up in evenly graded courses. Aside from this, the technique used is the same whatever the stone. Great emphasis is placed on 'keeping your heart up'. This means keeping the middle well packed, by placing the fillings at the same time as the face stones and by making sure the fillings are slightly higher than the level of the face stones so that the next course tips a little down and out toward the outside. An important point when beginning the dyke is to provide a proper 'scarcement' (in-set) between the foundation stones and the first course of doubles, to make sure the dyke sits on a firm base. Face stones are placed with their long edges into rather than along the wall, for strength. A feature is the use of the 'locked top' (p75) using heavy wedged topstones: fully one third of the wall's weight is

supposed to be in the coverband and coping. Scottish dykers accuse their northern English colleagues of placing the stones with their long edges along the wall and of filling in after rather than at the same time the course is placed, but this seems to be true mainly of competition wallers who are building for looks more than durability.

As with north of England walls, Galloway double dykes are well-supplied with openings for the use of the shepherd and trapper. Construction methods (p96) are the same as in England for 'pen holes' (rabbit smoots) and 'double water pens' (water smoots), but Prevost (1957, p99) says that 'lunkies' or 'lunky holes' (cripple holes) should be made narrower at the bottom than at the middle and top rather than rectangular as is usual in England.

Single dykes, built only one stone thick, are found in the granite areas of Kircudbrightshire, especially around Cairnsmore of Fleet. According to Rainsford-Hannay (1972, p45), they are often constructed in combination with double dykes to use up big stones. According to local legend, the 'real' or 'original' Galloway style featured single dyking from bottom to top but this proved too difficult for most later workers who started to build only the top half with a single thickness. Rainsford-Hannay (1972, p50) traces the written history of the half-single form back to early 18th century agriculture reports which mention them as march dykes running up into hills, while he attributes to John McAdam of Craigengullich, in the mid-18th century, the idea of building separate panels or 'sneaks' of single stones within the ordinary double dyke to create the 'butt and hudd' style, which is supposed to be tighter than either double or single dyking alone. Prevost (1957, pp86, 99) gives a slightly different story. The true 'Galloway-dyke', he says, was developed by McAdam and consisted of ordinary double dyking up to a coverband at about 1m (3′4″) (throughband at 530mm (1′9″)) topped by several courses of large single stones to a total height of from 1.6m (5′3″) to 1.8m (6′). He contrasts this to both the all-single dyke and the 'half dyke' where the double and single portions each occupy half the total eight.

Whatever its origin and exact form, the Galloway single dyke has several advantages over the more usual type of wall. Single dyking is faster to build than double and it allows the use of big rough boulders. In fact it requires tough coarse-grained stones to bind properly with friction, so it is most suited to granite country. It is surprisingly stable but looks so unsteady that all stock, including the notoriously adventurous black-faced sheep, are supposed to refuse to try climbing it. When single dyking is combined with a lower section of double dyking it adds shelter to its other qualities. The drawing below is of the all-single form.

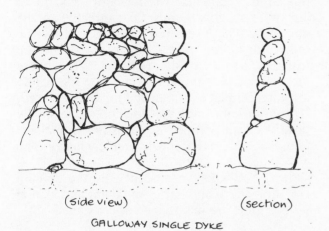

(side view)   (section)

GALLOWAY SINGLE DYKE

Rainsford-Hannay (1972, p103) says that the late 18th and early 19th century agricultural surveys report single dyking to be prevalent in parts of Argyll, Stirling, Dumfriesshire, Roxburgh and the Western Isles. The usual description is of an uncoped dyke, as shown, but the Roxburgh Survey of 1798 recommends a layer of turfs on top, placed on edge and 'condensed together' with a spade. The Hebrides Survey states that the single dyke originated in southern Scotland in 1720 and is generally the best type for the western sheep-grazing areas.

If single dykes were once so widespread, why are they seen today only infrequently? Perhaps because people in later years, not understanding the reasons for their see-through design, have pinned them up in misguided attempts to make them sturdier. But single dykes are said to be even steadier than double dykes, as long as their stones are rough and each stone has its centre of gravity on the stones below.

Galloway seems to have long been a centre for innovations in dyking methods and for the export of men and methods to other areas. The walls of the Isle of Man, mostly about 220 years old, were extensively rebuilt and improved in the 1880's by a pair of Galloway dykers with the help of local labour, according to Rainsford-Hannay (1972, p86). Slate-faced banks are prevalent but there are granite walls on the high ground and sandstone elsewhere. Rainsford-Hannay describes the sandstone as outcropping in good-sized slabs 50–75mm (2–3″) thick which are used both in free-standing walls and in stone-faced banks. Some of the banking takes advantage of the slightly wedge shape of these slabs where they are placed in vertical courses with their thick and thin ends alternating. In

this way the weight of the bank drives the stones ever more tightly together so that 'not a weed nor a blade of grass could show on the outside' (Rainsford-Hannay, 1972, p87). The banks are up to 2.1m (7′) high, about 1.8m (6′) wide at the base and 1.2m (4′) wide at the top and are usually faced with turf above the 1.2m (4′) level. In the north of the island, the easiest stone to find is water-worn beach cobbles. These are too smooth to use in the ordinary way but are placed edgeways-in to face earth banks. The Manx free-standing walls are coped with really big slabs, laid on top tilted slightly upwards at about a 15° angle from the horizontal with their ends overlapping 'like a neat lot of sandwiches laid on a plate' (Rainsford-Hannay, 1972, p87). Their great weight and gritty surface makes them immune to ordinary hazards but not, unfortunately, to the race spectators who remove them for roadside seats!

A final Galloway speciality worth mentioning is the 'Galloway hedge' or 'sunk fence', a combination drystone wall and thorn hedge rather similar to the Irish ditch with quicks (p21).

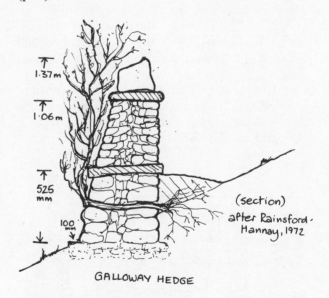

1.37m

1.06m

525 mm

100 mm

(section)
after Rainsford-Hannay, 1972

GALLOWAY HEDGE

The design is especially suited to fencing along the contours of valley sides where the climate is acceptable to hedgerow shrubs but where walling stone is available as well. In these situations, a wall alone would have to be very high on the lower side to keep sheep from jumping over it from the uphill side. If there were only a hedge it might well become gappy at the base unless frequently laid. The combination fence unites both types of barrier and eliminates their weaknesses.

Rainsford-Hannay (1972, p46) believes that the Galloway hedge was invented by Hamilton of Baldoon in 1730 and copied extensively by Lord Selkirk of St Mary's Isle. He goes on to describe how to create such a fence. First, make a horizontal cut along the slope to form a level platform. Throw the spoil uphill. Place the foundation stones and erect a double dyke with the uphill side vertical and the other side given a good batter. There should be a scarcement of at least 100mm (4″) on the downhill side but little or none on the other. When the dyke is raised to the top of the undisturbed soil, lay long thorn plants horizontally across the dyke with their roots in the soil. Finish building the dyke around the plants to a height of 1.3m (4′6″) including the locked top.

For the first year or so stock should be kept off the fields to both sides of the new Galloway hedge while the thorns turn up the fence and overtop it. After three years the plants should be big enough to defeat sheep and cattle. Although the combination of stone and thorn is hard to beat, the shrubs require trimming and general maintenance each year which may be why few sunk fences are now being built.

We turn now to the dykes of Aberdeenshire, which are designed primarily to fence cattle. There are two forms: the 'rough rubble' or 'dump and hole' dyke which uses field stones, untrimmed or with just their corners knocked off, and the 'course dyke' which uses trimmed quarry stones in neat courses. Both types are built to a similar design in each locale, but there are a number of local styles. The drawing below is of a course dyke built in the Dunecht style (OS grid ref: NJ774084).

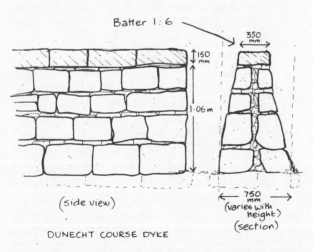

DUNECHT COURSE DYKE

The stones are massive, about 300mm (1′) thick and usually of granite. The dykes need not be as tall as sheep fences but they are carefully designed to offer no projections for cattle to rub against or push on. Normally no throughband is used since stones of the available thickness which could span the width of the wall would be too heavy to lift. Where thinner slabs occur they may be used as throughs as long as there is a minimum of 150mm (6″) of doubling above

them and below the coping and they are trimmed so that the dyke face is smooth. Aberdeenshire dykers never use the Galloway coverband: not only are cattle and deer supposed to be able to lever off the tops of walls built with coverbands but large rectangular topstones are said to sit less well on coverbands than directly on the doubling. The preferred topstones cross the full width of the dyke (350mm (14″)) and are trimmed so that they don't project. Where these are unavailable, smaller stones may be lightly mortared in place or a locked top may be used. It is more important that the coping be solidly positioned and pinned as necessary to make it immovable than that it be extremely heavy. The wall's height is typically about 1.2m (4′) as shown, but whatever the height, the 350mm (14″) top width and batter of 50mm per 300mm (2″ per foot) are maintained as constants.

As well as fully dressed boundary walls such as that shown above, the Dunecht area has many rough rubble walls which appear at first glance to be unconsidered heaps of boulders until one examines the care with which individual stones are placed. A few miles away to the north and west, the Cluny style takes over. This features low walls of small stones backed by post-and-wire fences. Still farther west, near Grantown-on-Spey, Morayshire, the dykes have a mixture of large and small stones in the courses and are topped by rough upright boulders.

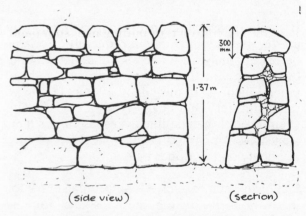

GRANTOWN-ON-SPEY RUBBLE DYKE

Whatever the local variation, these walls often require considerable work with the hammer and stone drill. More skill and patience are required to split granite, even roughly, than are demanded by most other stones (p58).

Moving to the far northeast of Scotland, one finds a very different type of wall – the Caithness Flag fence. Caithness Flags are a particularly interesting type of Old Red Sandstone, impregnated in many places, according to Hawkes (1951, p113) with bitumen from the compressed bodies of vast numbers of fish imbedded in them. The bitumen cements the finely laminated sandy particles and makes these stones exceptionally durable when used as pavings and stair treads. The Caithness fences are of flags placed upright and stapled together with metal clips set into the tops of adjacent stones. As in other districts where upright slabs are used, these walls are often backed by post-and-wire fences to increase their effective height.

Before leaving Scotland, we should mention that many of the dykes here seem to have accumulated a pointing of mortar, perhaps during repairs which may have been carried out years after their original construction. Many dykes, not only in Caithness, have a fence placed just behind the wall or built into the coping (see p103). Certain other features, such as a second row of topstones above the main coping, may be part of the original Galloway-dyke design or may be evidence of inadequate initial construction later corrected. Some dykes were originally built with inferior material. Prevost (1957, pp94, 100–1) documents oak throughbands used in dykes in Upper Annandale, Dumfriesshire and describes a method of coping dykes with sod tops in which two layers of tough stone-free turf are laid along the dyke, grass side together, to form a cover after which a layer of slightly smaller sods is laid at right angles across the cover to form the top. According to Wood (1973, p210), turf-topped dykes are still common in Selkirk and Roxburgh. Prevost also describes the practice, deceitful if in breach of contract, of putting in a 'split band' or 'false band', consisting of two stones laid alongside each other across the centre of the double, in place of the regulation throughband. He says that dykes were often changed in rebuilding, either lowered in height or 'thinned' to make them taller (another sharp practice if unacknowledged to the landowner). Given these facts, it is perhaps not surprising that some dykes have had to have later additions.

IRELAND

Evans (1957, p110) characterises Irish walls as untidy and cyclopean, mainly of rough glacial boulders and 'lacking the precision of those of north England or the Cotswold country'. This may be due to the absence of easily-shaped material (eg Jurassic limestones) as well as to the glacial drift covering so much of the country. Although a few walls or 'ditches', as all dykes or raised banks are termed in Ireland, are of Iron Age origin, most are from the comparatively recent enclosures of the 18th and early 19th centuries (Evans, 1957, p105). Throughout the lowland farming country, the hedged ditch

is most common, sometimes with a 'sheugh' or open drain running alongside it.

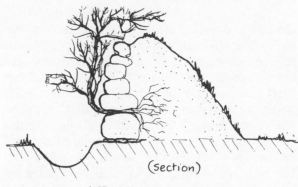

(Section)

HEDGED DITCH

Throughout the south and central part of the country dry stone ditches, where they occur, are usually built with far less batter and far more stones than their Scottish counterparts, according to Rainsford-Hannay (1972, p84), who goes on to list their typical dimensions as 1.8m (6') high and 1.2m (4') wide at the base. Throughstones are scarce but are sometimes used and the coping may be of mortar, sod, or small stones placed rather haphazardly on top. He relates that a County Galway enclosure contract of a century and a half ago specifies that the wall is to be 900mm (3') across at the base and 500mm (1'8") wide at a top height of 1.7m (5'9"); the wall has no foundation but throughs are used and it is coped with two tiers of sods.

In the west of County Clare and Galway, especially in the Burren district with its tiny fields and its outcrops of Carboniferous Limestone, single-thickness walls are built which closely resemble the Galloway single dyke in style and function. As in Scotland, sheep are said not to attempt to climb these unsteady-looking structures through which light can be seen. Evans (1957, p105) says these walls are typical also around fields on stony moraines and drift-boulder hillsides. In east Galway the limestone ditches are built double to a height of about 600mm (2') carefully levelled off and finished with a lace-work of single boulders to a total height of 1.2–1.5m (4–5'). It would seem that this similarity between Galway and Galloway walls may not be incidental and that the Irish version 'may well have been introduced by improving landlords or their agents' (Evans, 1957, p108). It would be interesting to know if other similar forms, such as the Irish hedged ditch and the Scottish Galloway hedge, are also directly related in origin. Many Irish dry walls are coped or even faced with mortar or cement. Significantly, the Irish language has no word for dry stone waller: wallers are always referred to as 'masons' according to Rainsford-Hannay

(1972, p85). These acts may further indicate the relatively recent importation of this craft into most parts of the country.

On Raithlin Island off the coast of Antrim, the idea of the unsteady-looking wall has been taken to a literal extreme. The ditches are low and loosely piled, and Evans (1957, p108) relates that he was told 'that animals give them a wide berth once having learnt that they collapse almost at a touch'. At the other extreme are the 3m (10') high demesne walls running for miles around the big estates which, according to Evans, are 'famine walls' built by destitute labourers in return for a pittance from the landowner.

Londonderry has examples of ancient head-walls, built to separate early farm enclosures from the rough outfields. These are known locally as 'Danish fences' and consist of irregularly piled stone slabs with standing stones set at intervals. Similar walls and walls with many stones set vertically or diagonally are found elsewhere in Ulster and Munster. Often only the standing stones remain today, buried in the peat which has overwhelmed the ancient fields (Evans, 1957, p106). Elsewhere in Ireland there are walls of almost inderterminate age – the wide granite accretion or clearance walls of the Mourne Mountains, for instance, which closely resemble those of the Lake District and Aberdeenshire (p25), and the walls of the Aran Islands shown below.

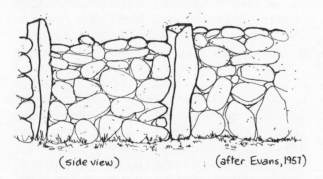

(side view)   (after Evans, 1957)

The 'phantom gates' of the Aran walls must be dismantled and taken down every time cattle are herded through a field, and we have been told of small grazing plots four fields in from the road. The reason for this laborious design, says Evans (1957, p105), is less the lack of wood and metal than the need to keep wind from getting into the fields. He reports that at one time this construction was also used in Connemara and County Clare.

Irish walls generally lack stiles because there are very few footpaths among the tiny fields while the narrow wall-lined lanes are plentiful. Short-cuts are seldom worthwhile in these con-

ditions. The acreage under stone is very great in some areas: according to Evans (1957, p112) fully one quarter of the land may be taken up with stone ditches.

Walls in History

Fascinating as it might be, this is not the place to outline the history of dry stone buildings or fortifications. We must pass by the gallery graves of the West, the stone circles and avenues of Salisbury Plain and the massive monuments of Hadrian's Wall; the beehive huts and chapels of the Dingle Peninsula on the southwest of Ireland and the black houses of Scotland's western isles; the village of Skara Brae in the Orkneys with its 3600 year old built-in dry stone furniture and the magnificent Iron Age brochs with ramparts thick enough to take a spiral ramp within them and to withstand any attack. We must restrict this history to the small walls, the field boundaries and enclosures built by farmers, husbandmen and labourers, the walls which are after all such an important identifying feature of the countryside which they traverse.

The walling-in of the rocky uplands of Britain began well back in prehistory, during the period when a nomadic pastoral and hunting life gradually gave way to settled farming. No precise dates can be assigned to this early agricultural revolution but it left a permanent if faint mark on the land in the form of stone circles and surrounding irregular patchwork of ditches and dykes which is the trademark of the 'Celtic' field system. In this simple non-rotational approach the 'infield' was enclosed, cultivated and manured while the 'outfield' or waste beyond was used for rough grazing. These early settlements were concentrated on the drier terraces and hillsides where woods and scrublands were most easily cleared – they now remain, often far above the present limits of cultivation, as evidence of a milder climate. In Ireland the earliest traces of walled fields have been discovered incorporated into megalithic tombs of late Neolithic age (Evans, 1957, p107). Here the pattern of small, apparently random-shaped fields survived the demise in the early 19th century of the transhumance or 'rundale' system and may still be found around the scattered farmsteads which replaced the old 'clachans' or tribal hamlets. The 'Danish fences' and 'Danish forts' which have been found in the peat of Ulster and Munster are not of military origin, according to Evans (1957, p106) but are the remains of Iron Age 'cashels' (circular farm enclosures bounded by dry stone walls) and associated 'raths' (earthen ditches). In Great Britain itself, similar settlements around the South Western moors, in the Lake District and on the limestone and gritstone terraces of the western Pennines are usually assigned to the Romano-British period, although occasional findings have been dated as far back as 2000 BC (Brooks, 1973, p14). Certainly it was around the time of the Roman invasions when fairly cohesive tribal federations developed, capable of erecting extensive fortifications and defensive earthworks. Sometimes these were later reused as boundaries: an example may be seen still standing west of Little Stainforth in Ribblesdale, North Yorkshire (OS grid ref: SD799675).

This wall is very massive, about 1.5m (5′) high and equally wide at the base with little taper. It uses large boulders of weathered limestone and has no throughs.

The next main period of wall building began in the early Middle Ages and continued, slowly and with many changes of pace depending on the economic conditions of the time, into the post-medieval period. It has been traced most thoroughly in Yorkshire where it is associated with the Anglo-Saxon and Scandinavian settlements of the 6th century AD onward (Raistrick, 1966, p6). It was then that the open-field system so characteristic of medieval English agriculture really developed. Typically, Anglo-Danish settlements, whether clustered villages or scattered homesteads, divided their holdings into three sections. On the fertile, flat and seasonally flooded bottomlands the 'leys' or 'ings' were located. These water meadows were set off from drier ground by a permanent ditch and fence, hedge or dry stone wall. Beyond this were the two or three common fields, similarly fenced off from each other and from the common pasture or waste which extended up the moors to the borders of the next settlement. Neither the meadows nor the common fields were subdivided except perhaps by boundary stones. These marked the individual farmer's scattered share-

holdings which, at least in theory, were re-allocated each year so that everyone had a chance of temporarily using the best portions. The common fields were quite large, often about 280 hectares (70 acres) at first, although they were later subdivided into smaller commonly held units (Brooks, 1973, p15). Where the medieval walls remain, they are of huge clearance boulders with little coursing of the stones and no throughs or topstones, but with some taper. They follow irregular alignments, in response to immovable obstacles or the waller's whim.

Although open-field walls can still be traced in some of the Yorkshire Dales villages, notably Linton in Wharfedale, the total impact of these enclosures was fairly small. Most of the land remained as waste, outside the bounds, although from the 12th century onward grazing disputes led in a few cases to the erection of fences between large holdings. These moorland walls or ditches are seldom traceable today but they remain among the earliest fences for which written documents are available (p27). According to Raistrick (1966, p7) some of the monasteries which held vast sheep grazing already favoured at this time the enclosure of small fields by stone walls to prevent sheep straying. But this was not the common practice of the period.

Meanwhile in the 'Celtic fringe', the older infield–outfield system persisted even where the earlier settlements were abandoned. In the granite areas of Cornwall and Devon, in parts of Wales and Scotland and through much of Ireland the story is one of continued nibbling away at the open land. Tiny garden-like plots fenced by massive clearance walls surrounded each farmstead, but these islands of cultivation remained virtually swamped in the vast expanse of open moor.

The next definable walling period, which particularly affected the Pennines region, started in the 14th and 15th centuries and continued until the 18th. It was at its height in the Elizabethan period when cottagers and householders for the first time were legally permitted to enclose small 'crofts' or private holdings. The fertility of the arable land was nearly exhausted by this period. To revitalize the land, it was necessary for individual householders to use their own stock to manure and improve their holdings. Crofts were small, about 0.2 hectare (half an acre) on average, with four or five scattered crofts held by each house. Crofts were walled by the individuals concerned using stone quarried or cleared from the common waste. Although the walls were still squat and poorly coursed, their lines were sometimes marked out by plough teams and so were rather more regular than the older piecemeal enclosures. By the 16th century also, attempts were being made to breed improved types of sheep for their wool and parts of the outlying wastes were enclosed to make this work easier. Despite this activity, Raistrick (1966, p7) indicates that the Elizabethan enclosures in the North were restricted to the vicinity of the villages, unlike the more extensive fencing which took place at this time in the South and Midlands. In the Pennines this period brought the completion of that 'maze of small enclosures, crofts and tiny fields, with scarcely a straight wall among them' which still surrounds many Dales villages (Raistrick, 1966, p6).

Already in Tudor and Elizabethan times population pressures were forcing some men to move into the waste and take up various types of piecework: walling, thatching, digging and stone getting. This, along with the enclosures and the consolidation of common fields into more cohesive individually owned strips, signalled the breakdown of the old openfield system. The population continued to grow in the 17th and 18th centuries. So did the cloth trade and, in certain areas, ironstone and coal mining industries. A phenomenon of this early industrial period were the 'intakes', rectangular fields from 0.4–1.2 hectares (1 to 3 acres) in extent, located beyond the old common fields on the moor sides. The land so enclosed could not be cropped but after liming and draining it would support a few sheep. These intakes provided the mining and textile labourers who farmed them with a source of protein as well as with the outdoor work which their employers considered beneficial (Brooks, 1973, p18).

This period also saw many far more extensive enclosures, which outlined the principal pastures of the community (often several hundred acres in extent) and divided adjoining townships from one another. They were made by common consent and involved all the shareholders in the construction and, frequently, the repair of the walls. Usually a shepherd was paid to tend the pastures and sometimes he had the duty of repairing walls and gates. Outside wallers or masons were seldom required, either for building or for maintenance. About 1780 the situation changed drastically. From this time, enclosures were promoted by large landowners or one or two private individuals in each area for their own benefit. These people had the means and the influence to engineer private Acts of Parliament which effectively stripped the smaller farmers of their common rights. Each Act appointed commissioners to survey the area in

question and to allot portions to every claimant, along with proportional responsibility for fencing the holdings. Since the set limit for walling the bounds was only a year or two, the specifications were very exacting and the length required was often many miles, the commissioners had to hire wallers or men free from the land to do the work. Only the wealthiest parties could pay for this labour; the others had to forfeit their shares to the commissioners. As Raistrick (1966, p11) concludes:

> 'The enclosures were a tragedy for the small man; he lost his right of pasturage on the common, lost his bit of land, and was compelled to become a wage labourer in a time of falling wages and rising cost of living. It secured the enslavement of the labouring classes.'

In 1801 the situation was further rationalised by the passing of a general consolidating Act of Parliament and by 1820 most of the work was done. The old common fields had been subdivided into small straight-walled rectangular plots of about 12 hectares (8 acres) or more in size (Raistrick, 1966, p11). There is no need here to list examples of the various specifications for these walls. Some indication of their dimensions is given on page 62. Visually they are unmistakable, with their precisely placed throughs and topstones, uniform batter and unvarying height, especially where they run for miles across the open moors. These walls were planned by city surveyors and built by professionals who often worked in gangs all through the clement months to finish the job. Although one often hears that Napoleonic prisoners of war built the Pennine walls, Raistrick (1966, p31) says that this is untrue. Parts of Dartmoor were, he adds, walled in this way and the tale may have been carried north by the Devon and Cornish miners who found work in Yorkshire later in the 19th century.

So far we have looked mainly at the Pennines enclosures. What is the story elsewhere? As CPRE (1975, p8) points out, taking the country as a whole, much more land was in its 'modern' form before the Parliamentary Enclosure Acts than is commonly thought. In the Midlands, perhaps the heart of the open-field system, at least 30% of the land was fenced by 1700, while in many counties including Kent, Sussex, Devon, Herefordshire, Worcestershire, Cheshire, Lancashire, Staffordshire, Northumberland, Durham, Suffolk and Essex the open-field system had never had a strong hold and piecemeal enclosures, often direct from the forest or waste, had taken place more or less continuously from the 12th century onward. This process was largely complete by 1800. In Northumberland, for example, Rainsford-

Hannay (1972, p24) says that only 2% of the land came under the Enclosure Acts. Similarly, in the South West and much of Wales the old Celtic field system had evolved gradually into one of separate farmsteads surrounded by small fields with large areas remaining as common moorland. Where fields in these regions are bordered by live hedges, botanical dating procedures usually put the enclosure at four to five centuries old and frequently much older. Where the fields are walled, dates cannot usually be assigned but the pattern often indicates ancient enclosures which sometimes still preserve what seems to be their original form, as for example at Zennor near Land's End (p17). In Wales, walling remained a matter for the small farmer even after he became tenant to an absentee landlord. Evidence given at Pwllheli, Caernarvenshire (now Gwynnedd), by a Mr Humphreys of Criccieth and summarised in the 'First Report of the Royal Commission on Land in Wales and Monmouthshire' (HMSO, 1894, p714), indicates that 'the stone walls in the neighbourhood were generally built by the tenant, except near the mountains, where sometimes the walls were long ones, and these were built by the landlord'. The Commission noted many complaints from tenants that landlords 'exhausted' the compensation for their work over a period of only fourteen or fifteen years whereas the walls were as good as new for twenty or thirty years or more.

Rainsford-Hannay (1972, p23) stakes a Scottish claim for the first 'comprehensive' enclosure walling. This, he says, occurred after the passing of an early Enclosure Act about 1710 and was organised by the McKies of Palgown in the west of Kircudbrightshire. The two brothers leased out pieces of land free to people who would move to them in the spring, set up huts reminiscent of the Highlanders' sheilings, work their plots and in return build enclosure walls. Within a year or two many miles of dykes had been raised, increasing the value of the land four times. This example was quickly followed, but not without opposition. In 1723 and 1724, bands of men and women known as 'Levellers' roamed the newly enclosed countryside, throwing down the dykes and even maiming and houghing the enclosed cattle (Prevost, 1957, p85). The authorities' response was to execute the ringleaders, and thereafter the enclosures proceeded virtually unhindered.

Most Scottish dykes were built according to strict and fairly standard specifications, the best and tallest being the march dykes which bounded the great estates, especially those built after about 1840 which took advantage of skills learned in earlier work. Occasionally, however, special problems resulted in unusual walls. Of special interest are the Monymusk clearance or 'consumption' dykes northwest of Aberdeen. Rainsford-Hannay (1972, pp68–72) traces their development in some detail, from the first improvements of the land in 1719 through the contracts of 1736 and 1741 which indicate that the tenant, William Denny of Dykehead, was to wall a certain area to a height of one ell, or 940mm (3'1"), using stones 'taken from within, as long as there are any, both great and small' and 'not to leave a stone in the enclosure, which three men cannot roll or four men carry in a hand barrow'. The first contract specified a coping of 'faile' or peat sods, but the later contract omitted this, probably because it robbed the land of important topsoil, and the dyke remained uncoped. Instead, Denny was paid to bring the wall up to a height of 1.4m (4'7½") as and when he wished, using stones which 'arose' after ploughing. Several other dykes were built at Monymusk to use up the immense number of stones encountered, the biggest by far being the Kingswell West Dyke. this structure 8.2m (27') wide at the top, 1.8m (6') high and 457m (500 yards) long. As an unknown Aberdonian enthused (quoted in full in Rainsford-Hannay, 1957, pp71–2), the dyke appears as:

'a monster mound,
Matching in size our long broad granite
* pier,*
Reminding us of Babylon's great walls,
For all along the middle of the top
The broader flatter stones designedly
Are laid to form a way quite passable
For gentle lady or fine gentleman.'

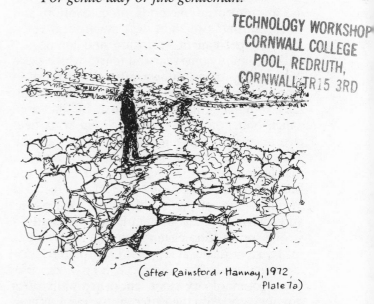

(after Rainsford-Hannay, 1972, Plate 7a)

Similar but slightly smaller clearance walls can be found in the Lake District, most notably at Wasdale Head. Here and elsewhere in Lakeland, Rollinson (1972, pp13–16) reports additional signs of walls which have been built primarily to clear the land of surplus stones, including the filling up and rounding off of corners and the piling up of 'clearance cairns' in the middle of fields.

Lake District enclosures were rather late on the whole. Until the Union of the Crowns in 1603, raids across the border from Scotland kept the area so insecure that the communal co-arration system of agriculture was long continued. Rollinson (1972, p23) quotes the description of this system by the local historian Thomas West, writing in 1744:

> '. . . the arable land being mixed (ie unenclosed) . . . several tenants united in equipping a plough, the absence of the fourth man was no prejudice to the cultivation of his land, which was committed to the care of three.'

Communal co-arration allowed tenants to leave the land at short notice for temporary military service. After the cessation of border troubles many of the common township fields were enclosed and improved by private agreement, but throughout the Cumbrian area farming remained generally backward compared to much of the country. Even as late as 1794, Rollinson (1972, p3) reports that three quarters of Westmorland was said to be waste or common. Most Lakeland walls were built after the Parliamentary Enclosure Act of 1801 and on through the 19th century.

Most Irish walls are also fairly recent, as mentioned earlier in this chapter. Evans (1957, p109) says that from the mid-18th century enclosure was advocated by land reformers to allow the use of improved methods of cultivation and stock rearing. But there was much local resistance to permanent enclosure and temporary ditches, mainly one-year sod fences which were deliberately thrown down after the harvest so that they could decay and replenish the soil, long remained throughout much of that area which had not been early enclosed with field clearance walls. It might be thought that the ancient megaliths would have suffered early at the hands of wallers. This occurred in the Mourne Mountains during the 19th century, but in other parts of the island, except near towns and quarries, there was until quite recently a strong superstition against splitting large stones for reuse or disposal (Evans, 1957, p107).

The history of dry stone enclosure walls does not quite end with the 19th century, even though little land remained to be subdivided after this period. Locally, as in some of the Yorkshire Dales, mining activities brought temporary bursts of walling in the affected areas. The recent efforts of county councils to rebuild walls after road widening is mentioned at the beginning of this chapter. During the depression in the 1930's this was done on quite a large scale, at least in the West Riding of Yorkshire, to make work for the unemployed (Brooks, 1973, p20). The Ministry of Agriculture, Fisheries and Food has employed wallers in conjunction with open-cast coal mine rehabilitation and the National Parks have provided work for craftsmen in recent years. Nevertheless, once the Parliamentary enclosure walls were up and finished there was little need for more than a very few full-time workers supplemented by part-time farm wallers able to repair the gaps. So it can be said with reasonable accuracy that the walled landscape of upland Britain is a monument to centuries of patient labour which stood complete, but for its finishing touches, over a century ago.

Wall Dating

If we understand a wall's geological makeup and design we can make an intelligent guess as to its history, the part it has played in the agricultural life of the country. But to become more certain of the picture we must learn the wall's date of construction. But walls are mute. They have no date stones. How can their age be assessed? (By age we mean the time since its original building, disregarding repairs and reconstructions which have not changed the basic design. A wall may be very ancient even if all its stones have just recently been replaced.)

Walls do in fact very occasionally contain hidden clues from the builders themselves, either their names and the date in a bottle or, in the case of some ancient walls, bits of debris or talismans inserted into the base of the wall. Dr Francis Turk suggests that many of these are token sacrifices made to the earth gods for disturbing the earth and putting weight on it, a practice which he believes to have been fairly widespread both in Cornwall and in South Wales at least until Tudor times. Other inclusions may mark unusual events. The most extraordinary item he has recovered is a 17th or 18th century hunting horn from a wall at Treswithian, Camborne, Cornwall, which he thinks marks the site of a fatal hunting accident in the late 18th century. Such items, of course, indicate a minimum but not a maximum age since they may have been placed during subsequent repairs rather than original construction. But usually the stones themselves are all there is to go on, with whatever written records are available for the area.

A combined approach of documentation plus observation is essential in the historical study of walls. There is, unfortunately, no simple rule of thumb by which you can date them as there is with hedges. Possibly the growth rates of lichens could be used to suggest an age for exposed faces, as they have already in the case of certain gravestones and also moraines. But it would have to be certain that the faces in question were fresh when the wall was built, ie that the stone was quarried and not derived from land clearance. Expert knowledge would be required as to the effects of the local microclimate, exposures and air pollution on the growth of the lichens. Even then, it is likely that rebuilding and restoration would mean that the largest lichens might not be found on the walls of earliest origin. In some cases wall plants might provide clues where they are remnants of interesting rare or local species which were more abundant prior to changes in ground cover, land use or climate, although village walls are likely to have a flora which is partly the product of gardeners who add or remove plants according to preference. D E Allen, in 'Hedges and Local History' (Standing Conference for Local History. National Council of Social Service, 1971, pp30–6), suggests that sod banks and hedgerows may be datable by the variety of bramble species growing on them; for the botanically meticulous observer this might prove a fruitful line of research. On the whole, however, the botanical approach seems of limited use, at least until a great deal of further preliminary work has been done.

Dr E M Yates, University of London King's College, says that a few Saxon land charters, eg Grundy, are of assistance in wall dating. Other than these, the oldest documents referring to walls are medieval monastic cartularies (property charters). These occasionally note boundary disputes which resulted in the erection of some sort of barrier, although the type of fence is seldom specified. Rollinson (1972, p18) says that the Rydale fence of 1277 is one of the earliest documented, but that it was probably a ditch and bank rather than a dry stone wall. Similarly, the Furness Abbey enclosures of the late 13th century in the Esk Valley headland consisted of a bank, probably topped by a wattle fence, since the aim was to restrict the movement of sheep but not of deer and fawns. The bank in this case can still be traced and it provides a convenient causeway for walkers through this boggy area. Some of the early Pennine enclosures can be located from other monastic records of about the same period. Later documents include a number of important 16th century maps, more recent estate deeds and maps, tithe maps from the 1840's, Parliamentary enclosure surveys and awards and the first Ordnance Survey maps. The 18th and 19th century maps are especially valuable, not only because in many cases they are accurate enough to pinpoint existing walls, but also because they sometimes mark out what were then considered 'ancient enclosures' which are probably of Elizabethan date or earlier (Rollinson, 1962, p21). The pursuit and interpretation of these documents is one of the special passions of the dedicated local historian. Hoskins (1967, especially pp117–35) provides an excellent introduction.

Walls which can be dated and tracked down from the written evidence may reveal general characteristics of the walls of their period. Such 'type' walls can then be used to evaluate others for which no documents exist. Although written documents are essential to decide exactly when the different phases of enclosure took place in any given area, the relative age of walls within a district can often be assessed purely from the shape and pattern of the walls themselves:

a In the 'Celtic fringe' of western Britain and Ireland the oldest walls are likely to be clearance walls forming small fields around farmsteads. In areas where the Anglo-Danish open-field system predominated, the oldest walls are those which separate the wet meadows from the common fields and the common fields from the original wasteland, forming enclosures from a few dozen acres up to several hundred acres in extent. In any case a continuous wall, unbroken except for gates, is older than all the walls which come to a head against it.

b The oldest walls usually use unsorted clearance boulders, sometimes including very large ones. There is little distinct coursing and no throughs or topstones. These walls are more pyramidal in section and in general thicker than later walls built of the same type of stone. Crawford (1936, p162) maintains that in the South West 'collapsed' walls, consisting of huge grounders between a 'confused and massive pile of collapsing material', are likely to be very ancient. He also asserts that the practice of placing stones in up-and-down instead of horizontal courses is a modern (but undated) innovation in the region.

c The oldest walls are haphazardly aligned and often change direction to take in large boulders or to avoid streams or other obstacles. Sections between obstacles tend to be curved, not straight. Old walls may have rounded or enlarged corners, like swollen joints, indicating accretion from field clearance over many years. (Note though that 'consumption dykes' were in some cases built to order during the Enclosure Era, as described on page 25.)

d Walls closer to a village or farmstead, or to habitation sites which are now abandoned, are likely to be older than walls farther away from the habitation. An exception are the few medieval boundary walls built by monasteries to restrict the movement of sheep, and these, unless they have been since rebuilt, are likely to stand out from later enclosure walls by their much cruder style.

e Walls built to strict specifications, unvarying over long distances and showing a consistency of style and craftsmanship, were probably built after 1750 as a result of a Parliamentary Enclosure Act. Throughstones were not used in walls until the 18th century, slate throughs, at least in Yorkshire, not until the 19th. Dressed stone was used by the Romans but then not again until the 17th century (Brooks, 1973, p123). The locked top was invented in 1753 in Kircudbrightshire (Rainsford-Hannay, 1972, p45) and spread gradually through Scotland and into northern England. Some innovations were later than the main enclosure period: Brooks (1973, p125) reports that the dressed, half-rounded topstones common along Yorkshire roadside walls seem to indicate a Victorian fancy that dates to no more than a 150 years ago, although it is possible that the walls themselves may be older than their copings.

f Occasionally the shape of the field bounded by a wall may reveal its relative age. Medieval 'reversed S' field strips are thought invariably to predate the year 1400, as discussed further in 'Hedging' (BTCV, 1975, p13). Walls dividing such fields were clearly constructed at some later date. Examples from the 16th century can be seen between Grassington and Hebden in upper Wharfedale. Elsewhere on the limestone of the Craven district of North Yorkshire there are 18th century walls built along the edges of lynchets (ploughed terraces) which may date from Anglian times. Walls forming L-shaped enclosures are likely to be from the 18th century too. Some of these were built on the lower hillsides to enable more fields to adjoin a stream for watering cattle (Brooks, 1973, p124), although Dr Francis Turk says that in Cornwall, where they occur occasionally, L-shaped fields are mainly a feature of higher ground. In all these cases, the field shape is more easily seen from an Ordnance Survey 6″ map than from the ground, although finds should be checked out in the field once located on a map.

g Sometimes the material of which the wall is built may be correlated with datable industrial, quarrying or mining activity. Often this is approximate and shows the period before which the wall is unlikely to have been in existence. For example, the slate fences of North Wales are associated with 19th century mining (Wood, 1973, p211). Throughs and other stylistic features have been mentioned under point **e**. Railway ties used as cripple holes suggest that a wall was built since the coming of trains to a particular area, the date of which can be checked against the documents. In Yorkshire, for example, such a wall would have been built in the 1840's in the south, a few years later north of Leeds and in the 1870's in the Craven area (Brooks, 1973, p122). Another example is provided by the sheep smoot built under the embankment of the reconstructed Ffestiniog Railway in North Wales (OS grid ref: SH679425), which could not have been built earlier than the advent of reinforced concrete pipe. In fact, the work was done in 1971 or 2. Whenever such clues are used, they must be placed within the total picture given by the wall as a whole, since they may simply represent later additions or repairs to an older wall.

h Occasionally, extraneous objects found within a wall may indicate a date by which it had been built. A 17th or 18th century hunting horn has been mentioned at the beginning of this section. The bowls of broken clay pipes are come across fairly frequently and these can usually be dated with some exactitude.

Wall dating is most productive when it combines a detailed field knowledge with the documentary research of the local historian. Raistrick (1966) has done this brilliantly for the village of Linton in Wharfedale. Volunteers should be able to help in such studies provided they coordinate with someone who can interpret their finds in the light of written evidence. The Cornish hedge survey discussed on page 108, although designed primarily to provide natural history data, could well be used as the basis for historical studies also. Such schemes, if adapted for use on dry stone walls, might provide a surprising amount of new information when combined with detailed notes of finds made during repair work.

2 Dry Stone Walls and Conservation

The Loss of Walls and Banks

Like hedgerows, dry stone walls and earth banks have come to seem something of a liability to many people charged with managing the land. They get in the way. They must be maintained. Building them new is usually out of the question due to costs. So the walls in many areas are allowed to tumble down or are carted away for landfill or are stitched together haphazardly with barbed wire and bedsteads to carry on a little longer.

No figures seem to be available on the mileage of walls destroyed or left derelict. Certainly they are less vulnerable than living hedges, which can be cut to the ground, burned or bulldozed out of existence without much trouble. And in some ways their loss is less significant since their wildlife habitat value is more restricted. Yet the total mileage which walls occupy must be immense. Margaret Brooks (1973, p2) estimates about 77,000km (48,000 miles) in the old West Riding of Yorkshire alone and the figure must be proportionately higher for the small earth-banked fields of the South West. The weight of these fences is even more staggering. Rainstrick's (1966, p27) estimate of 1.6 tonnes per metre ($1\frac{3}{4}$ tons of stone per yard of wall) suggests about 150,760,000 tonnes (147,800,000 tons) of rock in the West Riding walls, every stone lifted by hand. So walls cannot be dismissed lightly, whatever one thinks of their inherent aesthetic or conservation values.

Walls are left derelict or pulled down for many of the same reasons that contribute to the demise of hedgerows. These include the mechanisation of agriculture, the decline of the rural work force and rising wages, shifts in farming patterns so that many fields once under permanent pasture now serve the changing demands of ley management, which rotates pasture and arable use, and the miscellaneous taking of land for urban development, roads and other non-agricultural uses. These problems are discussed more fully in *Hedging* (BTCV, 1975). Here it is enough to point out that for walls it is the increasing cost and scarcity of labour that accounts for most of the decay, coupled with the fact that many walls are no longer required or, once derelict, can be replaced relatively cheaply by fences. These are problems faced not only by the individual farmer and landowner but also by parish, district and county councils that wish to preserve the traditional walls of roadsides and boundaries. But ultimately it is the farmer who is most concerned. Most walls were built to serve his needs and their maintenance is a responsibility bequeathed to him by earlier generations.

The Farmers' Viewpoint

Walls are of real use to the farmer only where the land is in pasture. Where the fields are ploughed there is little economic reason to maintain dry stone walls or earth banks except in areas such as parts of Cornwall where soil blow might otherwise be a problem. However, existing walls may be very costly to dismantle and cart away so it may be easier and cheaper to maintain them than to pull them down and put up fences.

WALLS VERSUS BANKS AND HEDGES

Before turning to a comparison of dry stone walls and stockproof fences it is worth noting briefly the advantages and disadvantages of walls relative to the other traditional farm barriers: earth banks and living hedges. These share many of the same advantages: shade and shelter; permanence; wildlife habitat and visual amenity. They also share some disadvantages: high initial cost, comparative inflexibility and greater taking of land. Hedges and banks provide some benefits which walls cannot. For example, a living hedge which is allowed to grow freely for a few years increases in shelter and wildlife value and also supplies useful by-products such as fruit and berries, faggots and various coppice and timber products. This is also true of earth banks crowned by live hedges, although banks can seldom support large trees without being damaged. And ditches, which are often dug to provide material for banks, help to drain the adjacent land. On the other hand, living hedges or hedge-topped banks may rob the field edges of nourishment, increase crop pests and diseases and harbour 'vermin', although these problems are often over-stated (see *Hedging*, BTCV, 1975, for a detailed comparison of hedges and turf-faced banks with post-and-wire fences). In addition, hedgerow maintenance costs are high compared to both fences and drystone walls.

Walls have several points in their favour over banks and hedges:

a They take up the least land. Walls usually vary from 600–900mm (2–3′) wide at the base depending on the type of stone. Hedges, even if trimmed, are usually at least 900mm (3′) wide, while earth banks are about as wide as they are tall, 1.5–1.8m (5–6′) being average.

b They use up unwanted field stones but do not take or deplete valuable topsoil as do banks and hedges.

c They may be more flexible in use than banks or hedges if provided with suitable openings (p11).

d They are stockproof when built, whereas hedges must be fenced off for several years against grazing and trampling and banks should be protected for some months until they become consolidated. Turf-faced banks should be permanently fenced from cattle.

e They require less maintenance than banks or hedges, except where particularly subject to damage as discussed on page 33. They are relatively unaffected by burning, atmospheric pollution, road salt and other special perils of turfed banks and living hedges.

Walls have three main disadvantages compared to banks and hedges:

a They are likely to prove more costly to establish, in terms of labour if not materials.

b Their upkeep requires a certain amount of skill, probably more than is needed for the routine maintenance of banks and hedges, although turfing and hedge laying are highly skilled jobs which must be done from time to time if banks and hedges are to remain stockproof.

c In general, they have less wildlife value than do banks and hedges where these are allowed to grow up fairly freely. However in certain cases they may be very important for some types of plants and animals (p34).

In most cases the choice between fencing with a dry stone wall, an earth bank or a living hedge is based on considerations of local climate and soil conditions. Walls are most suited to barren uplands or placed where stones are so plentiful that field clearance is a priority. In these situations hedge shrubs may grow poorly if at all and there may be too little soil to squander on earth banks. Banks are advantageous where some stone is available but it is too little or too fragmented to make solid walls and where ditching for drainage is worthwhile and provides soil for the bank. Banks probably yield the most shelter for their height if, as Rainsford-Hannay (1972, p55) and some South Western hedgers claim, the shelter effect is enhanced by a gradual or concave batter. With a live hedge on top their shelter qualities are greater still. Hedges are most suitable where the climate is mild, the soils are good and stone is lacking. Hedges can also be grown and trimmed into the best possible shelterbelts in special circumstances such as around orchards, hop gardens and flower fields where they still take up fairly little space.

In certain districts combination-type fences have evolved, notably the Irish hedged ditch (p21) and the Galloway hedge (p19). Stone hedges topped with thorn, beech, gorse or brambles, so characteristic of much of the South West, similarly combine many of the advantages of all three traditional types of fencing. Elsewhere walls and hedges remain separate but they may exist side by side in the same landscape, each being used where local conditions are most favourable.

WALLS VERSUS FENCING

In most situations where dry stone walls occur, the only practical alternative is a stockproof post-and-wire fence. Walls and fences are compared in detail below and in the sections which follow.

Advantages of walls

a They provide shade and shelter for stock in all seasons.

b They provide a windbreak for crops and help prevent soil blow.

c They can be made stockproof against all livestock but goats.

d They use native material which is usually ready to hand and dispose of field stones which might otherwise interfere with ploughing and reduce the area of grazing or arable on both sides.

e They require few or no tools and equipment to build.

f They are durable. With a minimum of maintenance they can be kept stockproof indefinitely. Breaks which do occur are usually limited and, if left unattended, spread only gradually.

g They provide a valuable habitat for certain plants, insects, small mammals and other wildlife.

h They provide a visual amenity, giving character to the agricultural landscape even (or so many people would say) when in a neglected condition.

Disadvantages of walls

a They shade immediately adjacent crops.

b They cannot be easily moved.

c They may block the efficient operation of farm machinery.

d They are laborious to build and, if stone must be purchased, the materials and transport costs may be very high. (Costs may be offset to some extent by farm grants.)

e They are subject to damage from a variety of causes (see p33) some of which, however, affect fences equally.

Advantages of fences

a They allow sun to reach crops near the fence line.

b They take up little space.

c They can be moved if necessary.

d They have low maintenance costs.

Disadvantages of fences

a They provide no shade or shelter.

b They can injure stock if the animals try to force their way through.

c They require some specialist tools to build and may be very difficult to erect in hard stony ground.

d They can be difficult to maintain in a stockproof condition in some terrain and are more easily damaged or weakened by storms, falling branches etc than are walls.

e They need to be replaced periodically at a relatively high capital cost. (This may be offset to some extent by farm grants.)

SHADE AND SHELTER

A wall significantly affects the surrounding area with its shade, but only to a distance of one or two times its height, ie about 1.5–3.6m (5–12′). Crops are affected in the strip next to the wall, grass less so. In fact, grass grows earlier in the shelter of a sunny wall and may provide important spring grazing for sheep in otherwise harsh conditions. Walls running east–west cast less shade overall then those running north–south, but their north side is shaded most persistently. Shade can be important for livestock in hot weather and walls often provide the only place out of the sun on open uplands.

Walls provide year-round shelter for crops and stock. The best wind barriers are about 40% permeable (eg hedges through which movement can be seen but objects not seen distinctly). Permeable barriers filter and slow air currents and cushion the air which is forced over the top, while solid barriers produce eddies which may be more destructive than the unimpeded wind. Dry stone walls are more solid than the optimum but they are much more effective than mortared walls and provide the best possible windbreaks where hedge plants cannot thrive, especially in winter.

The shelter effect of any barrier is significant for a distance of about eight to twelve times its height to leeward, although slight effects may be felt even farther. As with hedges, walls provide the greatest shelter for their height when placed along the crests of hills or ridges and across valleys. The least benefit is obtained from walls at the foot of or part-way up slopes which face the prevailing wind, which in most cases blows from the southwest.

The actual benefit of shelter to crops and livestock is open to debate (see *Hedging*, BTCV, 1975). Although recent studies cast doubt on the importance of shelter for liveweight gain and food conversion rates of stock, hill farmers still feel strongly that 'shelter is half meat', especially in lambing season when newborn lambs snuggle to sunwarmed stones out of the spring gales. Shelter also would seem of obvious value in winter when snow drifts deep over the grass and hinders the movement of animals. Of course walls themselves may cause drifting. Margaret Brooks (1973, p27) passes on the story told by a waller from Grassington, North Yorkshire of some sheep which were completely overblown by snow in a sudden storm. Forty-nine days later they were found – alive. They had eaten every bit of herbage around them and some of their own wool and had breathed through the chinks in the wall behind which they sheltered. Walls also clearly make good windbreaks around gardens and buildings and they are unexcelled for protecting new tree plantations and shelterbelts in difficult conditions.

LAND TAKING AND MACHINE EFFICIENCY

Walls take up land which might otherwise be put into production. They may also get in the way of efficient use of land already open. This applies particularly to arable land but increasingly also to pasture which may be periodically sown and mown for hay and silage. These problems have been explored in some detail in *Hedging* (BTCV, 1975) and in *Hedges* by E Pollard, M D Hooper and N W Moore (Collins New Naturalist, 1974, p200). The main conclusion is that the optimum field size, in terms of increased acreage per amount of wall removed and increased machine efficiency, is reached at about 20 hectares (50 acres). Beyond this it is probably not worth removing existing barriers unless the field shapes are awkward and can be easily rationalised with a few boundary changes.

Walls are most often in the way in lowland areas where land use has changed from pasture to arable. But with new farming methods the limits of cultivation are being extended onto higher and more difficult terrain, putting walls at risk in previously untouched areas. The introduction of paddock grazing and zero grazing also requires that existing fields be opened up and redefined for more flexible use. Despite these developments, most walls are on lands which are still rather marginal. Here it is just not worth the expense of knocking the walls down and removing their stones even if they have been allowed to decay.

Unfortunately, the smallest fields and most difficult walls from the farmers' viewpoint are also likely to be those with the greatest historical and amenity interest, especially those surrounding old farmsteads and taking up valuable bottomland around the dales and more fertile moorland edges. The problem is well put by Archer (1972), reporting on the bulldozing of Iron Age stone hedges on the Land's End peninsula in Cornwall. It is situations like this which bring the conflict between improving farmers and preservationists, naturalists and archaeologists to a head. Farming innovations undoubtedly require changes in field use. But while farmers are forced to think in terms of the immediate return on investment and are conditioned by short-run trends and policies, the skeletons of ancient field systems, once destroyed, can never be pieced back together.

COSTS

The farmer's main argument for neglecting walls, or for choosing post-and-wire instead of dry stone when a new fence is required, is cost. But while a new dry stone wall represents an enormous capital outlay it may be expected to last many times longer than a wire fence with little or no maintenance in favourable situations. So its real cost when pro-rated or amortised over the years is less than might be expected.

We have had reports of walls varying from 50 to 250 years in age which are as good today as when they were built, with no maintenance except the replacement of occasional loose topstones. Even when a wall is tumbled down its rebuilding cost is less than that of a new wall because the foundations are in place and only a little if any new stone needs to be supplied. Any estimate of the life of a wall is rather arbitrary and depends on the stresses of the particular site, which are discussed under 'The cost of maintaining a wall' on page 33.

Any costing must be taken as a rough guide only, since the prices of labour and materials increase so fast that estimates are soon outdated. Where fences replace walls, the cost of bulldozing, hauling away and disposing of the stone should be accounted for although it is not possible to include this factor here.

The cost of a new dry stone wall

The cost of any new dry stone wall varies drastically depending on whether or not the stone is commercially supplied or is already near to hand and whether all aspects of the job are done on a paid contract basis. At one extreme, a wall built with available stone by the landowner himself in his spare time or by volunteers costs nothing but the time required. Semi-retired craftsmen often charge less than the full rate and we have even known of men who refused all pay other than frequent libations of beer or cider (whisky is suggested north of the border). Farmers who hire professional wallers can save a proportion of the costs by digging the foundation trenches and setting out the stones themselves. But to give meaningful comparisons here, it is assumed that wallers are paid the full going rate for the entire job. Figures are given by the yard because that is how most wallers quote their charges.

Before the First World War a waller made about 1/3 (about 6p) per yard and was expected to build at a rate of a rood (6 or 7 yards, depending on the stone) per 14 hours working day. By the Second World War the rate had risen to around 3/6 ($17\frac{1}{2}$p) per yard and further progress remained slight until quite recently.

Estimates in 1988 for labour charges varied from about £10 to £15 per square metre (£8.50 to £12 per square yard), including digging the foundation trench and laying the footings. There may be extra transport charges, where the wall is at a distant or inaccessible location.

The cost of purchased stone varies enormously depending on the type, quantity ordered, haulage distance and site accessibility. Stone from demolition sites can sometimes be had free or almost free, especially if your wall happens to be en route to the disposal site. During 1988, the cost of ordinary rubble (untrimmed) walling stone varied from £15.00 per ton, inclusive of haulage, to £18.00 per ton with haulage an extra £12.00 per ton.

Before embarking on a walling project it is wise to get a written quotation setting out exactly what is covered by way of work, materials, transport and so on.

The figures below may be taken as average in 1988 for a 1.4m (4'6") wall. This is the typical height for North of England and Scottish subdivision walls suitable for enclosing cattle and most breeds of sheep.

Item	£ per metre	(£ per yard)
Labour, inclusive of digging foundations, setting out and cleaning up	16.00	(14.50)
Stone and haulage	25.00	(23.00)
	41.00	(37.50)

In some parts of the country, especially where cattle but not sheep are kept, the walls are built slightly lower. For a metre length of 1.2m (4') high wall the costs, based on the above figures, are: labour £13.50; stone and haulage; £21.50; total £35.00.

Walls which enclose black-faced sheep must be built to a height of at least 1.6m (5'3"). For a metre length of wall to this height the costs are: labour, £18.00; stone and haulage, £28.50; total £46.50.

The cost of a stockproof wire fence

The costs of stockproof fencing have not risen as fast as those for walling in recent years, due to a number of factors. Increasing use is being made of high tensile wire and netting, which requires fewer posts than conventional mild steel fencing. This results not only in a saving on the cost of posts, but in much quicker erection times, and hence a lower labour charge per metre. Increased competition and imports of wire fencing supplies have also helped keep prices steady. There has been an increase in the use of both permanent and temporary electric fencing, which has low material and labour costs per metre.

The most common type of fencing against sheep is stock netting, usually used with one or two top strands of plain wire. Various heights and grades of netting are available. An average price in 1988 for a high tensile stock netting fence is £1.00 per metre for materials and 75p per metre for labour; total £1.75 per metre. A fence of medium grade mild steel (ie non-high tensile) netting is more expensive at about £1.50 per metre for materials and £1.00 per metre for labour; total £2.50 per metre.

Cattle fencing usually comprises two or three strands of mild steel plain or barbed wire, and costs about 80p per metre for materials and 75p per metre for labour; total £1.55 per metre.

Permanent electric fencing, proof against sheep and/or cattle according to specification, costs about 80p per metre for materials and 50p per metre for labour; total £1.30 per metre.

For full details on the specifications and costs of all types of stock fencing see 'Fencing' (Agate, 1986), another handbook in this series.

It will be seen from the above figures that dry stone walling is many times more expensive than any form of wire fencing. A properly erected fence of good quality materials should have a life of 15 to 20 years before it needs replacing, hence even if compared over 100 years, or replacing the fence five times, walling is still the more expensive option.

However, as detailed on page 30, the comparison between walls and fences is not limited to their initial costs, and there are many other factors to be taken into account.

The cost of maintaining a wall

No figures can be quoted for wall maintenance costs since in every case local factors determine the amount of maintenance required. This may vary from no maintenance, or virtually none, where the wall is on flat, stable ground away from roads and other disturbances, to complete rebuilding every 20–30 years where the wall is subject to vibration or is on an unstable slope. The type of stone used and the skillfulness of the original construction also affect the wall's durability. In any case, you can keep maintenance costs down by inspecting the wall occasionally and repairing any damage as soon as you see it. This is far better than waiting until gaps grow too big to be ignored.

Walls are subject to damage in a variety of ways. When estimating the maintenance which a wall may require over the years, you should evaluate the likelihood of damage from such sources as you can foresee. These include:

a Livestock pushing on or attempting to climb the wall. Sheep and cattle seldom initiate a break in a well-built wall but they quickly take advantage of it. Sheepdogs are sometimes guilty of walking along walls and knocking off topstones when they are guarding penned-up animals. Cattle and horses tend to rub on the topstones, especially when bored. Deer can jump walls up to 2.1m (7′) high and may knock off stones in the process.

b Animals burrowing or hunting around the wall. Small mammals do little damage although moles and rabbits may loosen footings as they tunnel. Foxes sometimes disrupt stones when digging out their prey, but people and dogs digging out rabbits are likely to disturb foundations much more.

c People vandalising the wall. Damage may be from pure thoughtlessness or carelessness, as when walkers unskillfully scale the wall, knock off topstones and neglect to put them back. Picknickers may use topstones for seats. Children love to push off stones and roll them downhill and they even dig under the walls to get to the other side (walls with cemented copes near housing estates are especially prone to this sort of attack). Motorists may borrow stones to help jack up their cars when changing tyres. They may also look aside as unusually shaped topstones find their way into the boot and subsequently into the rock garden back home – this is a real problem for roadside walls coped in decorative water-worn limestone. And occasionally walls are deliberately pulled apart for no apparent reason. In all cases, the chances of damage are directly proportional to the number of people who can easily approach the wall.

d Vibration from vehicles passing the wall. Many country lanes, really just paved-over cart tracks, have no proper foundations and now take far more traffic than ever anticipated. Where lorries use roads which are designed only for light traffic the walls may need frequent attention.

e Direct hits from vehicles. These are all the worse when vibration has already weakened the wall. At least the cost of repairs can be recovered where vehicles have comprehensive insurance.

f Trees disrupting the wall. Trees near the wall may push it out of line as they grow bigger and they can weaken the foundations when their root-plates shift in high winds. Large trees which fall on the wall can devastate considerable lengths at a time. Tactics to minimise problems with trees are discussed on page 84.

g Storms may damage a wall directly, if strong gusts hit it face on. This is especially likely in exposed places and with walls which are poorly coped or built of small, light stones.

h Flooding may destroy walls in stream valleys, unless they are adequately supplied with water smoots (p96). Perhaps such a flood occurs on average only once a century or so, but if it happens at the wrong time you may be the one who has to pick up the pieces.

i In exceptional winters, driven snow may pile up against walls and damage them through sheer weight. This is likely only on hillside walls in open moorland which have been built with a too-steep batter on their downhill sie.

j Frost can niggle away at a wall, causing it to settle unevenly and become increasingly unsteady. Well-built dry walls are self-draining and have nothing to fear from this source, but walls with mortared copings are especially prone to this problem (see p63).

k Air pollution may weaken exposed stonework, especially limestone. In time it may become so crumbly that the wall needs rebuilding. More often, pollution damage adds to other problems which are the major causes of the wall's decay.

The Wildlife Value of Walls

It might be thought that dry stone walls would present a forbidding face to wildlife, that in fact they might be almost barren of living creatures. This is not so. Although the range of plants and animals which make use of walls is fairly limited, walls have considerable habitat value for certain species and in particular localities. Stone-faced banks are even more valuable, particularly if surmounted by a thicket of living shrubs. Their importance then becomes similar to that of hedgerows, which is evaluated in *Hedging* (BTCV, 1975).

The ecological study of dry stone walls and stone-faced banks is still in its initial stages, and the generalisations which follow have been pooled from a number of written sources and from correspondence with specialists in the field. Any conclusions must be considered tentative until more systematic work is available.

WALL FLORA

Walls of all types, except those backed by earth banks, are extremely well-drained habitats. But their particular aspect as much as their general situation determines just how dry they become.

The south face of a wall may present virtual desert conditions in summer while the north face remains cool and relatively moist. Thus south-facing walls support true xerophytes – plants which thrive in dry conditions – while north-facing walls are colonised by species more normally associated with the surrounding area.

Local sources of moisture play an important part in determining the point-by-point variation in wall flora. Studies of mortared brick and stone walls show how slight changes in slope, small ledges or even sections of crumbling masonry tend to retard runoff and allow plants a foothold, as do upright unmortared copings as opposed to those which are flat or sealed with concrete. Damp spots under broken gutters and drip lines below old roofs are favoured by a much more luxuriant plant growth than elsewhere on the same wall. Old colleges and churches are often important refuges for wall plants in towns and cities where most other stone surfaces are frequently replaced or renewed. Interestingly, throughout northern Europe the Protestant churches tend to have a much richer flora than do the Catholic churches because they are less used and so remain damper. The church of Altarnun on Bodmin Moor, Cornwall even has a plant of maidenhair fern (*Adiantum capillus-veneris*) growing on an inside wall!

Stone walls of all types are particularly important habitats for lichens, mosses and ferns. Though the flora tends to be rather uniform, this environment allows saxicolous (rock-dwelling) species to live in areas where there are few or no natural rock exposures. In many flat, lowland parts of Britain, walls extend or substitute for natural scree, cliff and open stone face habitats for many species of both lower and higher plants. This allows, for example, navelwort or wall pennywort (*Umbilicus rupestris*), which is common on non-limestone rocks and banks in the West, to reach its easternmost position in Britain on a wall in Kent. And rusty-back fern (*Ceterach officinarum*) is apparently only really abundant, in this country, on walls.

The type of stone is a major determinant of plant makeup: gritstone and other hard acid rocks support a completely different flora from limestone. The species of acid situations, very interesting in places, are nonetheless limited, especially in dry lowland districts; they are richer in wetter districts. Limestone walls tend to have a far richer flora, supporting for example many orange lichens of the genus *Caloplaca*. Mortared limestone walls, such as those of the Kentish ragstone belt from Sevenoaks to Hythe, are especially rich in mosses, particularly *Barbula* species, and in lichens such as species of *Collema*

which require more water-retentive calcareous substrates. A number of common and rare spleenworts and ferns thrive on limestone walls. In the Mendips, for example, two rarities, the brittle bladder fern (*Cystopteris fragilis*) and the limestone polypody (*Thelypteris robertiana*), the former typical of scree slopes and the latter of fissured rocks and walls, grow on scree-like derelict walls in the area.

Throughout southern England, earth banks with or without stone facings are particularly rich in lower plants, especially certain bryophytes which elsewhere occur on natural earthy rocks. Examples include *Reboulia*, *Targionia* and the apple moss (*Bartramia pomiformis*).

The saxicolous ferns mentioned above point up an important management consideration: old half-ruined walls should in some cases be left alone rather than rebuilt if their most interesting plants are to survive. In the Mendips it is estimated to take at least five years before lichens and ferns start to colonise a fresh stone surface, although Francis Turk reports that in parts of Cornwall which are even milder and sunnier ferns may, though rarely, start up in two and the larger and more conspicuous lichens in three years. (Tiny lichens such as the very common *Lecanora dispersa*, which is ubiquitous on limestone, cement and mortar, may appear in a year). The plants of mortared walls are most likely to suffer undue attention, since diligent repointing cleans out whatever is growing on them at the time and smooths over the cracks in which new plants can root. Although walls may be forced apart by woody plants, herbaceous species seldom do much damage and should most often be left in place.

Cementing the copings or plugging up holes in dry stone walls is also destructive of plant life. A R Perry of the National Museum of Wales says that, while very few if any species of bryophytes grow only on walls, several such as *Pterygoneurum ovatum* and *Plamellatum* and *Ceratodon purpureus* var *conicus*, once relatively common in eg Oxfordshire on soil-capped walls, are now extremely local owing to soil cappings being replaced by cement. He adds that the same probably applies to other species in different parts of the country, but emphasises that the value of dry stone walls and earth banks for mosses and liverworts is also dependent on the environmental context: for example, they are much more important in unpolluted rural districts than within industrial towns, where few interesting bryophyte species can survive. On the other hand, Frank Brightman of the British Museum (Natural History) points out that a number of lichen species, for instance *Lecanora muralis* and *Stereocanlon pileatum*, are now commoner on walls in towns than they are in natural habitats in the country. An important consideration from the conservation point of view is that these days new pointing and capping is usually done in cement rather than in a lime mortar as in earlier times. Cement finishes are too neat, smooth and durable for many plant species to gain rootholds. If mortaring is required, Frank Brightman recommends for botanical interest as sandy and weak a mix as possible!

Interestingly, a large proportion of the characteristic wall plants are introductions, many of them from Mediterranean countries. These are garden species which have escaped to flourish in crevices and crannies up and down the country. Examples include ivy-leaved toadflax (*Cymbalaria muralis*), Oxford ragwort (*Senecio squalidus*) and mind-your-own-business (*Soleirolia soleirolii*), a close relative of the native pellitory-of-the-wall (*Parietaria judaica*). The species name *muralis*, by the way, often indicates that the plant is usually found on walls. Native species which favour wall habitats include many members of the stonecrop (*Crassulaceae*), saxifrage (*Saxifragaceae*) and cabbage (*Cruciferae*) families.

While some wall plants such as Oxford ragwort grow also along the disturbed ground nearby or on waste and barren places generally, quite a few are limited almost exclusively to walls and earth banks and are increasingly at risk as these features succumb to changes in land use. Indeed, according to Dr Francis Rose of the University of London King's College, the destruction of stone walls and earth banks would appear to be even more serious botanically than the removal of hedges in many areas, particularly in intensively farmed lowlands where natural habitats are few.

WALL FAUNA

A variety of animals make use of walls and earth banks during part or all of their life cycles. Dry walls are especially valuable habitats for insects and spiders; as well as harbouring permanent wall-dwellers, their numerous crannies provide daytime resting places for nocturnal species.

Walls within or at the edges of woodlands are especially important as shelter. Limestone walls are good for snails (and the larvae of the glow-worm, *Lampyris noctiluca*, which feed on them) as well. Banks are extremely useful to reptiles, particularly adders which use them for hibernation, spring feeding, autumn nesting and as migration routes between dry wintering sites and wetter feeding areas. Walls and banks provide virtually the only places in which a variety of animals can overwinter as adults. South-facing limestone walls in particularly sunny parts of the country such as the Gower peninsula and Isle of Purbeck are unusually valuable in this respect.

A number of species of birds sometimes nest in walls, although they may normally choose other sites instead. Blue and great tits, pied and white wagtails, house and tree sparrows, spotted flycatchers, nuthatches and wheatears all use walls, while a few species such as redstart favour walls for nesting. Our smallest seabird, the storm petrel, is famous for its use of wall nesting sites in addition to rocky storm beaches and creviced cliff faces. It prefers the walls of the ruined field systems and abandoned dwellings of small and now uninhabited islands; sizeable colonies nest in the great broch of Mousa in the Shetlands and in the monastic beehive cells of Great Skellig, County Kerry.

Small mammals which make good use of earth banks and hedgerows often also inhabit walls, usually where there are holes or other damage to give them access. Field voles, house mice, rats, rabbits and hares all may seek safety in walls while red squirrels have been known to store nuts under the stones. Bank voles seem particularly to favour old ivy-covered walls for dwelling. Rabbits may burrow below very shallow foundations, and rabbits and rats wreak havoc by tunnelling into earth banks, but voles and squirrels do not dig below foundation level and so cause little damage. Weasels and stoats hide and hunt among the stones and polecats sometimes winter in walls, while foxes take advantage of whatever prey presents itself and may dig into a wall or bank for dinner. Larger mammals, including on occasion man himself, use walls for temporary shelter.

Walls and banks, like hedgerows, provide protected 'highways' for small animals to move between areas of favourable habitat. This is especially the case where the walls are bordered by strips of unmown and ungrazed vegetation. This plus the direct use of walls for habitat means that, while no animal species appears to be directly threatened by wall removal, several may find their usable habitat increasingly restricted as the stones disappear. Dereliction is less of a problem, since a low wide heap of stones is as good as a tall narrow one to most species.

The Future of the Walling Craft

It has often been said that walling, like many

another country craft, is dying. Indeed, this has been the case for so long that it is a wonder there are any wallers left. And yet there are, thousands of them; farmer-wallers who have the strong hands, common sense and good eye to repair their own walls, even if their only training was to watch their predecessors do the same thing years before.

But, as Margaret Brooks (1973, p22) says, 'there is a difference between the man who can wall a gap and the one who thinks about his work as a craft and who cares about the appearance of his wall because it will be there for so many years'. The number of such full-time craftsmen wallers has probably been low for a long time. Even in the Pennines, the Lakes and Scotland, where Parliamentary enclosure walling gave temporary employment to scores and even hundreds of wallers, the years since the 1840's have seen little need for new wall building, but only for repairs and realignments. However, C S Jardine of Auldgirth, Dumfries, says that in his locale there were still as many as 32 full-time dykers in the 1920's, which had dwindled to only four or five by the 1970's. The peripheral walling areas – the South West, the Mendips, Gower, Purbeck – probably never had many full-time wallers.

However, the immediate future of the walling craft is looking bright, as there has been a great upsurge of interest during the 1970's and 80's, with young people training in the craft, as well as a large number of volunteers becoming skilled in walling. This increase has been due to many factors, of which the most important is the value now placed on the maintenance of the traditional British farming landscape. Increased leisure time and tourism, which brings more people into the countryside, together with changing values in farming have meant that the traditional features of the countryside, walls included, are given a value far above their straight economic importance. Funding through National Parks, Country Parks, local authorities and other bodies, as well as through employment schemes has meant money invested in the craft of walling.

In the three years up to 1988, the number of professional wallers registered with the Dry Stone Walling Association (p110) quadrupled from 30 to over 130. Several of their Master Craftsmen are occupied virtually full-time in training, so investing further in the future of the craft, and an apprenticeship scheme has recently been started (p110).

Competitions and demonstrations of dry stone walling, from being almost moribund in the early 1970's, are now held virtually every weekend somewhere in the British Isles, as a glance at the programmes and newsletters of the Dry Stone Walling Association will prove.

Whether this trend will continue depends on continued funding for countryside management schemes, and on sufficient prosperity in farming to allow walling work to continue in the private sector. Most of the walling work done in National Parks and other areas is repair and rebuilding of existing walls, and in most areas there is still many years of work to be done. Some county councils and other authorities employ wallers for realigning and building new walls as part of road improvement schemes. Cornwall County Council has had a team of specialist stone hedgers for many years, with miles of Cornwall's newer roads and by-passes bounded by stone hedges built in traditional style. New walls are also needed for gardens and housing schemes, car parks, amenity areas and for footpath and bridleway management, so the future for those training now in the craft of walling looks reasonably bright.

3 Walls and the Law

Many of the legal considerations applying to the ownership of walls and responsibility for their maintenance are common to earth banks, ditches and fences of all types. Problems posed by shrubs or trees growing along a bank or hedgerow are dealt with in *Hedging* (BTCV, 1975).

The guidelines given below are general and may be subject to varying interpretations. Professional legal advice should be sought in any ambiguous or disputed cases.

Wall Ownership

a Where a wall or bank has a ditch on one side, the wall is presumed to belong to the owner of the field on whose side of the wall there is no ditch, unless deeds state otherwise. The boundary is the side of the ditch farthest from the wall.

b If the ditch exists but has been so damaged or neglected that the exact edge cannot be determined, the distance can sometimes be settled by reference to local custom. The usual width allowed is 1370mm (4'6") from the base of the wall or bank to the far side of the ditch. However, this 'custom of the country' may not necessarily be followed by a court of law.

c Where the wall or bank is ditched on both sides or on neither side, ownership is usually mentioned in the deeds. If the wall or bank is ditched on both sides, it usually belongs to both parties.

If the wall or bank is right on the boundary, half belongs to one man and the other half to his neighbour. The dividing line is taken vertically from the boundary line.

d Ownership and responsibility for the maintenance of enclosure walls may be indicated by the maps accompanying Parliamentary Enclosure Acts or by evidence built into the walls themselves:

(1) Enclosure Award maps often set out the portion to be walled by each party and show this by a small T mark placed with its foot on the wall line and its head into the field whose owner is to build and maintain the section of wall.

(2) Long enclosure walls often have heads built in at intervals, indicating the boundaries of the sections for which adjacent landowners are responsible. To show this, two heads are built immediately adjacent to one another with the coping carried across the gap to reduce weakness at this point, as shown in the diagram on page 78. When searching for boundary heads be sure not to mistake old walled-up gates for them. Boundary heads occasionally have initials or geometric markings carved into their footings, indicating the people originally responsible for the maintenance of each section.

(3) If throughstones, the coverband or topstones overhang one face only of the wall, this may or may not indicate ownership depending on the area and the situation. In some locales the 'face side' refers to the side without protruding stones and this is the owner's side. Elsewhere it is the side with projecting stones that faces the owner's land because the throughs, coverband or topstones have been placed to keep his sheep from jumping over. Local custom may indicate which is the case in the vicinity in question. However, garden walls are usually left smooth on the outside (the side away from the owner's land) for appearance, and roadside walls are almost always left smooth on the side facing the road, irrespective of who is responsible for the wall's upkeep, in order to lessen damage to vehicles hitting the wall and to keep passers-by from climbing the wall

e If a wall is built on a boundary line, any piers or strengthening buttresses must be built on the owner's side; otherwise his neighbour may claim ownership on the basis of this evidence.

f If there is a ditch on both sides or on neither side, and ownership is not clear in the deeds, it can be claimed by one party on the basis of 'acts of ownership' such as maintaining or rebuilding the wall or bank. In such cases it seems necessary to prove that the neighbour knew of or acquiesced in these acts and raised no objection to them. Twenty years of continual use is usually looked upon as an 'immemorial custom' conferring right of ownership.

g Where the origin of a wall or bank cannot be determined and there are no acts of ownership, the wall or bank belongs to both owners in equal parts.

h When land is sold the boundary may be based on Ordnance Survey field lines. These indicate the centre of a wall or bank rather than the true legal boundary, and to avoid later dispute the actual boundary should be determined before purchase.

Boundary Wall Maintenance

a The owner is responsible for repairing the wall or bank and clearing the ditch.

b If the wall or bank exists on the boundary line, the owner of each half is responsible for maintaining his half and can do what he likes with it.

c When a wall or bank belongs to both parties jointly, it is assumed to be divided down the middle and each party is responsible for maintaining his half.

d If a wall or fence falls on the neighbour's land and damages plants or property, the owner is liable for compensation except to any things which grow or rest upon the wall by sufferance (see 'Rights of use', point **a**, below).

e When digging or clearing out a ditch along a wall or bank, the owner must not cut into his neighbour's land. He must throw all topsoil upon his own land.

f The owner of a ditch can erect a fence at its edge, along the boundary line, to protect his ditch. He is then responsible for repair and maintenance of the fence.

g Many secondary rural roads are owned by the landowners along either side, with the boundary line taken as the middle of the road, even where the road is controlled and maintained by the county council. If the council widens or realigns the road it must replace the wall or bank, although not necessarily with a barrier of the same type. In all other ways, including maintenance after replacement, the wall is the landowner's responsibility.

When a motorway is built the Department of the Environment purchases a strip of land along either side of the route, along with the existing fences which then become the responsibility of the Department.

Obligation to Fence

a There is no law to compel a landowner to wall or fence his land. But if he fails to do so he cannot claim for any damage from the owner of straying stock, etc.

b Railways, however, must be fenced against cattle belonging to owners or occupiers of land adjoining the railway, to prevent them from straying on the line. The railway company is liable for damages to stock due to improperly maintained fences.

c Each man is responsible for his own trespass and that of his stock. So while he is under no obligation to fence in order to keep out his neighbour's stock he must prevent his own from straying on another's land. He cannot claim for damages if the cattle stray and injure themselves on a neighbour's fence.

d If the wall or bank between two neighbours is defective and only belongs to one occupier, the other neighbour must fence in order to control his own stock. He can put up any sort of fence but it must be on his own land.

e Where a wall or bank is owned jointly and it is defective, the owner of stock can place the fence in the wall or bank itself, along the boundary line.

f An owner or rent-paying tenant can claim damage done to his fences or gates by any trespasser, including a Hunt.

Tenant and Landlord

a The upkeep, maintenance and repair of walls, banks, ditches, gates etc is usually the tenant's obligation. In many cases the landlord must provide the necessary materials for the work. This should be stated clearly in the tenancy agreement. At the beginning or end of a tenancy the condition of the fences may be assessed and compensation is usually paid or claimed for improvements and depreciations to them all.

b In most cases the tenant cannot remove walls or banks or fill in ditches without the consent of his landlord.

c Any other fencing put upon a holding by a tenant, not necessary to the fulfillment of some obligation, is the tenant's property. He may remove it before or within a reasonable time after his tenancy ends, unless he has not paid his rent, but he must give his landlord one month's notice before removing the structure, during which time the landlord has the option of buying it. The tenant must make good any damage done in removing the fence.

Rights of Use

a A neighbour has no right to attach to his side of another's wall or fence any creeping, climbing plant or trained tree, or to fasten anything to the wall by nails etc or rootlets. Nor may he lean any loose timbers or heavy articles against the wall which may tend to damage it. If creepers or trained trees have been allowed to grow with no disturbance for a number of years, the owner's consent is presumed, but the owner is not responsible for any unavoidable damage to plants when the structure is repaired.

b When a wall or bank belongs to both parties jointly, each owner is considered to have 'rights of support and user'. This means that each can build upon his own side of the wall for support, but he has no right to go beyond the boundary line with any portion of his building.

c Where a wall or bank crosses a public right of way, the owner or tenant may or may not be responsible for the upkeep of the required stile or gate although he is likely to be if he is responsible for the repair of the footpath. Legal advice should be sought in any case.

d The owner of a roadside wall or bank or one beside a public footpath is responsible for seeing that the structure does not become a nuisance. 'Nuisance' is defined as something that may cause injury, damage or inconvenience to others.

Treasure Trove

Occasionally, objects of intrinsic or historical or archaeological value may be found within walls or banks when they are under repair. The law regarding ownership of field antiquities is rather complex and is well summarised in Wood (1973, pp296–8). In England, Wales and Northern Ireland, 'treasure trove' is deemed to be gold and silver that has been hidden in the soil or a building and of which the owner cannot be traced, and is claimed by the Crown. If there is apparently no element of hiding the items most probably belong not to the Crown but may belong to the owner of the land. In Scotland, however, all finds are deemed to be treasure trove, whatever their apparent mode of deposition and whether or not they are of gold or silver. In all cases, the most sensible course of action is to report any finds to the police, who can then inform you of any further procedure required.

4 Safety, Equipment and Organisation

Safety Precautions

GENERAL

a Have a suitable first aid kit on hand at the work site (see page 44).

b Be careful at all times when working with and among stones, especially on a slope. Keep the work area as clear as possible and watch out for loose stones underfoot.

c Avoid bending more than is necessary. Work from the downhill side on a slope.

d Carry as little as possible uphill. Collect stones from higher up and carry or roll them down to the wall.

e When climbing a wall, be careful to press down on the stones rather than pulling up or out. Put your feet as low as possible, on a solid ledge not a projecting stone. Don't put your feet on the coverband or coping. If you can get over without touching the coping at all, so much the better.

f Keep tools within easy reach but not where you may trip on them. Lean hammers etc against the base of the wall when not in use.

g Work far enough away from other people that you won't get in their way and if you drop a stone it won't hurt anyone else.

HANDLING STONES

Rainsford-Hannay (1972, p16) remarks that with a 50mm (2″) thick board, 1.2–1.5m (4–5′) long, and a knowledge of leverage, two wallers can manoeuvre and position stones as big as steamer trunks without strain. Fields (1971) details how to move slabs of mica schist weighing anything up to a ton. Hopefully you will never have to try this, but whatever the situation the important thing is to think of the dangers involved and to choose methods appropriate to the size of the task.

a Don't try to lift or carry stones which are too heavy for you. Use mechanical aid or get someone's help, otherwise you may damage your back or knees.

b To lift a big stone, stand comfortably with your weight equally on both feet and your feet fairly close together, not wide apart, so they will be under the stone when you lift. Wedge the stone underneath if necessary to allow you to get your fingers under it. Get a good grip on the stone with both hands. Lift the end which is not wedged first so that your hand won't be pinched. Keep your back as straight as possible, bending from the knees to take the strain on the leg muscles.

If you have to pause for a moment before placing the stone, move one foot back a little and rest the stone on your forward thigh.

c To place a big stone, stand sideways to the wall and swing the stone most of the way over it. Lower the outer end first, so that the stone comes to rest on its mid-section. This keeps your other hand from being pinched. If necessary, support the stone in this position while you place a temporary wedge under it which will allow you to manoeuvre the stone without catching your hand.

d The same lifting and placing techniques are used with two people working as with one. Make sure the stone is well wedged before you lift, to protect your hands. With a really big stone you should lever it up with a crowbar and push smaller stones or blocks of wood under so it is level and clear of the ground. Lay the stone on the wall at an angle, keeping the outer end down so that the person at the other end won't get pinched.

e Whenever you place a bigger stone on a smaller one, take care that the smaller one doesn't rise up and 'chock' your finger.

f When shifting a heavy stone more than a few feet, tilt it up on its end or side, straddle it and roll it along between your legs. Or, with a long rectangular slab, 'walk' it by pivoting it on alternate corners, aligned either horizontally or vertically depending on its shape. This saves carrying the stone, which jars the back and may be more of a strain than you realise.

g Shift a really big slab or boulder with the aid of boards and rollers. First use a crowbar and blocks or wedges to get the stone level and off the ground. Clear any obstructions from underneath with the crowbar. Lay solid (eg 50mm x 400mm (2″ x 8″)) planks from the stone to the wall. The planks must be level, otherwise the whole enterprise may get out of control. Put the near end of the second plank a few inches under the far end of the first plank to anchor it. Place wooden or metal rollers on the plank and nudge the stone along slowly, moving the rollers as they are left behind up to the front of the stone so that several are always available.

An even heavier slab can be moved by first manoeuvring the stone onto a short plank and then rolling stone and plank together towards the wall.

h To move boulders on a slope where rollers are impractical, use a Tirfor winch with the hook-and-line chain described below.

i The easiest way to move really heavy rocks is with a Land Rover and a chain having a flattened hook at the end which can fit around any of the links of the chain to form a quick and easy knot. First prop up the front end of the stone several

inches, wrap the chain around it as shown and pull the stone out onto level ground.

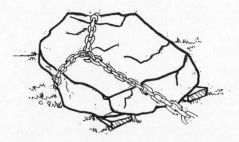

Next, block up each corner of the near end again and manoeuvre the hook-and-link knot until it is under the stone with the other end of the chain running forward between the blocks.

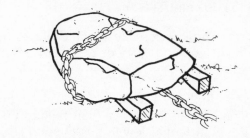

Back up the Land Rover until it is almost over the end of the rock and hitch the chain as tightly as possible to its trailer hitch or framework. Knock the blocks out from under the stone, leaving the slab raised at its front end so that it won't plough up the ground as you drag it away. On soft ground you can slide a plank under the stone to ease its journey.

j Although you should try to use really big stones low in the wall, preferably in the foundations, you may occasionally have to use one higher up. Set a plank against the wall at the most gradual slope possible and roll the stone up end over end. A heavier slab can be moved by means of rollers or a short plank plus rollers, pushed along a set of double planks which you have suitably levelled and supported.

k Big partly buried stones can be levered out of the ground with a crowbar. Use a small stone as a fulcrum, placed as near to the end of the bar as possible for maximum leverage.

It is safest to use just one bar. Often, however, two are required, each one alternately worked as a lever and then held steady to keep the stone in position while the other bar lifts. In any case, restrict the workforce to one person per crowbar, since the risk of someone being injured is much greater if extra people are around when the bar or stone slips.

l Don't use a pick to lever up a stone unless you are sure the stone is reasonably flat underneath. Otherwise the pick is likely to slip off it and throw you off balance. It is safer to lift it using a broad-bladed mattock and then, as soon as there is sufficient space underneath, to wedge the stone and finish lifting it with a crowbar.

m When breaking stones with a hammer, work away from other people so they are not in danger if the hammer head flies off the handle or if stone chips shower their way. Wear goggles when breaking or drilling stone.

n Hit the stone with the hammer head flat to it, not angled. This makes the chips fly out in front of you and lessens the chance of the shaft breaking. It also gives the most effective blow. Try to stand so that you can hit the stone with the hammer central to your body, neither to your left nor right but in line with the bridge of your nose. This way the hammer head itself prevents chips flying upwards into your eyes.

o Don't hold small stones in your hand to break them. Even if you don't smash your fingers, your wrist will get sore after a while.

p Don't push stones which stick too far out of the wall into place by hand. Tap them in with a hammer instead.

q Some types of stone are more difficult to handle than others and require extra care. Granite is particularly bad because it is coarse-grained, readily cuts the skin and tends to leave flakes of mica in the wound which then goes septic. For this reason it is important to clean out even minor scratches and abrasions well.

WORK SEASON AND WEATHER PRECAUTIONS

a Walling can be carried out in any season but it is best done when it is not too cold or wet. If possible, avoid working in frosty weather: foundations are hard to dig in frozen, snow-covered or muddy ground and you will have trouble placing the footings; stones stick to the ground and split in unexpected ways when you hammer them; permeable stones swell in frost so walls built with them will settle poorly. Walling in cold weather is very hard on the hands. And serious back problems are most likely to develop when you are cold and stiff.

b Try not to work when the stones are wet since they are slippery and dangerous to handle. If you work in heavy rain you get soaked directly or, if you work in waterproofs, you get almost as wet with sweat. Either way you become quickly tired and careless.

c Professional wallers, groups of volunteers and others who must generally carry on working whatever the weather, can make life much easier for themselves if they carry a portable windbreak or shelter for use in bad weather and exposed conditions. See page 49.

d Gapping is best done as soon as possible after finding a break, especially with hillside walls, although repairs may have to be postponed in the worst weather. On farms, late spring is usually a good time for routine repairs if they can't be done earlier. Lambing and winter feeding have finished, the days are lengthening and the weather is generally fair, and the walls can be made stockproof in time to keep animals off mowing grass or arable crops. Farm walling can be made more convenient if stones are stockpiled in advance against contingencies. They should be put well out of the way, though, since it may be several years before they find a use.

e The summer is the best time for major walling jobs because the days are longest and the weather is more likely to be fine. As one Scottish craftsman related, 'In the winter you work to keep yoursel' warm. In the summer time you step yoursel' out to keep yoursel' gettin' *too* warm. Now old dykers used to say, when the sun was shinin' bright and the stones were too hot to handle, you didna hold it so long, you put them on quicker.'

Clothing

The aim is always safety and comfort first.

a Comfortable work clothes, tough enough to withstand abrasion from rough stones. Scottish wallers used to wear aprons cut to knee length in front, with bibs designed to protect their waistcoats, and rolled up at the back so as to tie at the waist. These are sometimes still worn at demonstrations, but overalls or a boiler suit are more convenient substitutes.

b Boots. Heavy leather work boots with spiked or deep moulded soles and steel toe caps are safest. If you have an old but serviceable pair, work in them since new boots quickly become much the worse for wear when used for walling. Wellingtons are inadequate unless they have toe caps. Plimsolls and other light shoes are too slippery and do not protect feet from falling rocks.

c Gloves. Most experienced wallers wear gloves only in the coldest weather, and then often only for protection when handling very large stones. Normally you can tell the shape of the stones more easily if you work bare handed and can grip hammers and other tools better. If you only wall occasionally and for short periods, it is worth carrying sturdy, flexible leather work gloves to wear if your hands become uncomfortably sore and scratched. On longer tasks you should try to toughen up your hands gradually by wearing the gloves less and less as you become used to the work. You should find that you can quickly do without a glove on the hand which you use for hammering.

Some Cotswold craftsmen used to wear pads rather than full gloves, cut from leather or rubber (such as old inner tubing) with holes for the wrist, fingers and thumb. With these, a good waller could pick up and place stones keeping his palms down, without turning the wrists, thereby working more quickly with less strain. But in most parts of the country the stones are too big or awkward to be lifted one handed and even in the Cotswolds wallers today seem to feel no need for the protection which pads afford, perhaps because the pace of work is slower and the hours less.

d Goggles or eyeshields to protect your eyes when breaking and drilling stone. Although most wallers don't bother with these, they are well worth the inconvenience if they save you getting stone splinters in your eyes. Ordinary spectacles provide some protection and are better than nothing, although they do have the added hazard of being easily shattered by impact. Eye protectors should be manufactured to BS 2092 and should be marked with the British Standard kitemark and either the number 1 or the number 2, indicating that they are designed for impact resistance. Prices start at around £2.50 for general-purpose protective spectacles, which are available from ironmongers, d-i-y shops and builders' merchants.

Tools and Accessories

It is possible to build dry stone walls without any tools at all, especially if rebuilding from an existing foundation. But in most cases a few tools are useful and may be essential for working with some types of stone.

On group tasks enough hammers should be supplied so that one is within easy borrowing distance of every worker. Common sense should suggest the number of other tools needed for each situation. It is worth painting the butts of the handles of hammers and other inconspicuous tools a bright yellow, orange or pink at the beginning of the work season to make them easier to locate when they are laid down among stones.

FOR ALL TASKS

a First aid kit. Keep this available at all times. Pinched or crushed fingers present the most frequent problem. Stubbed toes and sprained ankles are also possible, as are sore eyes from dust and stone chips.

The BTCV can supply standard first aid kits which comply with the 1981 Health and Safety Regulations (First Aid). For six to ten people, the contents are as follows:

    1 guidance card
    20 individual sterile dressings
    2 sterile eye pads with attachments
    2 triangular bandages
    2 sterile coverings for serious wounds
    6 safety pins
    6 medium size sterile unmedicated dressings
    2 large size sterile unmedicated dressings
    2 extra large sterile unmedicated dressings

From experience on projects, the following 'welfare kit' is also found to be useful:

    100mm (4″) crepe bandage
    tweezers (round nosed)
    scissors (round nosed)
    insect repellant
    antihistamine cream for insect bites
    sunscreen cream
    mild antiseptic cream
    aspirin
    eye lotion and eye bath

Some wallers also carry home-made leather tube patches which may be slid over sore, chapped or scratched fingers and strapped around the wrist with a thong. The leather should be supple enough to bend easily. An eye sweep is another useful item. This consists of a thin metal stem, about the size of a matchstick, with a long soft elongated loop of platinum wire clamped onto the end. Stone fragments can be swept from the eye with this and there is no danger of scratching the eye's surface. Eye sweeps are available from welding suppliers.

b One or more walling hammers, the type depending on the stone (see p46)

c Sledge hammer 6.3kg (14lb) size

d Lump (mash or club) hammer, 1.8kg (4lb) size

e Heavy-duty garden spade, Devon shovel or

small round-mouthed shovel, for digging foundations, cleaning around the base of an existing wall or a retaining wall or stone-faced bank. This can also be used to mix any concrete or mortar required.

f Pick or pick-ended mattock, to supplement the spade or shovel and for digging up field stones. In the South West the 'digger' (a mattock with a single broad blade) is sometimes used instead.

A useful variant of the normal pick is the 'tramp pick' once common in Aberdeenshire but now available only through farm auctions and other sources of second-hand tools. This has an all-steel shaft and single pick blade with a wooden handle and adjustable wooden foot rest.

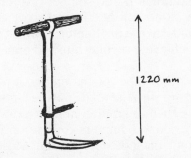

1220 mm

Unlike the ordinary 'shoulder pick' the tramp pick is used in the position shown, to lever and manoeuvre large heavy stones into place. The foot rest may be left on or removed as convenient. Tramp picks come in weights from 4.5kg (10lb) to 8.1kg (18lb) depending on the work they are designed to do.

g Batter frame, with lines and pins (see p48). Usually only one frame is needed, but a second may be required occasionally.

h Plumb bob and line

i Spirit level. Most wallers level up by eye, but a spirit level is useful for beginners to help keep courses of stonework running correctly on sloping or irregular ground and for work with cut and dressed stone. Use the level alone when checking the positioning of lines between walling frames. Fix the level to a 1.5m (4–6') long straight-edged board when checking the courses directly.

j Steel tape measure, for setting lines and checking the height of through courses, topstones etc

k Fencing pliers, for removing or constructing temporary wire fences across gaps.

l Windbreaks or shelter, for use on very exposed sites (see p49)

SHIFTING AND TRANSPORTING STONE

a Two crowbars

b Wooden or metal rollers, from 25mm (1″) to 100mm (4″) diameter for moving very large stones

c Several 50mm × 200mm (2″×8″) planks, 2m (6–8′) long, to use with rollers for moving large stones

d Wooden blocks 50mm × 50mm (2″×2″) or more, by about 600mm (2′) long, to prop up large stones for moving and shaping

e Buckets, barrow, sledge or trailer, depending on the amount of material to be transported to the work site and the distance involved. Buckets are useful for carrying small quantities of fillings and concrete or mortar short distances. Use heavy-duty rubber, not plastic or metal buckets which wear out quickly.

Traditionally, various forms of low, small-wheeled carts and simple sledges were used for shifting stones from local quarries down to the wall. A hand barrow, for use by two or four men, is good for moving small loads short distances over rough terrain.

A rubber-tyred wheelbarrow is best for a single worker to move earth and stones over fairly regular ground.

For larger jobs, a Land Rover or other four-wheel-drive vehicle with a trailer or sledge is best. You can make a simple sledge using 3mm ($\frac{1}{8}$″) thick mild steel plate, about 900mm (3′) wide and 600mm (2′) long, curved up at the front with a 25mm (1″) hole drilled to fasten a towing chain. From the back of this plate you should bolt four 50mm×200mm×2m (2″×8″× 6–8′) planks. Join the planks across their back ends with a 50mm×150mm (2″×6″) board and nail a 50mm×100mm (2″×4″) board at each side to provide raised sills.

g Chain, for fitting to the sledge and for use when winching large stones. This should have a flattened hook at one end which can fit through any link to secure it.

h Hand winch, for pulling in large field stones. The BTCV uses the 'Tirfor TU16' winch which has a 760kg (15cwt) safe working load, with 18m (60′) of 11.3mm diameter galvanised maxiflex cable, which has a 1620kg (32cwt) safe working load, fixed with a large eye hook. 'Tirfor' winches are made by Tirfor Ltd, Halfway, Sheffield S19 5GZ. An additional length of cable is useful, as are slings which can be used to anchor the winch.

CONCRETING AND MORTARING

a Mixing board, for small batches of concrete or mortar

b Bricklayer's trowel

CUTTING AND DRILLING STONE

These tools and their use are described more fully on pages 56–60.

a Cold chisel, various types for splitting slate

b Rock drills, various lengths, for splitting granite and setting metal posts etc in stone

c Cleaning tool, to remove rock dust when drilling. You can substitute a small bicycle pump or plasticine for this purpose if necessary.

d Steel shims (feathers) and wedges, for splitting granite

e Steel wedges of the sort used in tree felling, for splitting granite and schist. An old discarded axe head is also useful to aid splitting.

f Wrecking bar, for prying apart split stone

HAMMERS

Types

Hammers for use in dry stone walling seem to be adapted in the main from traditional masons' tools (see for example Jenkins, 1965, p163). This is to be expected, since stonemasonry requires that materials be carefully worked while rubble walling can make do with unshaped stone and did so at least until the 18th century, when steel became cheap enough for common use.

Hammers are necessary for relatively accurate splitting, trimming or shaping of most types of stone and for breaking large blocks down to a manageable size. The discussion which follows emphasises regional variations in the sort of hammers used, but for most purposes any single-handed shaping hammer, plus lump and sledge hammers for general use, should prove adequate.

Craftsmen show regional and individual preferences for various shapes and sizes of hammers, determined largely by the type of stone to be worked. Throughout most of northern England, especially in Carboniferous Limestone areas, hammers are carried but used sparingly if at all. Many craftsmen in this region consider it something of a defeat to have to break their stone. Elsewhere, where well-bedded stone is abundant, wallers routinely trim it to convenient shapes and break it into smaller bits for fillings. Cotswold stone can be shaped so readily that craftsmen there use the hammer almost continuously to achieve a regular finished appearance.

Whatever the type of hammer, it must be tempered to suit the materials. Hammers for hard stone such as granite, and general-purpose lump and sledge hammers for use on metal as well as stone, must be steel headed. Most walling hammers should not be used on metal. Cast iron hammers or mells should never be used for walling, since they may shatter or shed metal splinters when used on anything harder than wood.

Walling hammers may weigh from 0.45kg (1lb) to 11.3kg (25lb) with the heavier hammers used on harder, more massive stone. Most craftsmen carry at least two, a light hammer for splitting or trimming smaller stones and a heavier sledge-type hammer for breaking boulders into usable pieces.

Throughout the Pennines, the usual walling or 'scabbling' hammer has one square and one blunt end, usually with its axis parallel to the handle but occasionally perpendicular to it.

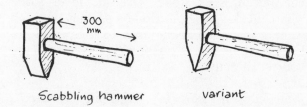

Scabbling hammer   variant

The square end is for knocking pieces off stones, the 'chisel end', as it is sometimes called, is for splitting stone along its bedding planes. The head weighs 0.9–1.3kg (2–3lb). In New England, Fields (1971, p61) uses two similar hammers, one weighing 1.3kg (3lb) and another with a

46

long handle and weighing 11.3kg (25lb), for trimming and splitting massive slabs of mica schist.

In areas of Scotland where the stone is well bedded, two types of hammer are distinguished. The usual type has both ends tapered with a square pein.

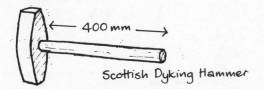
Scottish Dyking Hammer
400 mm

This weighs from 1.8–2.7kg (4–6lb), and is used for splitting and roughly shaping whinstone. The second type is the 'mason's hammer'. This is similar but smaller, for more delicate work, with one end tapered nearly to a wedge for cutting and splitting sandstone.

In Aberdeenshire, wallers must deal with hard granitic rocks which cannot be shaped with a tapered hammer. They must be drilled and split instead. Dunecht waller Frank Main uses a variety of hammers for this, starting with a 1.6kg ($3\frac{1}{2}$lb) 'hand mell' (lump or mash hammer, available from 1.1kg ($2\frac{1}{2}$lb) on up) for use with rock drills. Both his 2.7kg (6lb) 'cachie' or small mason's hammer and his 6.2kg (16lb) 'blocking hammer' or sledge hammer have symmetrical rectangular heads with squared ends.

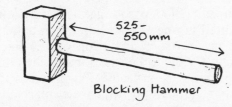
525–550 mm
Blocking Hammer
(cachie has smaller, narrower head and 300–350 mm long handle)

Blocking hammers are available from 6.3–9.9kg (14–22lb).

In the Cotswolds the typical walling hammer has a symmetrical tapered head with two 'polling edges' about 6mm ($\frac{1}{4}$") thick for rough shaping of the stone, or one polling edge and one 'dressing edge', which is thinner, for fine cutting. These hammers are available in several weights, with 1.6–1.8kg ($3\frac{1}{2}$–4lb) being usual.

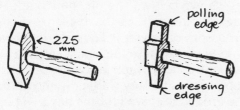
225 mm
polling edge
dressing edge
Cotswold hammers

The drawing above right shows another Cotswold hammer, very nicely balanced and less head-heavy than the usual type. This was made by J Rathbone, Blacksmith, Kingham, Oxfordshire.

Marshall (1960, p14) recommends a 1.8–2.2kg (4–5lb) square-faced 'stone maul' for breaking large stones and a bricklayer's-type hammer with one end 31mm ($1\frac{1}{4}$") square and the other tapering to a flattened or pointed pick. He appears to be writing about Cotswold walling, but this hammer is more typical of the South West. (See diagram below.)

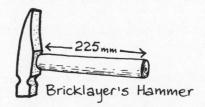
225mm
Bricklayer's Hammer

Archie Radmore, working near Plymouth, Devon, uses the square end of his bricklayer's hammer to break stones while the pick end serves to cut down the stone hedge's earth fill for firm bedding of facing stones or to scrape in the fill behind the stones. He also uses a mason's hammer, which is similar to the ordinary tapering Cotswold hammer shown above. Rule (1974, p26) says that stone hedgers in mid and west Cornwall use the same sort of hammer but use the pointed end for breaking off small chunks of rock and the squared end for tamping the earth fill. Such hammers are known in her district as 'walling' or 'hedge hammers' or more picturesquely as 'biddicks', 'tubbals', 'gads' or 'slaves'. Square-ended sledge hammers, available from 0.45–6.3kg (1–14lb) are used for driving wooden wedges to split granite; after the stone is weakened the walling hammer is used to break off the correct size piece.

Maintenance of hammers

Hammer heads tend to wear more at the front than at the rear corners, because even when trying to hit a stone squarely one tends to swing a bit too far.

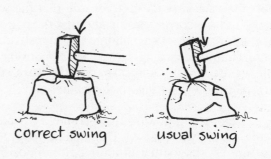
correct swing
usual swing

After the front corners have worn about 6mm ($\frac{1}{4}$") they become too rounded for accurate splitting and the head should be reversed to bring the other corners into play and promote more even wear. The head is much easier to remove if it is held by a large staple instead of a wedge because you can simply knock a punch under the staple and pry it out whenever the head or handle needs changing. If the head is the least bit loose you should soak it in a bucket of water each night before using it, to swell the end of the handle and prevent the head flying off in use.

A badly worn hammer head can be squared by a blacksmith, but he must take care to retemper it properly; if it is too soft it will flare, if it is too hard it will chip. Unfortunately, not many smiths now know how to temper hammers for use on stone.

A hammer shaft should last about 6 months of continuous use, provided you don't drop a stone on it. Once a handle becomes badly frayed or splintered it should be replaced. Be sure that the new handle is long enough, otherwise you will have to grip it awkwardly far up. Wallers traditionally made their own handles out of ash, cut to the correct length and split rather than sawn to shape before being trimmed with a spokeshave. This allowed them to choose a comfortable grip and length. Whether it is home-made or not, the handle preferably should be somewhat oval rather than circular in cross section to prevent it twisting in your hand, and it should be tapered so that it is slightly larger at the bottom to avoid slipping when the handle is wet.

BATTER FRAMES

Batter frames are also known as 'walling or dyke frames', 'patterns', 'wall gauges' and 'templates'. Walls of different specifications require different frames, although within any district there are usually only one or two standard specifications. Frames are unnecessary for minor gapping work, and in the north of England they tend not to be used except on local authority and other exacting jobs, but for beginners they are very useful to ensure that the wall is built to the correct profile and that the courses are kept level. They should be constructed beforehand according to the specifications of the wall to be built and carried to the work site. See page 66 for setting up the frames.

For free-standing walls, the frame is usually built as shown below. The height, top and bottom widths, batter and number and position of ties vary according to the design and dimensions of the wall concerned.

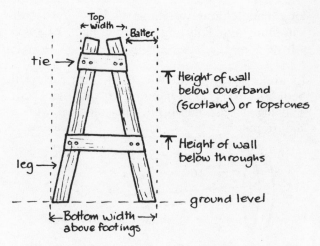

Cotswold walls often lack throughs, and here the frame or gauge is constructed as shown below.

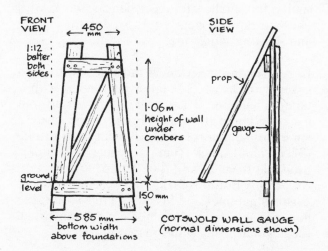

Marshall (1960, p15) suggests using a long prop, pointed at one end and driven at an angle into the ground so that its top end is the correct height for the top of the coping when the frame is positioned vertically. He provides the prop with a groove in which he places the line indicating the top of the coping.

Guidelines should be nylon rather than hemp, which stretches and soon rots when wet. Metal pins are useful for securing the lines to an existing section of wall or for tightening them where they are fixed to the frame. You can substitute thin wooden wedges or even bricklayer's trowels for these pins if necessary.

South Western stone and turf hedges usually have a concave batter which requires a more complex pattern. Rule (1974) describes two types, shown below. The one on the left is held up against the side of the bank from time to time as work progresses. The right-hand pattern may be held against the end elevation of the bank as it is being built or, preferably, can be set up like an ordinary walling frame at the end of the ground prepared for the day's work. Prop it vertically with a pole lashed to the highest

48

cross-bar to hold it in place. Pin guidelines to it in the same way as with an ordinary walling frame.

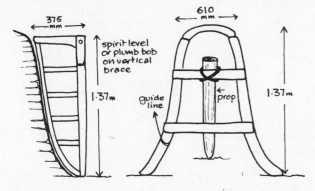

The pattern on the left is made of wood, while that on the right is of metal tubing bent to the correct shape and held by flat bolted metal bars and a curved tubular top end. Typical dimensions are shown.

WINDBREAKS

On exposed work sites, especially in winter, it is very helpful to erect a windbreak or shelter. A simple windbreak consists of a piece of sheet metal about 1.8m (6′) high, lashed to poles driven into the ground a couple of yards to the windward side of the wall to leave room for a supply of stones. A wattle hurdle is better, since a somewhat porous windbreak is better than a solid one. A thatching of straw gives some additional protection from driving rain if you position the windbreak nearer to the wall and fetch stones from around the ends. A single sheet or hurdle will do for two to four wallers. Extra sections can be added in series to provide for larger groups of volunteers.

For extended tasks on exposed sites, the shelter shown below and on the next page provides a much better solution to the weather problem. It was designed by Eric Boyes, a dyker from Dumfriesshire. Despite its high initial cost it is well worth consideration by both professionals and volunteers who must often work whatever the weather. The shelter is spacious enough for four to work in comfortably in high wind, driving rain or even a few inches of snow, with the supply of stones held inside, yet it can be slid easily along the ground by two men and can be taken apart to fit into a Land Rover.

The frame is made up of round-section pipes welded to form eight side pieces (two upper and two lower each side) plus four curved top pieces. The material used is hollow galvanised iron water pipe 25mm (1″) in diameter except along the bottom where it is 37mm ($1\frac{1}{2}$″) in diameter. Where durability and lightness are the prime factors, stainless steel or aluminium pipe may be used instead but this is much more expensive. Each joint is formed by means of a section of large-diameter pipe welded to one of the frame pipes as shown in the detail below. The loops, which are used to tie down the canvas cover, are made of flat steel strips welded to the bottom pipes.

Six iron pins are carried to hold down the frame in high winds or when the shelter is left up over night. They are also used to lever up the frame when it is set up on a slope. For this, the pins are driven in on the lower side just far enough to hold the bottom pipe on that side level with the other side when the pipe is resting in the cup of each pin. The frame is flexible enough that the base width can be adjusted to account for any small obstacles or local irregularities in the ground.

Three large sheets of canvas cover the frame: a

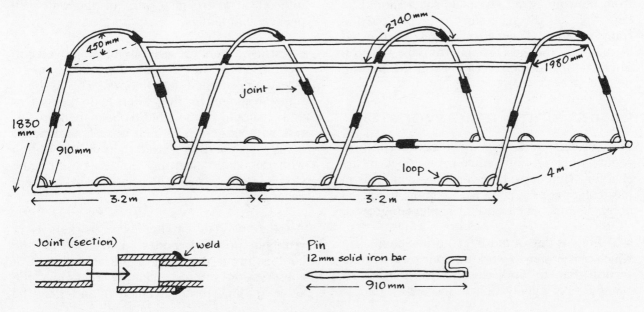

49

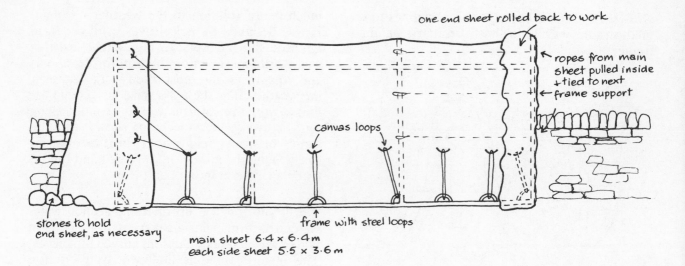

one end sheet rolled back to work

← ropes from main sheet pulled inside + tied to next ← frame support

canvas loops

stones to hold end sheet, as necessary

frame with steel loops

main sheet 6.4 x 6.4 m
each side sheet 5.5 x 3.6 m

main sheet and two end sheets. Their dimensions and the method of fixing them to the frame are shown in the sketch above.

The canvas must be waterproof, but it should also be thin enough for light to shine through. Plastic sheeting, although a great deal cheaper, cannot be used since it soon tears. It is possible to cut costs by substituting triangular end flaps instead of the capacious rectangles shown, but experience suggests that the more extra material the better to keep out draughts. If sewn-on flaps are used, they should be left with plenty of overlap all around, including at the base so that stones can be piled on when necessary, as when the shelter is left up over night. It is possible to save on replacement costs by cutting a worn-out main sheet in two to use for end sheets.

One end of the shelter should always be covered when in use – otherwise it acts as a wind tunnel. Normally the end away from the wind can be left open, with the end sheet rolled back as shown below. Over night, it should always be closed down and the frame pinned to keep it from blowing away. The main sheet should be kept tight all the time since it helps hold the frame together. The main sheet can be adjusted by means of the guys running from the sewn-on canvas loops to the steel loops on the bottom pipes.

Organising Group Work

Most wallers work alone or in pairs. The procedure when working alone is described in the chapter. 'Building a Free-Standing Wall' (see in particular page 69, point **h**). Keep the following points in mind when working in pairs or groups:

a Walling is one of those territorial activities in which it is easier to work on your own definite section than to work closely with another. It can be very aggravating if too many people crowd onto a section of wall since inevitably your neighbour takes all the best stones or misplaces those which you are keeping an eye on or puts his stones where you plan to place superior ones. Whatever the size of the working group, each person should have at least 1m (a yard) to himself or rather more if he is working opposite a partner. The more skilled the worker, the greater the length which he is likely to feel comfortable constructing himself.

b It is best for two people to work opposite each other rather than side by side. This way each can build up one face of the wall using the stones laid out on that side and can more easily keep out of the other's way. Paired workers can also help each other with the placing of throughs and other heavy stones. Professional wallers, especially in Scotland, often work in pairs this way since it saves time and makes for greater efficiency. With volunteers, it allows more experienced wallers to work opposite and help those of lesser skill. When working this way, the partners should be especially careful to build up the courses at the same rate, otherwise it is difficult to keep the centre of the wall well packed with fillings.

c Extra workers can usefully be employed collecting fillings and placing them between the already positioned face stones. This is quite time-consuming for the wallers to do themselves and it should be possible to help them in this task without getting in their way. Traditionally, many farm children started their walling tuition with this chore, learning how to position the stones rather than throwing them in haphazardly.

Another way to employ extra workers is in grubbing up field stones, provided that the land is primarily of agricultural and not of conservation interest (see p9 regarding the value of limestone pavements) and that the landowner has agreed to this. They can also bring stones within easy reach of the wallers. They shouldn't actually hand stones to the wallers, though, since it is easier for the people on the wall to pick out what they want by eye.

d When several people are working on adjacent sections of wall, they should bring their sections up to the same height before placing throughs, coverbands and topstones. This allows the courses to be levelled properly before these bridging stones are placed.

e When walling with other people be careful to work over or under the guideline. It is very annoying to them if you constantly bang into the reference marker.

f Work rates are difficult to specify, but professional wallers average about 2.7–4.6m (3–5 yards) per person for an 8 hour day, depending on the type of stone, height of wall and site conditions. The rate is much slower in rain. Amateurs working alone can expect to complete rather less than half as much in the same length of time, although well-organised groups of volunteers who are used to working together might begin to approach the professional rate. In competitions, professionals and experienced amateurs must usually build 2.7m (3 yards) per person and novices 1.8m (2 yards) in 6 or 7 hours, including stripping down the existing wall. It is possible from this to judge the sort of hours which wallers traditionally worked in order to average their rood (6 or 7 yards depending on the stone) per day. Gapping tends to be quicker and, if you only have to rebuild from about the middle of the wall up, 18–27m (20–30 yards) per day is possible for an experienced worker.

g From an organisational viewpoint, the most suitable walling work for large groups of eg a dozen or so volunteers is gapping, especially where the gaps are fairly small and conveniently spaced along a given length of wall. Where the task requires a considerable length of wall to be rebuilt, the leader must co-ordinate the work carefully, ensuring that the courses are laid down at an even rate so that lines of weakness do not appear between sections, keeping the courses level and overseeing the position of throughs and topstones. Where separate lengths are started in order to employ extra volunteers, it is important that the ends of each length are left rough (see diagram p87) so that they can be knit together when they meet.

5 Know Your Stone

These notes are intended as a general guide. To learn more about the type of stone in your locality it is worth talking to local wallers, masons and especially quarrymen, who know the stone as it comes from the ground and who take a professional interest in its strengths and weaknesses. Local terminology for various types of building stone is often complex and confusing, so it helps to be able to recognise major types and place them according to their geological features.

Building for Durability

CHOICE OF STONE

Characteristic walling stones are described later in this chapter. Given the usual limited choice in any area, a few points are worth keeping in mind:

a Avoid highly fissile rock when possible. (Good quality slate is an exception. See page 57.) Fissile rock tends to split or fragment easily on weathering and so flakes away piece by piece. If you must use it, keep it in fairly thick blocks rather than splitting it into thinner pieces which will break and crumble.

b Avoid using very large stones, eg bigger than about 300mm (1') on a side or 200mm (8") high, other than for foundations, throughs and coverbands. Even foundation stones should be, if possible, just high enough to come up to ground level from the bottom of the foundation trench, eg about 150mm (6"). Although large stones speed the building process, they are hard to work around and reposition and they may settle unequally relative to smaller stones in the wall. The massive stones found in many old walls are there because of the need to clear adjacent fields or to incorporate immovable boulders, not because they add strength to the wall.

c Avoid using water-washed stones, if possible. Although one occasionally comes across very beautiful walls of rounded river-bottom stones which show the work of a master craftsman (an example is shown on page 79) this challenge should be avoided by amateurs since rounded stones are hard to use, are too smooth to grip properly and may have fine cracks which cause them to break apart in frost. Large rounded stones should be split with the hammer to give them flat beds and faces. Where this is difficult they should be broken up for fillings.

PREVENTING DECAY OF STONEWORK

Stonework, whether dry or mortared, is attacked by a number of agents, including:

a Wind-borne dust or sand, which abrades the stone. This is especially severe in coastal areas.

b Fluctuating temperatures, which cause the stone to flake at the surface or split due to differential expansion and contraction within the stone.

c Frost, which forces the stone apart along cracks as the water freezes and expands.

d Rain, which penetrates cracks in the stone and may lead to frost damage, and which also dissolves certain types of stone directly. Limestone, which is over 90% calcium carbonate, is especially easily affected by the dilute acids found in rain and ground water. Industrial air pollution, which may increase the acidity of rainfall, is responsible for the rapid deterioration not only of limestone but of sandstone as well.

Sedimentary rocks in the ground contain 'quarry sap', a dilute acid having silica, lime and other chemicals in solution or suspension. If the stone is allowed to dry naturally for a year or more before use, the quarry sap forms a hard protective coating on the surface. Because of this, stone which is to be worked should be shaped before curing, when it is softest.

The weather resistance of cured sedimentary stone is reduced if the surface coating is removed in building. Naturally, stone used for dry walling is not given the careful treatment of masonry stone, but it is worth remembering that limestone and to a lesser extent sandstone may last longer if the protective skin is left intact. This is an argument against using the hammer too actively when building with these materials.

Cotswold stone is very subject to frost action, and the most durable stone of this region is dug by hand and left in the open to weather over a winter. This ensures that any bad stone breaks up before use. The topmost layer in the quarry is always the hardest, since it has been exposed to frost over millenia. Nowadays most quarried stone is blasted out and is left with minute stress fractures which may show up only in the first hard frost. If the stone must be purchased when still 'green', ie moist from the earth, it is wise to give it time to dry out before building with it. In other parts of the country less care is usually taken than in the Cotswolds, but Rainsford-Hannay (1972, p61) reports that some Clydesdale wallers used to cart their stone to the building sites in autumn to weather through the winter, again with the idea that the bad stone would be broken by frost before it could be used in the wall.

An important consideration when walling with most types of stone is its bedding. As used in walling the natural 'bed' of a stone is the plane on which it was originally laid down (in the case of sedimentary rocks) or along which it has developed planes of cleavage or foliation (in the case of metamorphic rocks). Since layers of rock are frequently tilted or contorted over the course of geological history, their bedding is not necessarily horizontal when the rock is found in the quarry. Nevertheless, all stones with a laminate bedding should be placed on this natural bed when incorporated into walls and other structures (this is shown in a diagram on page 71), except in upright copings where there is usually no alternative to placing the bedding vertically. Placing the stone on its bedding gives it the greatest resistance to decay.

Stones which are quarried in large blocks with no tendency to split in any particular direction are termed freestones, and can be given any orientation when placed in a structure. Freestones include granite and other igneous rocks and a few extremely fine-grained sedimentary rocks such as Portland, Bath and some of the other famous building stones.

Characteristic Walling Stones

The most important types of walling stones are described briefly below. Wallers often use loose generic terms to describe the rock found in their area. For example, 'whinstone' walls are built through much of Scotland. The Oxford English Dictionary describes whinstone as 'a name for various very hard dark-coloured rocks or stones, as greenstone, basalt, chert or quartzose sandstone', but as actually used the term seems to be a catch-all for hard dark stones which cannot be easily described in terms of the more clearly defined types listed below.

SANDSTONES

Sandstones consist of grains of sand, mostly quartz, cemented most commonly by silica, carbonate of lime or iron oxide. The resulting material may vary considerably in hardness. Colour ranges from white through yellow and brown to red depending on the cementing minerals. The main types of sandstone from

the point of view of walling include quartzite, consisting mainly of quartz grains cemented into a hard continuous mass by silica; grits, which are hard sandstones especially those where sand grains are mixed with small pebbles so that the rock breaks with a very rough surface; (the coarsest grits were once widely used for millstones) and flags, including thin-bedded sandstones which split readily parallel to the bedding.

Sandstones of widely varying ages are found in walls in many parts of the country. Perhaps the oldest is the Precambrian Torridonian Sandstone of Sutherland and Wester Ross, but the earliest widely-used sandstone is the Old Red Sandstone of Devonian age found for example in many parts of eastern Scotland. Caithness Flag fences (p20) use stone of this type. Through large areas of the Pennines and the North East of England, Millstone Grit and other coarse dark Carboniferous sandstones dominate many of the walls. Around Carlisle and in Dumfriesshire the warm New Red Sandstone of Permian age is trimmed into blocks to produce masonry-like dry walls.

LIMESTONES

Limestones are calcareous rocks formed from solidified masses of whole or broken shells, from the remains of coral reefs, from chemical precipitates or evaporates or from the redeposition of eroded materials from older limey beds. Most limestones are formed almost completely of calcium carbonate, but magnesium limestone contains much magnesium carbonate. Chalk is a peculiarly uniform limestone made up of minutely divided shell fragments and other calcareous detritus, often with layers of flints. All limestones are more or less readily weathered by rain and ground water containing dilute carbonic and sulphuric acids, particularly where the stone has been cracked or has developed bedding due to the pressure of overlying strata. Limestones often intergrade with sandstones and shales so that the division between calcareous sandstone and gritty or sandy limestone, for example, is not always clear.

In Britain the oldest really widespread limestone is Carboniferous Limestone, which forms part of the Derbyshire Peak District and the area to both sides of the Craven Fault in the western part of North Yorkshire. This pale grey, lumpy stone is immediately recognisable wherever it occurs, not only in the walls of the north but in the Mendips and the Gower Peninsula as well. North of Wensleydale the Carboniferous Limestone becomes increasingly sandy and the walls are more mixed. Jurassic limestones of many different varieties colour the buildings and most of the walls in the Cotswolds. In Oxfordshire, Stonesfield 'slate' (really a sandy flaggy limestone) provided until recently an important local roofing material. The Jurassic Limestone belt runs north-northeast from the Isle of Purbeck to the Cleveland Hills in North Yorkshire and has been widely used for building. Chalk, of Cretaceous age, forms the downs of southern and southeastern England and parts of East Anglia. It is too water soluble to be used in dry stone walling, but the flints which it contains are widely used alone or banded with bricks in the mortared walls of this part of the country.

SHALE AND SLATE

Shale beongs to the group of argillaceous or mud rocks, made up of very fine particles of rock flour, clay etc which have been dried and hardened by compression. Shale is distinguished from other mud rocks by its well-developed lamination, and it tends to split readily into thin slabs parallel to the original bedding. Most shale is soft and weathers readily, forming a generally subdued landscape where it is widespread or representing gentle slopes or valleys where it occurs in series with more resistant sandstone or limestone. Most of central Wales is covered by Ordovician and Silurian shales which are often tough enough to form moderate rolling hills. Only when the shale has been further metamorphosed into slate does it begin to make a reasonably durable walling stone, however.

Slate is mudstone or shale which has been metamorphosed under intense pressure. This has so compressed the original material that flaky minerals such as mica have formed and been shifted so that their flat surfaces lie approximately at right angles to the direction from which the pressure came. The metamorphosed material may retain traces, often highly distorted, of the original bedding, but it can now most easily be split along the new cleavage planes.

Most slates or slatey shales are low grade and have little use in building, but it is these stones which are used for walls in much of central and north Wales, the Skiddaw Slate area of the northern Lake District and elsewhere where preferable walling stone is not readily available. The common feature of these walls, whether of true slate or simply highly compressed shale, is their fissile nature – that is, the stones tend to split further and further along their cleavage planes or laminations. Unless another type of stone is available to form a heavy capping, these walls often tend to flake away layer by layer, or settle sideways if on a hill or next to a roadway.

High-grade slate, eg waste from slate quarries, can be trimmed into rectangular blocks which are much more resistant to splitting than the more open-jointed materials and can even be used to make fences of cut slate uprights or flags (pp13, 15).

GRANITE AND OTHER IGNEOUS ROCKS

Granite is formed by the slow cooling of acid molten rock deep in the earth's crust. It is often, but not always, coarse grained and is made up mainly of felspars and quartz with considerable mica and small percentages of other minerals. True granite grades into granodiorite, quartz-diorite and diorite as the balance of minerals changes. Here, however, the terms 'granite' and 'granitic' are loosely used to include the related family members as well.

Granite is the toughest and most durable of the building stones. It forms the resistant bulk of many of Britain's wildest moorlands: the Cairngorms and Rannoch Moor as well as other parts of northern Scotland, mainly in Caithness, Aberdeenshire and Inverness-shire; Cairnsmore of Fleet in Kircudbrightshire; The Cheviot; parts of the Lake District; and in the South West, Dartmoor and Bodmin Moor, Land's End and much of the rest of Cornwall lying above 150m (500′). Detached blocks of granite have been used locally from prehistoric times for tombs and standing stones and, later, for Christian crosses. But it was not until the 18th century, according to Hawkes (1951, p109), that granite was quarried for anything more than rough local purposes, so difficult was it to prise from the quarry face. The clearance walls of Zennor, Cornwall (p17), may date back to the Iron Age while those of Aberdeenshire, the other area where granite walls dominate the scene, are of late 18th, 19th and early 20th century date.

The extrusive igneous rocks form a widely varying group including everything from obsidian (volcanic glass) to pumice (puffed and solidified ash) to dense and fine-grained black basalt. Basalt is crushed for roadstone but has little other use in building, although it is found with other dense stones in many rough Scottish walls. In the Lake District, walls of Borrowdale Volcanics, composed of varied Ordovician lavas, ashes and agglomerates, are characteristically coarse and warmly coloured compared to the dark slate walls to their north and south.

SCHISTS AND GNEISSES

Schists and gneisses are metamorphic rocks which represent an intermediate between sedimentary formations and granite. A distinguishing feature of both schists and gneisses is their foliation, like the tightly packed leaves of leaf-mould. Schists have the foliation closely spaced throughout the body of the rock, so that almost any part of it can be split into flakes. The most common type is mica schist, so called because mica is the mineral chiefly responsible for foliation. In gneisses the foliation is open and interrupted. Highly micaceous layers alternate with bands or 'eyes' (lenticals) that are granular and more like granite in texture. Many gneisses, unlike schists, contain felspar as an important mineral and are like granite or granodiorite in composition.

Schists and gneisses are usually ancient rocks, Precambrian in Britain. In Highland Scotland, mica schist occurs widely, but interfolded with other rocks, in a belt stretching from the island of Kintyre northeast to the Aberdeenshire coast, with other areas inland in Ross and Cromarty and Sutherland. Hornblende schist, a type which develops from basaltic rocks, is more limited in occurrence but is distributed similarly. Gneiss covers most of the outer Hebrides and parts of the Inner Isles and the northwest coast, in places cut by inliers of epidiorite and hornblende schist. The other main areas of occurrence of these rocks are Anglesey, the Lizard in Cornwall and Start Point in Devon. While some schists produce even rectangular blocks of walling stone, gneisses tend to be rough and irregular. But even the roughest gneisses are easier to use than granite in rubble dry stone walls.

Sources of Stone and Amounts Required

In general, the best stone for use in walling is that which is local. Even if other stone can be had more cheaply, local stone preserves the continuity between the natural landscape, the older walls in the vicinity and the new work. Occasionally local stone is not to be preferred, however, such as when it is extremely fissile and weathers poorly or when it must be taken from areas of limestone pavement or other sites of special geological or botanical interest.

There are four sources of stone to consider when collecting material for a new wall:

a Surface field stones (other than limestone pavements). Early farm walls were often built in part at least to clear the land. Often in areas of rough grazing there are still ample supplies of stone near to hand, requiring only picks and crowbars to remove. Even where bedrock does not form convenient outcrops, glacial till often supplies stones large enough for walling although these tend to be less easy to work with than quarried stone.

b Stone from derelict walls and buildings. Old stone should be reused in new walls when possible, although some Cotswold stone and fissile shales and slates may become unsuitably soft and crumbly through weathering. Where there are plenty of other dry stone habitats, existing derelict walls and stone outbuildings often provide the cheapest and least laborious source of stone, although highly dressed building stone is not good for dry stone walling since the faces are too smooth to bond securely. Always check with the landowner before using stone from old walls or buildings no matter how decayed they may seem.

c Stone from abandoned quarries or self-quarried stone. 'Vest pocket' quarries often dot the line of long enclosure walls, usually as near as possible in their uphill side. Sometimes these can be worked again without much trouble. Limestone faces usually produce good-sized though irregular chunks with just a little pick and crowbar work, but outcroppings of weathered sandstone often yield unusably big boulders. Weathered granite is very difficult to extract, but schist is less troublesome. Whinstone and slate or slatey shales can be taken from rock faces without too much difficulty. If road haulage of stones is no problem, you may find rather larger abandoned quarries within a few miles of the walling site, often with much split stone or quarry waste ready to hand. Seek out the owner and see if you can remove the rubble or work the face for your needs.

d Professionally quarried stone. Council, estate boundary and decorative garden walls often call for cut stone from commercial quarries. But this is expensive and so is seldom considered for ordinary farm walling. And regular trimmed blocks, whether of slate, sandstone, limestone or granite, may look incongruous if the surrounding walls are of rough rubble.

Where the adjacent walls are of quarried stone it may be worth trying to match them for style and type. There are a number of associations representing the interests of quarry owners, masons and others involved with natural stone, from whom details of stone supplies in any area may be sought. Preliminary inquiries should be made to the Stone Federation, 82 New Cavendish Street, London W1M 8AD, or the Building Research Station, Bucknalls Lane, Garston, Watford, Hertfordshire WD2 7JR.

AMOUNTS REQUIRED

The weight of stone required to build a given length of dry wall depends primarily on the wall's height, top width and bottom width, but also on the density of the rock used and the amount of air space left in the completed wall. The last factor depends in turn on the size and regularity of the stones used.

Raistrick (1966, p27) estimates that rather more than 1.6 tonnes of stone are required per metre length of wall (1.75 tons per yard) for a wall 1.8m (6′) high, 910mm (3′) at the base and tapering to 400mm (1′4″) high at the top. This includes the weight of the fillings but allows for the assumption that one third of the volume of the finished wall is empty.

Scottish wallers give a figure of about 1.1 tonnes per metre (1 ton per yard) in the 'standard' double dyke, ie a wall 1.4m (4′6″) high with a 100–150mm (4–6″) deep foundation, 810mm (2′8″) wide at the footings, 660mm (2′2″) wide at the first course above the footings tapering to 350mm (1′2″) wide immediately below the coverband and coping. The standard locked top type of coping (p75) is said to contain fully one third of the weight in this type of wall.

Beddall (1950, p78) gives a figure of 2.5 tonnes per metre length (2.25 tons per yard) for a 1.5m (5′) high wall (1.8m, 6′ from the bottom of the foundations) with an average width of 760mm (2′6″). It is not clear whether he makes an allowance for air space in reaching this rather high estimate.

Beddall (1950, p77) also states that South Western granite-faced stone hedges require 1 tonne of stone per 3.3 square metres 'super' (1 ton per 4 square yards). This means that it takes 1 tonne (1 ton) of granite to face a 0.9 metre (1 yard) length of 1.8m (6′) high hedge on both sides. Assuming the hedge is 1.3–1.5m (4′6″–5′) wide at the base and 760mm (2′6″) wide at the crown, it requires about 2.2 cubic metres of material, inclusive of stone, packed earth and turf for every metre run (72 cubic feet per yard) or nearly 46 cubic metres (60 cubic yards) per chain (20m, 22 yards).

Breaking and Shaping Stone

Margaret Brooks (1973, p46) once talked to a Yorkshire waller who said he used his hammer only

> *'with something of the feeling of giving way, something of a feeling of defeat. One ought to be able to fit all the stones, make use of all the stones whatever their shape and size.*

> *One should manage with the stones as they are, especially stones from an existing wall that's fallen. They have been used before; it should be possible to use them again.'*

This is a sentiment that many wallers would agree with, not only in Yorkshire but throughout the North of England and in Wales as well. Nevertheless, breaking and shaping stones is often a necessity either to provide material of a usable shape and size or to trim it to a more regular finished product.

GENERAL POINTS

a Be careful when breaking stones, especially when quarrying rock faces or getting big boulders out of the earth. Goggles are essential to protect your eyes when hammering or drilling. See the precautions on pages 41–44.

b Examine each stone before hitting it to see how it will break. Almost every stone, even granite, has some lines of weakness along bedding or cleavage planes or in areas of frost damage and other weathering stress. It is along these planes that stones break most easily and predictably. If there is no obvious crack to work on, hammer away until one appears and then concentrate your efforts on this crack.

c To quarry slabs of bedded or cracked stone, enlarge the cracks with a pick until you can drive in wedges with a sledge hammer or pry the rock apart with a crowbar. See page 58 for methods of drilling smooth slabs of granite.

d Most types of walling stone can be split with a hammer of an appropriate size and weight for the size and type of stone (see page 46). Hit the stone 'fair on' or you will just chip it away and round it off, although if you can't split it as far in as you want to you may have to cut it in several stages working back gradually to the correct shape. Hit with the full face of the hammer head as shown below.

This is most effective, causes least wear on the hammer and helps prevent chips from flying up into your face. Use a full, solid swing except when doing careful trimming. Hit very slightly away from the line of proposed fracture so that the correct part of the stone breaks off, as shown above.

If the stone doesn't split immediately, keep hammering away at the dust which you create. The dust acts as a wedge to force the stone apart.

e Experiment with each type of stone to find the way in which it splits most readily. Sometimes it works better to hit at right angles to the grain than to strike in the usual way along the grain.

f Break stones on the ground, not on the wall, which will disrupt it, or in your hand, which will hurt it. Support the stone against another stone and hold it firmly with your left foot.

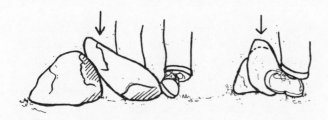

It is easier to split the stone when it is positioned more or less on edge, as shown, rather than flat on the ground.

g Before you break up a big stone, make sure it won't be needed as a through, cover, topstone or gate post. Try to break it so as to produce several usable face stones or one useful face stone plus fillings. Don't waste effort and stone trying to shape it exactly – in rough rubble walling it is better to use what you've got where you can find a place for it.

Except in the Cotswolds and a few other places, small regular stones are considered an unnecessary luxury. (See the first chapter in this handbook for more on regional practice.) Although a wall of small stones may be tighter than a very coarse wall, it is unlikely to be any tighter than a wall of medium-sized stones and it must be built with very level, well-graded beds for strength and appearance. As well as involving extra effort, such a wall may look out of place next to rougher neighbours.

h There are various ways by which stone can be shaped more precisely when required. Cotswold and other soft stones can be chipped away with a hammer having a narrow or pointed pein for dressing. Other methods include scoring and wedging apart big slabs, drilling and wedging freestones and splitting finely bedded or foliated stones with a hammer and chisel. Techniques are described in the following sections for slate, granite and schist and gneiss. These can be adapted for use on other types of stone as necessary.

SLATE

Slate can be cut into square-cornered blocks of the desired size and split down to almost any thickness using a cold chisel and lump hammer. Unfortunately, the best chisels for the job are no longer available because they were made by slate quarry blacksmiths who knew the exact shape and temper of tool required for different processes and even for different faces or veins in the same quarry. An ordinary commercially made cold chisel can be substituted with some effect even though it is too small and is designed for use on metal rather than stone. You can also use a bricklayer's bolster to break slate across the grain. If you manage to acquire second-hand slate-cutting chisels take care of them since they are virtually irreplaceable. They are usually shaped as shown below. Their flanges are easily broken off if they are misused.

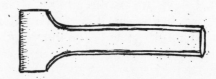

Quarrymen often work with a set of three identical chisels, allowing two to rest while the third is in use. The set should be sharpened and retempered about once a month if in constant use.

A block of good-quality slate can be split easily and precisely in two but not all three planes. It can be cleaved, ie forced apart along a cleavage plane. It can also be split along the grain, ie the original bedding plane which lies roughly at right angles to the cleavage. But it cannot be as easily split perpendicular to both the cleavage and the bedding. Lower-quality slate, more often encountered in rough walling, can be cleaved but not so easily split along the grain.

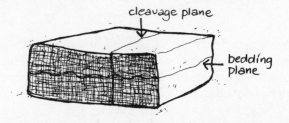

To cleave slate, place the stone on end with its cleavage planes running vertically. Hold the chisel or bolster in one hand, perpendicular to the surface as shown below, and tap it firmly but not heavily with the lump hammer. If cleaving a narrow block, hold the chisel in the centre of the line which you wish to cleave. If cleaving a wide block, start near one end and work gradually along the line.

If the block is too large it may not split, but a crack should appear which you can gradually force apart with further light taps of the chisel or by gently prying with a wrecking bar.

To split slate along its grain, start with the chisel or bolster at one edge of the slab and move it along the line of the desired cut, tapping it in the same way as described above. At first you may have to go over the line of the cut more than once, but with practice you should be able to split it with two or three blows. It helps if the ground below the line of the cut is soft enough to absorb some of the shock and distribute it through the slate.

To split slate perpendicular to both the grain and the cleavage, first cut a groove with the chisel along the line which you hope to split. In quarries special chisels are available, but you can use an ordinary cold chisel to carve out a line about 6mm ($\frac{1}{4}''$) deep and wide. Now tap along this groove in the same way as when splitting along the grain.

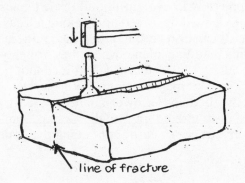

line of fracture

You may have to hit quite a bit harder than when splitting the slate in other ways, and the break will probably occur not at right angles to the end of the block but slightly off it.

In commercial cut work, slate is sawn along this line rather than split with hammer and chisel to achieve a more exact result, but for general walling or building purposes it doesn't matter if the cut is a bit off.

GRANITE

Fields (1971) goes into detail on how to split large blocks of granite and schist, and the information in this and the following section is based largely on his experience. He suggests the following tools for use on granite:

a 375mm (15″) grinding chisel with a three-quarters-square shaft with a flat top for striking, tapering to an 18mm ($\frac{3}{4}''$) wide arrowhead grinding surface. A star drill may be used just as well.

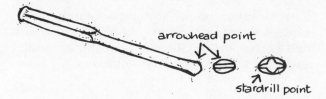

arrowhead point

stardrill point

Drills may also have waisted shanks, which are particularly useful on wider drills to keep them from jamming in the holes.

For drilling a hole in which to set a metal post etc, it is best to have several drills, graduated in length so that as the hole deepens you can use progressively longer drills. This is easier than using a long drill from the start. Drills for this purpose should be 6mm ($\frac{1}{4}''$) wider than the post to be set in, so that there is space around the post to pour in lead or cement for fixing. Electric stone drills are made but their expense is prohibitive for the amateur or occasional user and they require a mobile source of power.

b Cleaning tool to remove rock dust when drilling. This is a light metal rod, 150–175mm (6–7″) long and about 5mm ($\frac{3}{16}''$) in diameter, with the last 12mm ($\frac{1}{2}''$) flattened and curved as shown.

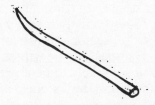

You can also use a small bicycle pump to blow out debris, or push in lumps of plasticine to which the dust and stone chips will stick.

c Six sets of shims and wedges. Each set consists of a pair of metal shims or 'feathers', narrow at the top and flaring outward so that you can grip them, and a metal wedge.

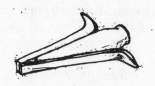

d Lump and sledge hammers

e 150mm (6″) steel wedges of the sort used in tree felling

f Crowbar and wrecking bar

To split granite:

1 Drill a series of holes along the line to be split. Their distance apart is set mainly by the length of stone to be split with the available shims and wedges. Holes can be spaced up to 300mm (1′) or more apart but the closer they are the more accurate the results. Rule (1974) says that Cornish stone hedgers drive their wedges in as close together as 75mm (3″) for exact results.

To drill each hole, hold the grinding chisel or star drill in one hand with the shaft perpendicular to the rock. Rest the drill point on the rock and hit the drill smartly with the lump hammer. Do not use very heavy blows, however, since these will not necessarily speed the work and, if attempted on other types of rock, may shatter the stone. Then turn the drill 60°. Continue hitting and rotating the drill until the hole is 200–225mm (4–5″) deep (less for a small slab). Flick the dust out of the hole from time to time with the cleaning tool. Drilling granite is a very slow, tedious job so don't exhaust yourself by trying to rush it.

2 When all the holes are drilled, insert a pair of shims in each with a wedge between. Pound each wedge once, moving down the line in consecutive order. Return to the first wedge and repeat the operation until a thin crack forms between the wedges.

3 Insert one or more large steel wedges into the crack. Retrieve the shims and small wedges. Then hammer the big wedges a few times until the split is wide enough to insert the crowbar or wrecking bar. Remove these wedges and lever the slab apart.

SCHIST AND GNEISS

Schist has definite planes of foliation and along these it splits much more readily than granite. Mica schist is the easiest type to split. Gneiss can be split using the same tools and methods but the results are less easy and predictable. Extremely irregular and tenacious gneiss may require drilling before it is split.

To split small slabs of these rocks all you need is a lump hammer and cold chisel. To split and trim big slabs you need:

a Two heavy sledge hammers, one square-peined and one with one square and one bevelled pein. The latter should be as heavy as possible, up to about 11.3kg (25lb).

b Lump hammer

c Hand hammer with one square and one bevelled pein, about the same size and weight as the lump hammer

d Thin steel wedge. An old discarded axe blade is ideal.

e Crowbar and wrecking bar

It is easiest if two people work together to split a large slab of schist:

1 Prop the slab up on edge using wooden blocks or stones.

2 Mark out a straight line parallel to the grain of foliation.

3 While one person holds the bevel-pein sledge hammer with its edge alone the line to be split, the other pounds it with the square-pein sledge. Starting at one end of the slab, move along it striking one solid blow in each position. Repeat the sequence until a crack shows along the line which has been marked out.

4 Tap the old axe blade into the crack until it can stand without being held. Then drive it in farther with the sledge.

5 When the crack is wide enough, insert the

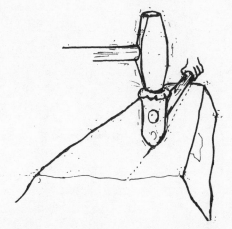

end of the crowbar or wrecking bar and pry apart the slab.

To trim schist to a more precise shape:

1 Prop up the slab and wedge it in position with stones.

2 Hold the small bevel-pein hammer against

59

the bottom of the surface to be cut away, with the head angled downward about 30°.

3 Hit the bevelled hammer with the lump hammer to chip away at the face of the slab.

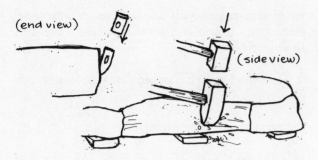

Remove the face bit by bit, gradually moving

the bevelled hammer higher on the face as the lower part is cut back sufficiently.

4 As you near the top edge of the slab, remove the props. Finish squaring off the top face by removing small chips of stone. To do this, hit the bevelled hammer while holding it perpendicular to the top face as shown.

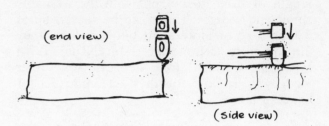

6 Building a Free-Standing Wall

This chapter covers design and construction procedures basic to all free-standing dry stone walls. It leaves to the following chapter the additional problems to be considered when using stone to face or retain an earth bank.

Every locale has its own terminology, which tends to hide the fact that similarities in their walling methods are far more important than differences. The usage given here, and the procedures where different from other regions, are those general to the old West Riding of Yorkshire, that is basically the area of Pennines limestone, Millstone Grit and Coal Measures. The first chapter, 'Walls in the Landscape', should be read for regional variations in walling design and technique.

General Features

The diagram on page 62 illustrates the construction of a typical Pennine wall, a design which is followed with fairly minor modifications throughout most of Britain's walling country. Note the range given for the height, width and other specifications. These vary according to the wall's purpose, its age and the type of stone in which it is built. Garden walls may be any height, but those which fence cattle are usually about 1.2m (4') from the grass to the top of the coping, while those which fence sheep, particularly moorland varieties, are usually at least 1.6m (5'3"). Old walls pre-dating the Parliamentary Enclosure Acts are usually more coarsely built, wider at the base with a more gradual batter and with fewer throughs, while the most highly-designed examples are invariably the major enclosure walls, or march dykes as Rainsford-Hannay (1957, p23) calls them. Whatever the age of the wall, the more regular its stone the less batter or taper is required. Fields (1971, p36) builds his walls with vertical sides, 'so that each stone casts a shadow', but while this is fine for low garden walls built of Vermont mica schist it would never work in other situations. The right batter for the stone at hand is sometimes specified in the walling contract, if there is one. Otherwise, choose a good example of an existing local wall for your guide. The diagram of the Pennine wall shows the optimum number and spacing of throughs-tones for its height (less than 1.5m (5') under the topstones). Where, as often happens, fewer throughs are available, they should be set out as explained on page 72.

The Use and Abuse of Concrete and Mortar

In a masonry wall, concrete or mortar is usually essential to bind the stonework together. But a dry stone wall is designed to settle into a durable structure without any cement at all. The fact that many miles of completely unmortared walls have stood intact for centuries, often with no repair or attention, proves that with proper construction and materials no binding substance is necessary. Yet old walls occasionally and new ones much more often incorporate concrete or mortar into what is by design dry stonework. This is not always a mistake, since mortar does have its uses. These include:

a To strengthen the coping on an otherwise dry wall. Buck-and-doe copings and upright or flat copings using small, light stones are especially vulnerable to being dislodged by animals, vandals or traffic vibration on an adjacent road. Here, and where a stile is built into the wall, it may be necessary to mortar the coping.

b To strengthen the entire wall against vibration from heavy traffic. New council walling is often mortared throughout and given a solid concrete coping or a heavy layer of mortar below the topstones.

c To strengthen walls made of too-regular or fissile stones which would otherwise tend to slip apart on settling.

d To make a sturdy coping easier and faster to place.

e To provide a solid foundation when suitably large footing stones are unavailable.

f To strengthen a wall head made of small stones, or a stile which uses stone stoops or wooden posts.

g To anchor fencing standards into the wall (p104).

h To create a horse jump (p8) or other special feature.

In most cases the disadvantages of concrete and mortar in dry walls far outweigh their advantages. Drawbacks include:

a Materials and transportation costs are considerably higher if cement is added to a dry stone wall. (continued on page 63)

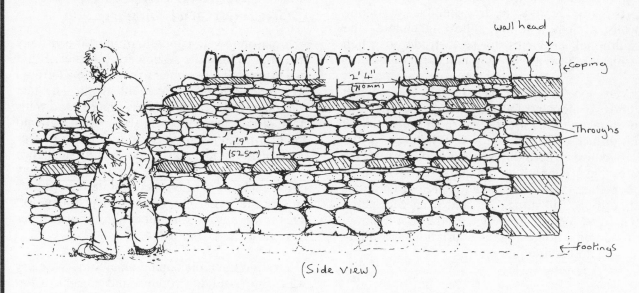

wall head

coping

Throughs

2'4"
(710mm)

1'9"
(525mm)

Footings

(Side View)

Courses are horizontal. The stones are roughly graded with the biggest at the bottom and the smallest at the top under the coping. Where available, thin flags (preferably throughs) are used to make a continuous base for the topstones.

Enclosure Era walls often have twenty-one throughs per rood (5.5m or 6.4m, 6 or 7 yards, depending on the stone). Throughs are usually in two rows, often with twelve per rood at a height of 0.6m (2′) (525mm centres (1′9″)) and nine per rood at 1.2m (4′) (710mm centres (2′4″)) as shown above. If the wall's height

under the topstones is 1.2m (5′) or more, the same number of throughs should be used but in three rows. Low walls, eg under about 1.2m (4′) excluding the topstones, may have a single row of throughs placed halfway up the body of the wall. Throughs in different rows should be staggered for greatest strength. Throughs may be flush with the wall faces or may project a few inches on one or both sides.

The coping is often upright with even-sided topstones, but various styles are possible (p73). A large secure topstone is required for the wall head (p79).

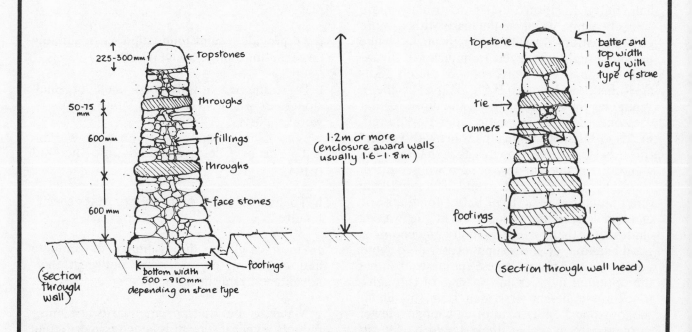

225-300mm — topstones

50-75 mm

600mm — throughs

— fillings

600mm — throughs

— face stones

— footings

(section through wall)

bottom width 500 - 910mm depending on stone type

1.2m or more (enclosure award walls usually 1.6-1.8m)

topstone — batter and top width vary with type of stone

tie —

runners —

footings

(section through wall head)

b New walls settle by about 75mm (3″) in their first few years. As this happens, dry walls increase in strength and cohesiveness, since every stone shifts into the tightest relationship with its neighbours. But dry walls with solidly mortared topstones tend to settle away from the rigid copings and without the weight of the topstones to anchor them the other stones below are easily dislodged. All too often the result is as shown.

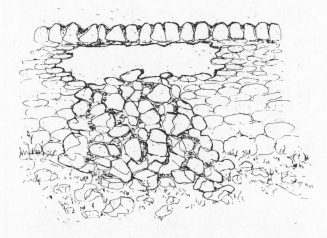

Vibration from traffic may cause greater-than-normal settlement in dry walls, so the likelihood of gaps forming beneath a cemented cope is greatest on a roadside wall.

If mortar is used in the body of the wall, the coping may settle along with the wall but the wall itself may develop humps or bulges due to reduced flexibility. According to Chantree (1971), this problem is less likely if an old wall is mortared during repairs, since most of the settlement will have already taken place.

c Water expands by $\frac{1}{12}$ when it freezes. Dry walls are built so that water drains freely through and into the subsoil. Concrete or mortar can trap rainwater which may break and dislodge stones when it freezes.

d Gaps are more difficult and dangerous to repair if a mortared coping is still in place, bridging the gap. It is sometimes necessary to break away the concrete bridge with a sledge hammer.

e Vehicles which hit partly mortared walls are likely to suffer more damage than those which run into dry walls. At the same time they knock down extra yards of walling since the wall tends to be dragged out in a unit.

N C Butchart, an authority on walls especially in the Lake District, points out that cement-based mortars are rigid and brittle and are especially prone to poor settlement. And in some cases cement mortar is stronger than the walling stones themselves, causing the stones to deteriorate before the mortar. Therefore, except when concrete slabs must be laid as substitutes for foundation stones, any mortar used should be composed of lime and sand rather than cement and sand, to retain some flexibility. This is also preferable from a botanical viewpoint (p36). However, where a wall head or other part of the wall is to be mortared throughout, a small proportion of cement can be added to the mix for extra durability (see page 77 for specifications).

Walling Procedure

Dry stone wall construction has four rules which are so basic that they apply to any situation. These are:

a Place the biggest stones at the bottom, except for throughs and topstones.

b Cross (break) the joints.

c Keep the middle full.

d Taper the wall, following the correct batter for the type of stone.

Walling techniques based on these rules are virtually the same whether the work is done by one person, a pair or a group. But pair and group work involve a few considerations additional to those given below (see page 50).

The work sequence outlined below is covered in detail in the sections which follow. For simplicity, it is assumed that the wall is on level ground and its ends are already secured by wall heads. The problems of building heads, of walling on slopes and of repairing or rebuilding existing walls are discussed later in the chapter.

To build a dry stone wall of the sort illustrated on page 62:

1 Line out, clear and dig the entire foundation trench (p65).

2 Set out the supply of stones along the trench, leaving room to work (p65).

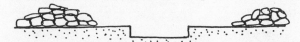

3 Put in the footings (foundation stones) along the entire trench. Place fillings between them as you work (p68).

4 Set up the batter frame or frames for the estimated day's work (p66). Place the guidelines about 300mm (1') above ground level.

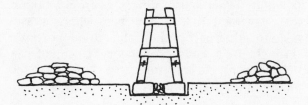

5 Build the courses to the 300mm (1') level, following the four basic design rules given above (see also pages 66–68).

6 Raise the guidelines to the height of the bottom of the first row of throughs, normally about 600mm (2') above ground level but proportionately lower for a low wall or if three rows of throughs are planned.

7 Build the courses up to the lines and level them off to take the throughs. Follow the basic design rules at each course.

8 Lay the first row of throughs (p72).

9 If a second row of throughs is planned, raise the guidelines to the height of the bottom of this row, usually about 1–1.2m (3'6"–4') above ground level. If no second row is planned, go to step 16.

10 If you need to move more stones in to where you can reach them easily, this is a good time to do it. But keep back suitable topstones for use later.

11 Build the courses up to the guidelines and level them off to take the second row of throughs. Follow the basic design rules at each course.

12 Lay the second row of throughs.

13 Raise the guidelines to the height of the bottom of the third row of throughs, if there is to be one. If not, go to step 16.

14 Build the courses up to the lines and level them off to take the third row of throughs.

15 Lay the third row of throughs.

16 Raise the guidelines to the height of the top course, ie to the top of the wall minus the topstones.

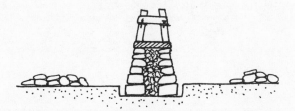

17 Build the courses up to the lines and level them off to take the topstones.

18 Normally the topstones are placed after the entire wall is brought up level, in which case you should repeat steps 4–17 until this is done. However, for long stretches or where the wall may have to be left unfinished for some time it is worth placing topstones on shorter finished sections to protect them. The method used depends on the style of coping (p73).

19 Clean up at the end of the day's work, and shift unused stones to the section to be built next (p87). Leave the end of the wall in stepped courses, unless you have finished the section at a head, so that the next day's work will bind in well.

The Foundation

A wall is only as good as its foundation. Poor footings are the source of most serious collapses, and no amount of careful building higher up can correct for problems at the base. A proper foundation:

a Provides a stable base for the rest of the wall. With from one to two tons of stone in every yard length of wall, the foundation must be suitably wide, solid and firm to resist unequal settling.

b Keeps the fillings in position in the centre of the wall. Otherwise they tend to wash or settle out.

c Allows water to drain out the base of the wall, minimising disruption due to frost.

d Prevents soil erosion under the wall due to running water from rain or snowmelt, which might cause subsidence.

LINING OUT

Follow this procedure:

1 Clear woody plants, coarse tussocky vegetation and stones from the line of the proposed wall. Don't bother trying to move solidly embedded boulders.

2 Mark out one edge of the proposed foundation trench. Stretch a nylon guideline tightly between stakes or metal pins at either end.

3 Stake or pin a second guideline parallel to the first at the correct width for the proposed trench. This should be about 300mm (1′) greater than the specified foundation width, to allow room to manoeuvre and make adjustments.

4 'Nick out' along each line. To do this, face the line, holding the spade vertically with the back of the blade against the line and parallel to it. Push the blade straight down to the estimated trench depth, using the foot if necessary. Do this along the entire line.

5 Dig the trench down to firm subsoil or bedrock. This is usually between 100mm (4″) and 310mm (12″) deep, with 150mm (6″) about average. Footings, unless you must use very large ones, should come up to but not above ground level. If they are too high they provide a convenient step for livestock investigating a way over the wall. Cut the trench sides vertically, otherwise you may have trouble placing the footings.

SETTING OUT

Set out the day's supply of stones alongside the foundation trench and about a yard away from it. This minimises the walking and carrying but at the same time gives you room to work without stones underfoot. Set additional stones a bit farther away, rather than piling them up, so that you may see to choose from as many stones as possible.

Set out wall stones and fillings on both sides of the trench unless you prefer to work from one side only, in which case you should set out all the stones on the preferred side. If you are unloading and setting out by hand, you can sort the stones roughly as you go, just as when stripping down an existing wall for repair (p86). In this case, keep likely throughs and topstones to one side and a little back from the other stones. Don't bother sorting stones already on the ground, though: just keep your eye out for good throughs and topstones and avoid using them elsewhere.

PLACING THE FOOTINGS

a Use the biggest stones in the foundation, except those which would make good throughs or topstones or which you want to reserve for wall heads, cripple holes etc. While it is best to use stones which come up to but not above ground level, if you have to use very large stones use them here rather than higher up where they would rest on smaller stones.

If the bottom of the foundation trench is irregular bedrock, build up a regular bed for the footings with small flat stones, closely spaced. If the bedrock lies just an inch or so below ground level, don't bother with big footings but lay the first course of wall stones directly on the prepared bed. In this case the bedrock acts as a foundation.

b Lay the footings in two parallel lines along the foundation trench with their long edges into, not along, the line of the wall.

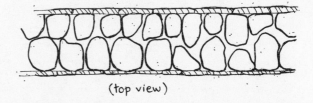

(top view)

Stones placed this way are very hard to shift,

once weighted from above, whereas stones placed along the wall may easily rotate out of position. Very big footings, however, may have to be placed long edge along the wall to avoid widening the trench or interfering with the footings on the opposite side.

c Be sure that each stone sits on a good bed or base. Check them for steadiness. They should not need to be wedged, since any wedged stones are likely to tilt or slip as the wall settles. Avoid round-backed footings since it is hard to build firmly on top of them.

With each footing, choose the smoothest edge or the one most nearly at right angles to the bed to use for the outside face. You should do this with the face stones in succeeding courses as well. The smooth outer surface looks good and deters climbers, while irregular inner edges bind best with the fillings. Raistrick (1966, p19) reports that the bed and face or 'end' of the footings and lowest courses are 'often just roughly scappelled with a three or four pound hammer' to make them flatter and more perpendicular to each other, but few Pennine wallers bother with this in our experience unless the stones are hard to use otherwise.

d Allow at least 25mm (1″) between the inside edges of the footings to promote drainage within the wall. Normally the space is considerably greater because of irregularities in the stones.

e Pack between the two rows of footings with angular, free-draining fillings (see page 68).

Use of Batter Frames

Batter frames are described on page 48. Pennine wallers tend to dispense with them, except when walling long sections or working to precise specifications, but beginners and groups of volunteers should use them to insure accurate results. The only time there is no need for frames is when repairing small gaps.

When building from an existing section of wall or wall head, only one frame is needed. It is set up at the end of the estimated day's section and guidelines are run from it to the existing wall.

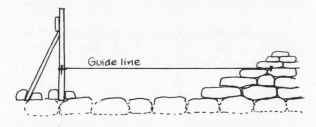

Occasionally two frames are necessary, one at each end of the day's section, eg when starting a wall on its own because the stones for the head are unavailable or are to be built later with masonry.

To set up the batter frame and guidelines:

1 Set the frame squarely across the foundations so that its feet are at ground level and its centre line is over the centre of the trench.

2 Check the frame for plumb in both directions and prop it up with a board placed against the upper crosspiece. Anchor its feet and the end of the prop with stones.

3 Tie the ends of both guidelines to metal pins or wooden splints or pegs.

4 Fasten the lines to the legs of the frame about 300mm (1′) above ground level. To do this, bring the lines outside the legs, wrap them around the legs twice and push the pins or splints down the back to secure.

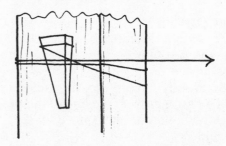

5 Set up the other frame and fix the lines to it in the same way, or fasten the lines to the existing wall by pushing a pin, splint or trowel into a convenient crack at the correct level and wrapping the lines around the ends. Make sure the lines are taut.

6 On a long length, where the lines are under their own weight, build a wall up to the correct level at about the midpoint of the section. Then wrap a rag or twist a bunch of grass around the lines to keep them from chafing and anchor them temporarily with a stone placed on top.

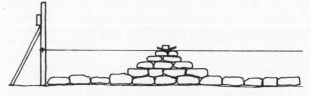

This is helpful in group work, to limit the movement of the guidelines if they are accidentally knocked about.

Courses

Dry stone walls are built up in more or less

regular courses not only for appearance but to insure the greatest possible symmetry and stability along the length and across the section of the wall. Although there are a number of points to keep in mind, most of them are just applied common sense and become second nature with practice. Once you understand how to build courses you should have little trouble with other aspects of dry walling.

GRADING

Place the biggest stones at the bottom, except for throughs and topstones.

There are three reasons for this rule. First, small stones on top of big stones are less likely to slip or settle badly than big stones on top of small stones. Second, it is much less tiring and hazardous to use the big stones near the base than to heave them up to waist or chest height. Third, stones should be placed with their long edges into the wall if possible, and to do this without interfering with stones on the opposite face it is necessary to use the big stones lower down where the wall is widest.

The following points should help you grade the courses properly:

a Determine the height of each course by the biggest stones which you plan to use in it, discounting the occasional misfits which must be accommodated in more than one course. Try to keep to this established height along the whole course, making it more than one stone tall in places if necessary.

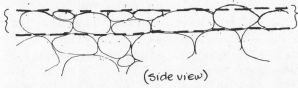

(side view)

Take extra care to level up the courses on which throughs and topstones are to be placed. You may have to use thin flags to make good any small discrepancies in the heights of stones in these courses.

b The regularity of grading which can be

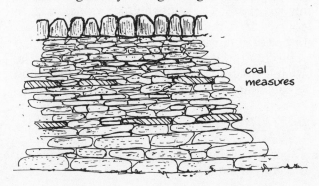

coal measures

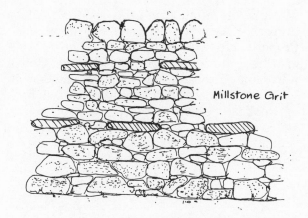

Millstone Grit

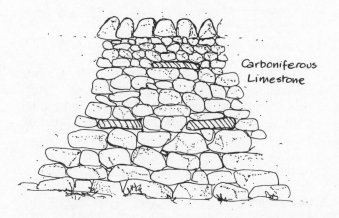

Carboniferous Limestone

achieved depends on the type of stone available. The drawing shows three examples of proper grading and good construction for three types of stone.

c Use stones of roughly equal size and weight for each face of the wall at any given point in the course.

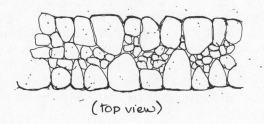

(top view)

Even if you can't always follow this rule, avoid putting all the biggest stones on one side of the wall in any given length or the wall may settle unevenly across its section at this point.

d If you have to mix big stones with small ones to complete the course, try to space the bigger stones fairly evenly along both faces of the course rather than putting them all together, which looks bad and which might cause the wall to settle unevenly along its length.

JOINTS

Cross (break) the joints, to achieve a good bond between courses.

This rule is often expressed as 'the waller's prayer': 'One upon two and two upon one'. Properly crossed joints, as in a brick wall, distribute the pressure from each stone downward and outward evenly over the entire wall. Uncrossed joints channel this pressure into lines of weakness which show up as seams which widen as the wall settles. The weakness increases geometrically with each additional uncrossed joint in vertical line.

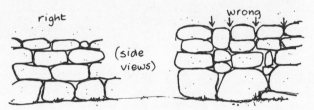

Even an expert waller must sometimes leave one uncrossed joint to make the stones sit firmly or to bring up the course between two taller stones, but the hallmark of what one Yorkshire

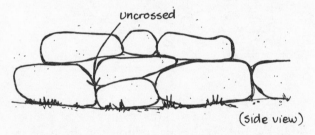

craftsman calls 'slap work' – hasty or careless walling – is a seam of two, three or even four uncrossed joints.

The same consideration applies to the joints across the wall's section. Hidden but crucial, these are easy to cross with most rough walling stone but, if you are unlucky enough to be using very regular or cut stone, it takes a conscious effort to keep to the rule. Without proper crossings the face stones may not bind with the fillings and both sides are liable to belly out and collapse.

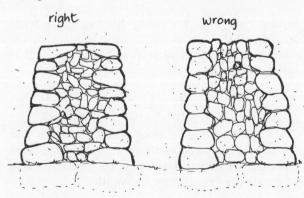

FILLINGS

Keep the middle full, or as the Scots say, 'keep your heart up'.

Fillings or heartings are invisible but essential components of every dry stone wall. Without them, face stones settle inward and the wall collapses in the centre. Fillings should be used at every course to help bind and steady the face stones, provide drainage and create a base for the courses above.

a Use solid rocks, not topsoil, earth, sand or fine gravel, for fillings. Too fine material washes or settles out of the wall.

b The size of fillings required depends on the type of face stones – larger for irregular walls, smaller, down to very coarse gravel at least 25mm (1″) in diameter, for the most regular walls.

c Fillings should be angular to bind properly under pressure. Split water-worn and other too-regular fillings with a walling hammer before using them.

d Although you should avoid making fillings by smashing up potential face stones which may be needed later on, you can convert very big, awkwardly shaped or rounded stones into fillings if you know you have plenty of better face stones. You are likely to create some fillings as you shape face stones to produce a better fit.

e Use large fillings between the foundation stones and in the lowest courses and smaller ones in the upper courses. Fillings usually grade down less quickly than the face stones so that by the top course the fillings may be almost as big as the face stones.

f Place fillings in position carefully, one at a time. Do not throw or shovel them in haphazardly, since this produces a poorly consolidated centre and also tends to include soil with the fill which eventually washes out of the wall. The aim is not to get the wall up quicker by using fillings, but to provide a sturdy structure that tightens as it settles. Make sure the fillings don't dislodge face stones and that each is held by its neighbours so that it cannot settle or be washed out of the wall.

g Keep the fillings at the same height or a little higher than the tops of the face stones in each course. It is best to add fillings as you work, rather than finishing a course of face stones and returning to fill in between. Take a look at the completed course before starting the next one, to see if any low spots need additional fillings.

BATTER

Taper the wall, following the correct batter for the type of stone.

Batter is necessary to allow for slight differences in settling which cause vertically sided walls to develop an overhang, especially when assisted by leaning cattle or the pull of gravity on a slope. Walls made of irregular, poorly bedded stones require more batter than walls of more regular blocks or slabs, especially if the number of throughs is limited. But too much batter means the wall is wastefully wide at the base or becomes too narrow and weak near the top.

To achieve the correct batter:

a Set the first course in about 62mm ($2\frac{1}{2}''$) from the outside edges of the foundation stones on each side. This in-set, or 'scarcement' as it is known in Scotland, is necessary to provide good weight distribution and to make sure that no stones slip off the foundation as the wall settles.

b Set in each succeeding course by a constant but lesser distance, usually 12–25mm ($\frac{1}{2}$–1$''$) or finger width. The batter may be specified in the walling contract or determined by the batter frame used for the job. In the absence of these indicators, estimate the batter based on that of the best-built wall of similar stone in the neighbourhood.

c Keep to a straight batter, neither concave nor convex. Think ahead so that the batter can be distributed evenly over all the courses. This can be done most easily by building to guidelines strung from a batter frame. Avoid large in-sets which give footholds to animals and people.

d If you are using guidelines, bring up the courses so that the stones are about 6mm ($\frac{1}{4}''$) inside the lines. They should not push the lines out of position. Push in any stones which project too much, or tap them in with a hammer if you have already placed additional courses on top. Make sure you don't unsettle any stones as you tap others back into line. Where the stone is irregular be prepared to allow occasional non-conformists to break the smooth face of the wall.

POINTS ON TECHNIQUE

General

a It is usually best to place each course along the entire day's section before beginning the next course above. If you do this, and at the same time always look for the biggest stone to use next, you should have no trouble grading the courses.

b Build up both faces at once and keep them well filled between. Never put stones on suc-ceeding courses until the wall immediately below is complete and steady.

c Work on a short section of 1m (3–4') at a time before continuing the course to either side. Pick up a likely stone from nearby and then look to see where it will fit in this length. Remember that if it doesn't go where you had imagined, it will probably fit nearby. Instead of throwing it down in disgust or carrying it up and down the wall looking for the best place, just experiment by trying it in different ways in the immediate area where you are working. This saves time and effort and is usually more successful. As you become more experienced you will find it progressively easier to place stones correctly at the first try.

d Face along the wall when placing courses. This is easiest and is a comfortable position from which to lift and position large stones.

e Use both hands to pick up and place stones other than fillings or very small face stones. This is safest and gives you the best sense of shape. After positioning each stone, test to see how easy it is to shift with a downward and outward pressure from your hands. It should be steady so that succeeding courses make it sit even more firmly.

f Place, don't drop, the stones on the wall. This is healthier for the wall and for your fingers. See page 41 for further safety information.

g Use the best stones for the face. Awkward or misshapen stones can go in the centre. Break them up only if they are too big to use whole for fillings or if they are too smooth to 'bite'.

h When working alone it is at first easy enough to build from both sides, stepping back and forth over the wall to use stones laid out on either side. When this becomes difficult, you may be able to adjust stones in the opposite face by putting one hand on a stone on the far face and leaning over. This is better than stepping on the wall to cross it, which tends to disrupt both faces.

Once the wall is a few feet high, you can either work mainly from one side or continue to cross over or walk around it at frequent intervals. Experts work as much as possible from one side and set out the stones accordingly. They first build and wedge the far face from the back, and then place the near face and fillings, repeating this process for each course. From time to time they go around to the other side to check the results.

For beginners, it is best to work equally from each side, concentrating on the near face each time. Where you have to cross over the wall, as when rebuilding between existing sections, step carefully on a face stone on the far side and check afterwards to be sure it has not been displaced. Do not put your weight on the fillings.

Placing the stones

a Place face stones with their long edges into rather than along the wall, just as with footings (p65), unless they are so big that they would interfere with face stones on the other side. If they are too long to place into the wall and seem likely to swivel out of position if placed along it, they should be broken into smaller pieces.

b Place each face stone so that its top is either level or slightly higher towards the centre of the wall than at the outside.

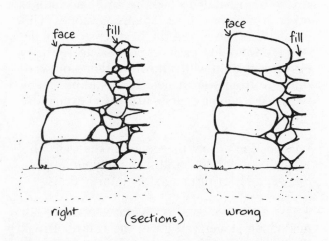

right   (sections)   wrong

Never place the stones so they tip down toward the centre, since they tend to tilt more and more as the fillings below them settle. This brings their weight and that of the stones above them more and more onto the fillings rather than the face stones and foundations below. Inward-tilting stones also feed rainwater into the vulnerable heart of the wall, increasing the likelihood of frost damage. Both processes are likely to cause the wall to collapse inward eventually.

Wallers in some regions, particularly the Cotswolds and to a lesser extent Scotland, stress the need to keep the stones slightly higher in the middle to ensure that the wall sheds water. Pennine wallers agree in principal but their stones are often too large and irregular to carry this out. They are always careful, though, to make sure the stones do not tilt down on the inside.

If you do build the wall with outward-tilted stones, make sure the angle is very slight to prevent them being pushed out as the wall settles.

c Try to place each face stone with a flat side downward so that it is solidly bedded. Even if this means that the upper surface is rounded, it is usually easy enough to create a good bed for the next course by placing small flattish stones to either side.

(side views)

Don't put the round side down, since the area in contact with the stone below is smaller this way and it may be hard to wedge the stone so that it sits firmly.

d Don't place stones so that they act as downthrusting wedges.

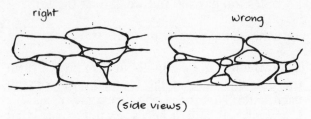

(side views)

This is especially tempting when using irregular blocks of limestone but it tends to force neighbouring stones apart and weakens the wall.

e Given the above restrictions, place each stone so that the flattest edge or the one most nearly perpendicular to the bed is outermost, to form the face of the wall. This looks best and also helps ensure an irregular inner edge to bind with the fillings.

If possible, each stone's face should be in alignment with the wall's batter, as shown in the diagram at the top of the next page.

The overhanging face is wrong not only because

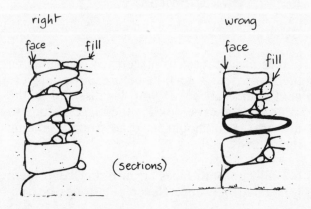

(sections)

it looks poor but because it provides less support for the stone above.

f Avoid placing stones so that they project beyond the general face of the wall, if possible. Where this has to be done with large stones which do not otherwise sit properly, make sure they are really solid, as shown below left.

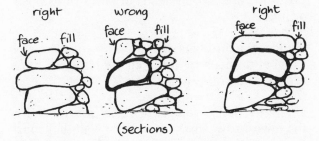

(sections)

The middle sketch shows a stone which should never be placed sticking out from the wall, because in this position it will be forced down and out by stones on top. Place this type of downcurved stone farther back so that it is driven strongly against the stone below by the weight of succeeding courses, as shown above right.

g Most sedimentary and metamorphic rocks have a definite grain along the bedding planes or lines of cleavage or foliation (p54). Try to place face stones so that their grain runs horizontally, even if the upper surface is tilted because of this.

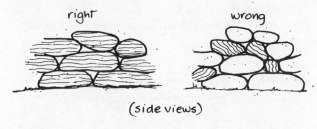

(side views)

Stones best resist weathering when aligned in this way. Competition judges look out for this and once you begin to think of it you will be surprised at how poorly stones look when their grains run the wrong way.

h When you use a small stone to bring up the level of the course between two large stones, be sure that it is level with or a little higher than its neighbours. Otherwise it cannot be held firmly by the stones above and is liable to slip out.

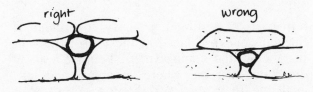

i When finding a stone to fit against an awk-

wardly shaped neighbour, it may be easier to feel the needed shape than to estimate it by eye. Experienced wallers often toss or shuffle the stones around in their hands while looking at spaces in the wall, to get a better idea of the required fit.

Wedging

Often a stone which does not sit firmly by itself can be secured with a small wedge-shaped stone tucked underneath and behind it.

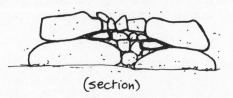

(section)

Wedges are also useful to raise face stones at their backs in order to make sure their top surfaces are level or tipped slightly down and out rather than in towards the centre. Wedges may be any size and shape as long as they have a sharp angle to fit snugly in position. Test the face stone after wedging to check that it doesn't rock back and forth or loosen when weighted down. If you need to break up big stones to get suitable wedges, make sure you have plenty left for the wall face.

Pinning

Pinnings are wedge stones which are forced into gaps in the wall face or between topstones to create a locked top (p75). Wallers in the Pennines dislike the use of pinnings for a number of reasons:

a You may disturb face stones or fillings in an effort to push in the pinnings.

b Pinnings, even if tapped in with a hammer, are unlikely to be really secure. Often they are forced out as the wall settles or frost disturbs the face. Even with gentle tapping the pinnings often crack, allowing water to seep into them so that they soon fragment.

c Pinnings are usually unnecessary as long as the face stones are properly placed and wedged from behind.

Sometimes pinnings are used to fill cracks or holes which the waller feels are signs of bad building. In fact cracks and gaps are fine as long as every stone sits tightly and the openings are too small for fillings to wash out. There is no need to have every face stone snug against its neighbours when this might cause them to sit poorly.

71

Scottish wallers tend to use pinnings quite often, but they stress that it is much better to pin as you work rather than to patch up the wall face afterwards. If you do need to pin at any time, remember the motto, 'One stone to one hole'. Several small pinnings in a single hole are unlikely to stay tight.

Throughs

'Throughs' or 'throughstones' straddle the wall, connecting one face with the other. They help keep the wall from bulging outward as it settles by:

a Tying the two faces together into a single unit.

b Maintaining the wall's equilibrium by distributing the weight of upper courses equally onto both faces below.

Not all walls have or need throughs, but where they are lacking the stones must be chunky and irregular to bind well and the wall must be made wider at the base and built with greater batter than would otherwise be necessary. The number and spacing of throughs shown in the diagram on page 62 ensure a very strong wall. Where throughs are scarce and the wall is tall enough to take more than one row, you should increase the distance between the throughs in each row rather than use them in a single row. If you are building several walls, save the greatest proportion of throughs for the highest walls or those most liable to damage. It is worth using throughs even if you must place them as much as 2 or 3 yards apart or more.

Keep the following points in mind:

a Be especially careful when lifting and placing throughs. Your back and fingers are at risk (see page 41).

b The best throughs are sandstone flags about 50–75mm (2–3″) thick. Slate throughs are also good though a bit more liable to fracture. Other more irregular stones may be used provided they don't split too easily.

c Throughs must be long enough to straddle the wall, but it doesn't matter if they stick out an inch or so on either side. In a few areas, such as around Derbyshire High Peak and in slate areas of Wales and the Isle of Man, throughs which project as much as 175mm (7″) are used to dissuade sheep from jumping. Most wallers think this is a bad idea because it encourages cattle to rub and people to climb the wall, which

puts weight on the projecting edges and may lever the top of the wall out of position.

Don't bother to shorten excessively long throughs if you can't find better ones. Throughs are too laborious to cut and you may upset the wall's innards if you break off their ends after they are positioned. Very long throughs are best saved for use in wall heads or stiles or as posts or lintels.

d Place the throughs so that they project equally from both sides of the wall, unless you have reason to do otherwise (see p39).

e The hardest throughs to select are those for the lowest row, since to span the wall they must be longer than throughs used higher up. So use your longest throughs first. As these are also the heaviest, it is best to get them out of the way early so that they don't have to be lifted very far.

f Before placing the throughs, bring the course below them level with the guideline. Fill this course well to make a secure bed. Place each throughstone with its flattest side down. Try not to wedge it – shift it as necessary or adjust the fillings if it doesn't sit securely at first. The through's weight must rest as much on the face stones on both sides as on the fillings between.

g After placing the throughs at the correct spacing along the entire section, build up the wall between them with face stones and fillings.

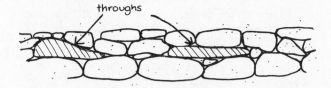
throughs

Choose stones that fit around the throughs rather than shifting the throughs to fit the face stones. Continue to add succeeding courses in the usual way, using the tops of the throughs as beds for the stones above.

h When you reach the next row of throughs, level off the course as before and place the throughs so that they are staggered with the ones below, as shown on page 62. This makes the wall stronger than if they are placed directly above the other throughs.

i In parts of Scotland, a heavy coverband of throughstones is placed at the top of the wall just below the coping (p18). Pennine wallers don't do this, but where suitable stones are available they level off the top course with small, thin flags laid side by side to make a good bed for the topstones. Depending on the stone, these may or may not be throughs, but except where local practice suggests otherwise they should not project more than a little beyond the wall face.

Coping

The coping consists of a row of topstones which straddle the top of the wall. It is important for two reasons:

a It weighs down the courses below and bonds both faces together so that the wall settles into a solid unit.

b It protects the face stones and fillings from the weather, animals and people. Without copings, walls tend to flake away course by course, especially if they are made of small or fissile stones.

The coping is the part of the wall which needs most frequent inspection and repair, since once a few topstones are dislodged a gap may soon start which is likely to grow larger and larger unless rebuilt.

There are many types of copings and with most stones a choice is possible based not only on practical requirements but on personal preferences as well. Where there is no good reason for doing otherwise, it is usually best to follow the example of the surrounding walls. The pros and cons of each of the main types of copings and some of their variations are discussed below. Procedural details follow (pp76–77).

TYPES OF COPINGS

Flat

The simplest coping is a plain flat top, using throughstones placed side by side along the entire length of the wall.

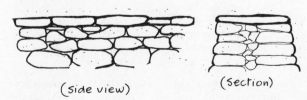

(side view)   (section)

Advantages:

a This type provides a way of using extra throughs, if you have them.

b It is quick to build and uses less stone than other types.

c The finished result is neat and tidy, especially

where the stones can be trimmed easily to form large rectangular slabs.

Disadvantages:

a Stones must be large, heavy and regular to make this coping as secure as other types. Such stones, even if available, are hard to lift and position on a high wall.

b The coping is lower than other types which means that extra courses may need to be built to achieve the required total wall height. This is slow and requires extra face stones.

c A flat coping is easily disrupted if the stones project from the wall's face where cattle can rub on them or if children use them for stepping stones.

d As the wall settles the stones may tilt so that some of the finished appearance may be lost.

This type is usually seen capping village or garden walls where looks are important and disturbance is minimal. Where they are likely to be knocked about by animals or children they are often lightly mortared in place. Infrequently, they are anchored by large squarish boulders as shown below.

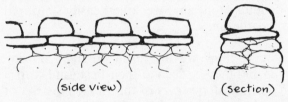

(side view)   (section)

A variation of this type is used to make wall-top flower beds for gardens. Small flat (or occasionally vertical) stones are concreted along both faces of the wall, leaving a central well in which plants can be grown.

Tilted

Tilted copings vary from nearly flat to nearly upright, and are found constructed in many types of stone. A few examples are shown below.

(side views)

73

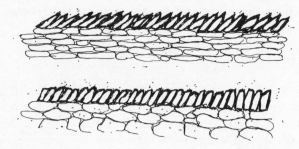

Advantages:

a Less stone is needed than for an upright coping, although more than for a flat cap.

b Each stone holds down its neighbour. This makes individual stones harder to dislodge.

c The coping tends to bind ever tighter because individual stones slip past yet stay in contact with each other as the wall settles.

d On slopes, this coping is easier to build and more secure than other types (p82).

Disadvantages:

a Less height is achieved than with a vertical coping.

b It is less strong than a locked top if the individual stones are weak and easily shattered by weathering.

Tilted copings are the norm on steep hillside walls and may be seen at their best (and worst) on the limestone scars of the Craven district of Yorkshire and in the Lake District.

Rubble Finish

Rubble or rough-stone copings use any size and type of stone, arranged loosely according to circumstances. The only requirement is that the stones span the width of the wall.

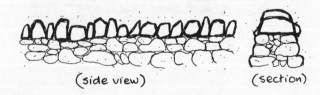

(side view)   (section)

Advantages:

a This type is quick and easy to make and does away with some of the bother of reserving good-quality topstones as you build the wall.

b It provides a way to use up mixed lots of stone, including shale, slate etc which would make a poor coping if used alone.

Disadvantages:

a This type tends to be less secure than copings using more regular topstones.

b It is not particularly attractive.

Most rubble-finished walls predate the Parliamentary Enclosure era, or form less important subdivision walls within more neatly coped boundaries.

Upright with even-sized topstones

This type usually uses stones which are thinner than they are tall with a flat base which beds well across the width of the wall. The regularity of finish depends on the local stone.

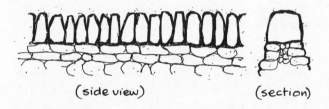

(side view)   (section)

Advantages:

a With many types of stone it holds more tightly than other copings.

b It achieves the greatest height for the stone used.

c With care, it is possible to produce a very neat job.

Disadvantages:

a This type requires more stone than other copings.

b It may be necessary to trim or wedge the stones for a proper fit.

c Some stones may come loose as the wall settles. Over the first few years at least it should be checked more frequently than other types.

This type is generally favoured for ordinary walling throughout the Pennines. Dressed topstones, frequent on roadside or estate walls, are almost always placed upright.

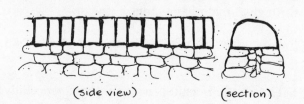

(side view)   (section)

Locked top

Most craft innovations are anonymous, their origins lost to local memory. But Rainsford-Hannay (1972, p45) attributes the locked top to John MacAdam of Craigengullich, and even pins a date to its invention: 1753. It has always remained a Scottish speciality, although it is occasionally seen in other areas including Ireland, where the stones used are thicker than in Scotland and of varying height.

The locked top is a variant of the upright coping described above. It is usually of whinstone, the toppings about 250–300mm (10–12″) wide and tall and seldom more than 50mm (2″) thick. After the stones are carefully bedded and tightly placed along an entire section, specially selected thin pinnings are driven down between some of the topstones to lock them even more firmly together.

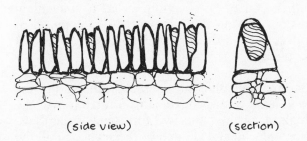

(side view)   (section)

Advantages:

a This type of coping is very strong, as long as the stones are rough enough to grip well.

b If it loosens a bit on settling, it can be easily restored with a few more pinnings.

Disadvantages:

a This type is perhaps the most difficult and slowest to build, which is probably why Rainsford-Hannay (1972, p89) mentions in his description of the locked top that dry coping is the hardest and most important aspect of dry stone walling.

b As mentioned above, it tends to loosen as the wall settles and unless maintained may lose most of its value.

c The locked top cannot be used on highly finished copings of regular or trimmed topstones, or where suitable thin pinnings are unavailable.

d If it is over-pinned or pinned poorly, the topstones may be loosened and the coping becomes weaker than if no pinnings are used.

Buck-and-doe

The buck-and-doe coping, also known as 'cock-and-hen' in the Cotswolds, alternates tall and short topstones to give a castellated effect. The stones are usually but not always placed upright. A few of the many variants are shown below.

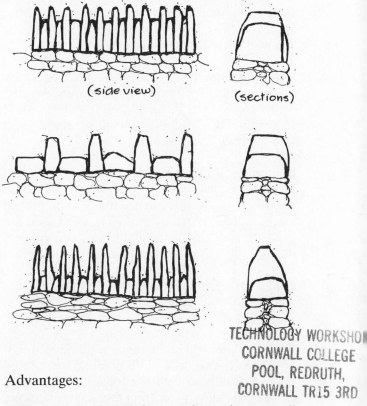

(side view)   (sections)

Advantages:

a With a buck-and-doe coping, the overall height can be as much as with other upright copings even when the supply of tall stones is limited.

b According to some wallers, sheep are disinclined to try to jump walls with this type of coping because it looks insecure.

Disadvantages:

a With this type, it is necessary to carefully sort the topstones and considerable trimming may be required.

b It is a relatively weak type, although it can be strengthened by bedding the stones in a light mortar or by using stones which are more even in height. It is most at risk where cattle are kept, since they may knock off the topstones by rubbing on them. Bullocks and heifers, when frightened, often try to jump low walls and can wreak havoc to the coping in the process.

Buck-and-doe copings are usually found only where the decorative touch is most wanted, on garden, roadside and estate walls.

BUILDING THE COPING

Technical points

a For an expert, placing the topstones is no slower than building the rest of the wall. But for beginners it is worth leaving plenty of time and working carefully to achieve good results. In competitions, more points are won or lost on the coping than on any other single part of the wall, which reflects its importance in terms of the wall's strength and appearance.

b If topstones are too wide at the base they usually should be roughly trimmed back to the wall's top width. Place a stone on the ground to trim it – you will disturb the other stones if you hammer it in place.

Sometimes projecting topstones are used on purpose to deter sheep from jumping. Do not try this, though, if cattle are likely to be grazed in the field. Where overhanging topstones are used on a boundary wall they should project only on the owner's side, against his own sheep.

c The end topstone is constructed as part of the wall head and should be as big and solid as possible (p79).

d On a slope, tilted copings should lean uphill (p82). At the crest of a hill, place an extra large coping stone and lean the topstones against it from both sides as shown in the diagram below.

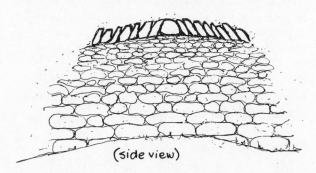

(side view)

Elsewhere, tilted copings should lean against the stone which tops the wall head. Note that where a head occurs in the body of the wall, eg to denote a change of ownership between different sections, the coping should be carried across the gap (point **d**, p78).

Procedure

The following steps produce a neat result when building a coping of even-sized stones. This procedure can be modified as necessary for other types.

1 Determine the height of the coping. This may be set by the building specifications and is usually 250–300mm (10–12″) for upright copings. Note that it is the overall wall height which is important, not in most cases the height of individual topstones, which should be varied slightly as necessary to make up for any irregularities in the wall's top course. Where the topstones are very irregular, judge their height from their topmost parts since this determines the profile of the finished wall.

total height

Choose a stone of proper height to cap the wall head and then use this as a guide. This stone should sit securely with no wedging required.

2 Place a stone of the determined height at the other end of the section, or at a convenient distance along if it is too long to cope all at once. Wedge this stone as necessary to hold it in place.

3 Pin a guideline into a crack at the end of the wall head where convenient. Stretch it over the highest parts of the two topstones which have been placed at each end of the section. Pull the line taut and pin it at the far end.

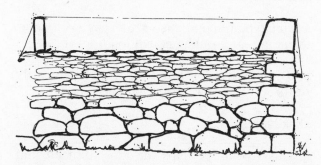

4 If you are working on a section longer than about 3m (10′), place a third topstone approximately half way between the end stones and wedge as necessary to hold it in place. Check that its top is at the correct level. To prevent the guideline sagging at this point and to keep it steady as you work, wrap the line in a rag or twist of grass and anchor it to the centre topstone with a small stone.

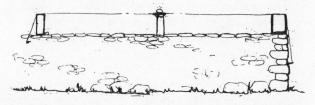

5 Build the rest of the coping, starting at the

wall head. The top of each stone should come to just below the guideline. Depending on the finish required and the time available you can shorten stones which are too long, but try to minimise the use of the hammer by developing an eye for the right size stones. If one doesn't suit one place it may be perfect a little farther along.

Unless you are building a locked top (p75), avoid pinning the coping from above. The topstones should fit tightly without this. A few stones may need wedging from below, but try to find stones which bed securely on their own instead.

Where you lack enough stones of the right height, make up the difference by first placing another course of small stones properly bedded and filled as usual.

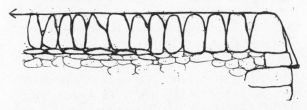

Often this degree of finish is unnecessary, eg where the topstones are very irregular anyway and a rough rubble top is all that is required.

Mortared copings

Although Pennine and most other walls are usually best left with their copings unmortared, Cotswold copings are very often held by mortar because their topstones are usually too small and light to stay secure by themselves. The preferred 'combers', as the topstones are called in the Cotswolds, are semicircular and wide enough at the base to bridge the wall. When these are unavailable, smaller stones are placed to give the same overall effect, although for strength it is best to have at least one full-width comber between every four or five sets of paired combers.

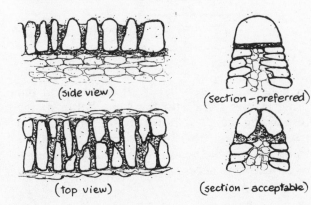

(side view)

(section – preferred)

(top view)

(section – acceptable)

To mortar the combers:

1 Mix up mortar in a proportion of 1:3 lime to sand by volume. Where extra strength is required, as on mortared wall heads or stiles, a small amount of cement should be added to the dry lime-sand mixture in a proportion of 1:6. If you must use all cement instead of lime, make the mixture 1:4 cement to sand if mixing by hand, or 1:6 if using Readymix or mixing by machine.

2 Add water slowly to the dry mortar until it becomes workable. The mortar should be stiff enough to stay on the trowel.

3 Put a bed of cement about 25mm (1") deep along a foot or two of the wall's top.

4 Position the first comber on the wall and bed it down. Then mortar the edge against which the second comber will be placed.

5 Push the second comber tightly against the first, making sure that there are no air pockets between the two. Then mortar the edge against which the third comber will be placed.

If you have trouble keeping the mortar on one comber before placing the next, put them on unmortared and dribble mortar between them, being sure to fill up the space between using the edge of the trowel.

6 Continue to place combers in the same way. Add mortar as necessary so that they sit upright, not tilting over.

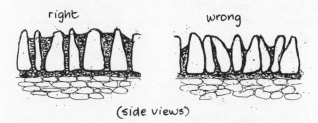

right   wrong

(side views)

7 Ordinarily the mortar is left rough, but for garden work you can smooth between the stones using a wet sack or rag.

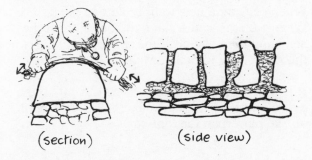

(section)   (side view)

Wall Heads

The wall head is a specially constructed pillar

which acts like a huge bookend to strengthen the wall faces and to protect the centre, which would otherwise weather away and collapse. Heads should be built at the start and finish of every distinct section of wall, including:

a Where gates and other openings are taken through the wall.

b Where a new wall butts up against an existing one. While it is stronger to interlock the two, this requires tearing down a section of old wall and so should only be done where the old wall is to be rebuilt anyway.

c On steep slopes, to provide stability and limit the formation of gaps (p80).

d In certain cases to indicate changes in ownership of different wall sections (p39). Here, two heads are built against each other and the coping is built across the seam to reduce its weakness.

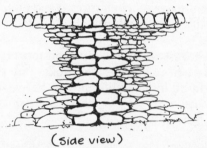

(side view)

The ends of a dry stone wall are the parts which are most exposed to damage and the stones here are only supported on two sides rather than three as elsewhere. For this reason the head should be built of the biggest, most regular stones available. These should be selected and kept apart from the other stones. They may have to be brought in specially if the local stone is inadequate. Large granite or sandstone blocks are best, preferably with smooth square faces on the two or three sides where they are exposed. Be particularly careful when handling heavy stones. See pages 41–43 for methods of moving big blocks.

When starting a new wall, build one head first. When you near the far end, build the other head and then complete the wall behind it. Use this procedure to build a wall head:

1 If you have a boulder which can cross the entire width of the wall, use this as a through or 'tie' placed on the footings.

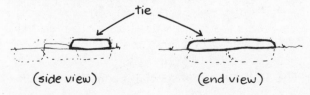

(side view)   (end view)

Do not bother shortening ties which are longer than required unless a trimmed finish is necessary. If no suitable stones are long enough, start the head with two big 'runners' placed along the line of the wall. If these don't meet in the middle place large fillings securely between them.

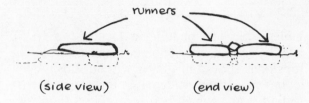

(side view)   (end view)

2 Build up a short section of wall to the height of the stones just placed, using ordinary face stones and fillings.

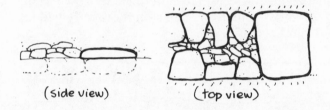

(side view)   (top view)

3 If the bottom course uses a tie, place two runners on top of it to form the second course of the wall head. If the bottom course uses runners, place a tie on top of them. Continue to build up courses in this way, alternating ties and runners and building up a short section of wall behind the head at each course.

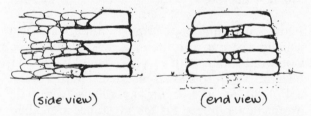

(side view)   (end view)

If at any course you cannot find a tie to extend through the wall, fill the space with two similar but smaller stones, which must join and be fully supported over a runner, not over the fillings.

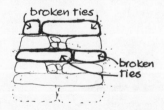

As you build, keep the head end vertical but bring up the sides with the same batter as the rest of the wall, as shown by the drawings on page 62. Check this by holding up the batter frame against the head as you place each course to adjust it as necessary. The head should not need pinning.

4 If you can arrange it, bring up the courses so

that the last one before the topstone is a tie. This gives the strongest bed for the topstone.

5 Finish the head with a large square topstone, as shown on page 62. This must be heavy enough to resist the push of the rest of the coping against it and should sit firmly without wedging. Too small a stone here and the coping can never be really secure.

Occasionally one comes across unusual wall heads, especially where suitable large rectangular blocks are lacking, such as the milestone heads of Little Langdale in the Lake District (p12). An interesting recent example is the section of demonstration wall built by I Fyfe for the Countryside Commission for Scotland's Battleby Display Centre. A large cut slab is used to finish a superbly constructed 1m (3'6") high wall of rounded boulders in which the usual throughs are lacking.

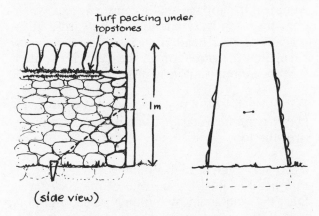

turf packing under topstones

1m

(side view)

The slate was fixed by drilling two holes half way up it, looping galvanised wire through the holes and pegging the ends of the wire angled down into the wall base. The wall was then built around the peg and wire. By the time the peg and wire rot the wall should have finished settling and be quite stable, although it seems likely that if this design were tried on a slope the weight of stone behind the slate would eventually topple it.

Changes of Direction

CURVES

It may be necessary to curve a wall in order to follow a boundary line, avoid a tree, pool, hollow or other difficult spot or incorporate an immovable boulder into the wall. Gradual curves are preferable to corners where both are possible, since they are easier to build and likely to prove sturdier in the long run. However, a tight curve can be tricky to build due to problems judging the batter, and in this case a corner may be required.

Usually it is adequate to mark out the curved section by eye. Garden or park walls designed with regular curves for decorative effect can be more carefully lined out using a long garden hose or rope. After you have laid out the hose so that it simulates the required curves, 'nick out' along it (see point **4**, p65) to mark one edge of the trench, taking care not to damage the hose. To line out a circular section for a view platform etc, stick a crowbar vertically into the ground at the circle's centre. Tie a rope loosely onto it, hold the rope at the desired radius and swing it around to mark the circle. To line out a circular section around a tree, tie the rope loosely around the trunk and swing it around in the same way. Be sure to keep the loose end of the rope at the same level as the tied end.

No changes in walling method are necessary to build a curve. Just follow the alignment of the trench and fit the stones together in the usual way. The outer face of the curve will receive more stones than the inner but you don't need to concentrate on this to achieve the correct shape. Be careful, however, that the wall has the correct batter in the curved section as well as in the straight. You won't be able to set up the batter frame and guidelines on curves, but you can still hold the frame up against the end of the section to help judge the batter by eye.

CORNERS

An abrupt change of direction is accommodated by building a corner into the wall. This need not be 90° but it can always be distinguished from a curve because each stone used in the outer face of the corner has one end as well as its face exposed.

To build a corner, overlap each course with the one below, crossing the joints both back to front and left to right. Use large stones with two good outside faces if possible.

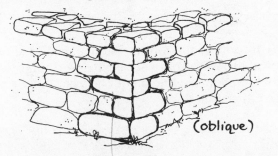

(oblique)

As the drawing shows, the face of one section of wall forms the head of the other and vice-versa. Pack the centre with fillings at each course in the usual way, and check that each stone in each course binds well with the stones at its back and side as well as above and below it.

Do not build a corner as a junction with two wall heads. As the wall settles the seam is sure to widen, especially on a slope.

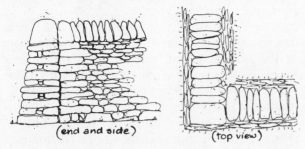

(end and side)   (top view)

A weak corner may devastate the wall by triggering a collapse at both sides. If you must build the corner as two heads, at least bridge the gap with topstones.

Walls on Slopes

A few common-sense adaptations of basic walling technique are all that is required to build walls even on very steep slopes. It may be misleading to follow existing examples, however, since it is surprising how many design faults they often have. Gravity has the advantage here, and poorly built hillside walls betray themselves in frequent serious gapping and eventual collapse.

DIRECTION OF WORK

Start at the bottom of the slope and work upwards.

This is especially important where it is steep. This way, gravity keeps the stones together and tightens completed sections of the wall as they settle.

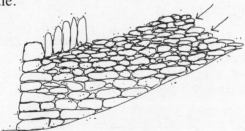

If you start at the top, the stones tend to slide downhill away from you as you work and the whole wall loosens no matter how carefully you place the stones.

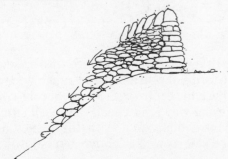

The easiest way to work is facing more or less uphill, choosing stones laid out to your side or just in front. This saves bending and back strain.

USE OF WALL HEADS

Additional heads must be built into walls on steep slopes to strengthen them and to limit the extent of gapping if it does occur. Follow these suggestions:

a Build a wall head at the base of a steep slope or at a sharp upward break in slope. This head helps support the weight of the wall above it. Build the head after laying the foundations but before building the courses of the section uphill of the head.

b The more heads the better, where a wall runs up a steep hillside. Gaps are more of a problem on slopes than on the flat, both because the wall is subject to slippage and because any gap which does form tends to extend ever upward until it reaches a solid head. If a head is built every chain 20m (22 yards) or so, the gap is prevented from becoming ruinously large.

c Build a head at the top of a steep slope to keep a gap which starts downhill from continuing over the top.

d To surmount a high outcrop, build the wall to a head against the bottom of the rock face. Start the wall again by building a head right on top of the outcrop, so there is no room for livestock to edge past.

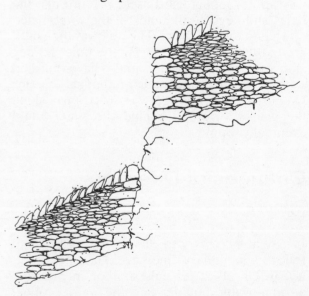

When you build a head on a slope, it is most important to bind it to the wall on the uphill side. Given suitable head stones it may be possible to use some to bind with the wall downhill as well. Always carry the coping across the break.

80

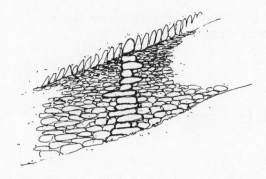

LEVEL COURSES

Lay the stones on the true horizontal, whatever the slope.

This is most important, even though it is tempting on slight or moderate slopes to lay with the curve of the ground.

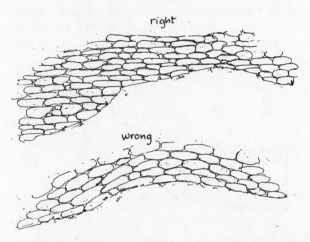

right

wrong

Stones which are not laid on true level are likely to slide over each other. The bigger and more regular they are, the easier this is. You can test this yourself by placing a flat slab weighing 50kg (1cwt) or more on a level base. Try to shift it laterally. Now bed the same stone on a hard, sloping surface and see how it is comparatively easy to edge it downhill using a crowbar or other lever.

Follow these points to achieve level courses:

a Level bedding starts at the foundation. Dig the trench as usual and then dig out the bottom a little more as you place each footing stone.

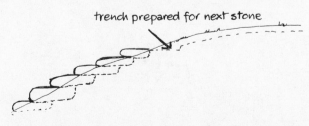

trench prepared for next stone

b Once the footings are in, place the batter frame at the uphill end of the day's section or,

on steep slopes, at a convenient distance along so that you can run guidelines between it and the wall head as shown. Check the guidelines with a spirit level.

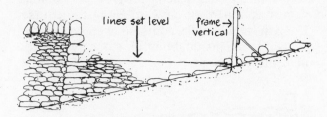

lines set level   frame vertical

On really steep slopes the batter frame is useless but you can still set guidelines at convenient heights by pinning them under stones at the uphill end. Since the wall must be built wider at the hillside end of each course than at the outer end, as explained below, the guidelines when set up taper in plan as shown in the diagram.

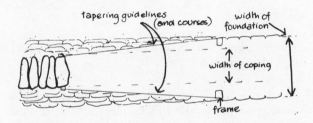

tapering guidelines (and courses)   width of foundation

width of coping

frame

c The best way to check the bedding of large, flat slabs is with a spirit level fixed to a flat-edged board.

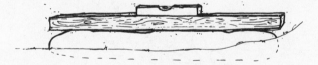

With practice you should be able to align the stones by eye, although it is always worth checking occasionally to make sure you are not being fooled by the slope.

GRADING THE COURSES

Grade each course so that the biggest stones are against the hill and the smallest away from it.

This is very different from the situation on the flat, where each course contains stones more or less of the same size. On a slope, each course starts with a footing stone at one end and ends with a topstone at the other.

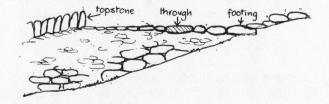

topstone   through   footing

Notice that if you look at the wall on the true vertical, the stones grade from bottom to top in the normal way. To achieve this grading in both directions, start at the footing and add the largest face stones, placing progressively smaller stones as you work outward along the course. Keep the height of the course as even as possible, even if it means doubling up stones when you near the outer end.

On gradual slopes the courses may be too long to build easily one at a time along their whole length. Build them up in convenient sections, trying to keep the stones graded both ways as shown above for a steep slope.

COPING

Always place the topstones on the true vertical or slanting uphill.

Topstones tilted uphill bind most strongly on a slope, because as the wall settles they are pulled more tightly together and held by friction. If one stone is dislodged its neighbours remain firmly in place.

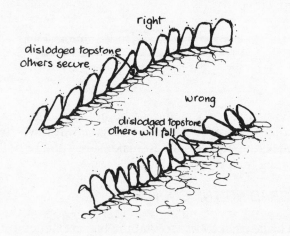

As shown by the right-hand sketch, topstones which slant downhill are poor because once one is dislodged all the others above it are liable to fall in turn.

Upright copings may be necessary on very steep slopes where there is not enough surface for tilted copings to grip properly. Otherwise they are less good, since they tend to lean gradually downhill as they settle. The locked top (p75) is best in this situation.

Always start at the bottom of the hill and work up. Never work the other way, since if you do the topstones will loosen and slip away from you in the process.

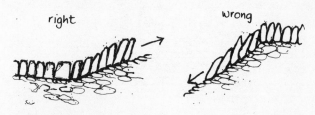

Place a heavy square topstone first, even if you have not built a wall head, to support the coping above it. Once a few stones are placed, tilting uphill, they help support each other. You don't have to hold them all up as you work!

HEIGHTS OF THROUGHS AND THE WALL TOP

Except on very steep slopes, the height at which the throughs and topstones are placed on the level should be maintained on the slope. In other words, the true vertical dimension of the wall is kept constant.

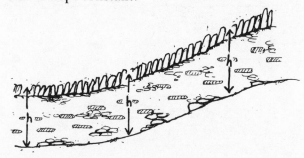

Place the throughs as shown above, so that each row forms a staggered line, rather than all on one course as when building on the level. Check the heights with a plumb bob on a line knotted at the height of each row of throughs and at the wall top below the coping.

On the steepest slopes, a problem occurs if the true vertical height is maintained as on the level. Here the direct distance from the base of the wall to its coping may become small enough that sheep may be able to scramble over the wall. To prevent this, use a notched stick or rule to measure the wall's height perpendicular to the slope as shown below.

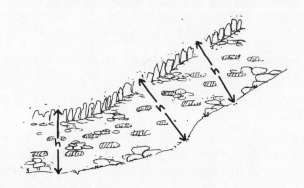

If this distance is kept equal to the vertical height of the wall on the level, the wall on the slope should prove easily high enough to deter livestock.

Occasionally the rule about maintaining a constant height is broken where the wall's appearance is of prime consideration:

a In garden-type walls which have no stock-proof purpose, the top may be stepped up the slope. Walls built this way are usually of flat, regular slabs which form, in effect, a series of partial heads.

b In walls on irregular ground it may be desired to keep the lines of throughs and the wall top at a given overall height for appearance sake. Although this usually requires extra stone it is sometimes done on estate boundary walls.

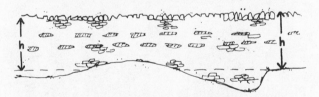

To build to a set height in this situation, choose two points of reference along the wall line, set up batter frames and check that they are perpendicular. The frames must be close enough to run a guideline between their tops without the string sagging badly. Move along the line, measuring down the predetermined height of the wall. If the ground level is low the wall must be built up to the indicated point before you start to count height toward the throughs and top course. If there is a hummock, subtract its height from the overall height when measuring the placement of throughs and the top course.

If a wall of this type is required to be stockproof, make sure it is high enough along its entire length. Otherwise you must either raise the overall height, build it higher at the hummocks or cut the hummocks away.

WALLS ALONG SLOPES

Where a wall runs along a slope, ie with rather than across the contours, increase its batter on the downhill side and decrease it on the uphill side in proportion to the slope. Otherwise, the wall may come to overhang the downhill side as it settles.

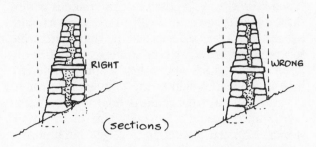

Build the bottom half of the wall from the lower side facing uphill, to save your back. When it becomes difficult to lift stones to the wall's height, move to the uphill side to finish.

Obstacles

BOULDERS

The best thing to do with large boulders near the wall line is to incorporate them in the wall. If they can be moved with the use of crowbars, winches and boards or rollers, haul them in as foundation stones. If they can't be moved, swing the line of the wall to take them in.

Don't build wall heads at the boulder, but fit the wall to it by shortening or lengthening each course to conform to the boulder's contours. Use pinnings for a close fit. If the boulder is lower than the top course, continue the courses straight over it when you have reached its top height.

If it is higher than the top course, use the boulder as a base for the coping.

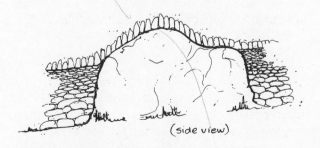

(side view)

WET GROUND

In areas which are too boggy to be grazed at any time of year, it is easiest to bring the wall to a head on either side and leave the wet patch unwalled. If the wall must be carried across the bog, dig the foundation trench deep enough to reach a firm base, if possible, and make it wider than usual to give the wall more support and protect the base from erosion. The bigger the footings the better. Extra stone is needed with deep foundations, but this is preferable to having the wall collapse due to uneven settling. If you don't have particularly big footings, pack below and around them with gravel or small stones. Construct water smoots (p96) in hollows or wherever water may try to drain across the line of the wall, remembering that the wall itself becomes a channel as it settles into soft ground.

Once or twice we have heard people assert that what look like old ruined foundations are really the tops of walls which have sunk in deep peat. We have also been told that on some of the Welsh slate railways, embankments have sunk as fast as they were built. But we have not as yet had the chance to get to the bottom of these claims.

TREES

Trees and walls make poor neighbours. As large trees shift in the wind their root-plates disturb the ground above them, buckling the foundations and loosening the wall for several yards to either side. Large surface roots can force apart the footings directly. Big trees immediately next to the wall gradually push it over as their stems thicken.

For the wall's sake, it is best to clear all trees within about 2m (6') of the footings or even more for pines and other shallow-rooted trees which are subject to wind-throw. For the sake of the trees, curve the wall by this distance to avoid them.

Where it is desirable to preserve both the trees and the wall line, or to plant trees near to a wall, the following tactics should lessen the inevitable damage and uneven settling:

a Bridge robust roots with small smoots (p96).

Room must be left for tree growth but preferably not enough to let sheep through. The usual smoot construction is shown above, but a few examples occur where the root or tree buttress is bridged with a low arch in mortared stone.

b Leave a gap for the tree, building the wall to a head at either side and erecting a short section of post-and-rail fence in front of the tree itself.

c Build the wall with only one face where it abuts the tree. As the trunk thickens the fillings should compact up to a point without pushing out the face.

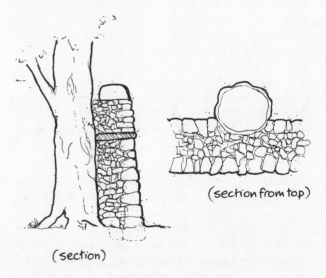

(section)

(section from top)

This method is less good than the preceeding two, since eventually the growing tree will disturb the face and the roots may still lift the foundations in high winds.

Gapping and Rebuilding

Well-built walls are largely maintenance free, unless subject to unusual stresses such as vibration (or direct hits) from heavy traffic, wind-shake from trees or vandalism or accidental damage from passers-by. How often a wall should be checked depends on its situation and whether the likely sources of trouble (discussed further on page 34) are infrequent and unpredictable, such as violent storms, or more or less constant, such as attrition by livestock.

The sooner you repair any damage the better, since gaps once begun inevitably grow bigger due to animals or people climbing over the weak place or to erosion of the centre or both. Too often, it seems, gaps are plugged with old bedsteads, planks, sheet metal: anything which comes to hand except the obvious material, stones. This makeshift policy creates more work in the end since it cannot keep gaps from spreading.

ANALYSING THE PROBLEM

Whether you decide simply to gap the wall, ie repair only the existing breach, or to undertake a major rebuilding job depends on the nature of the problem and the available time and work force. The following list of typical situations should help you decide the best course of action. The situations are ranked in order of increasing severity.

a One or a few topstones have fallen or are knocked off, usually followed by a few of the upper courses. This is the most frequent problem and is simply repaired by replacing the stones after making sure that the stones below them have not been disturbed.

b A gap has formed a few feet or yards long, extending downward for several courses. This is the usual result of the above situation remaining uncorrected. But check the stones which remain in the highest course in the gap. Often one or more of these has settled badly or was poorly placed originally, causing the stones above to come loose. This sort of gap often occurs where a wall settles out from under a mortared coping.

c The gap extends well down in the wall or the wall below it has bellied out, has courses which are much more uneven than those in adjacent sections of wall or leans heavily to one side. These problems are often caused by poorly placed stones low in the wall, probably at the foundations. The gap should be stripped to the foundations and rebuilt.

d The wall has frequent major gaps and the standing sections look insecure. Complete rebuilding is the only long-term solution, although gapping can be attempted where time and labour are short.

PROCEDURE

General points

a Except for the smallest gaps, you are likely to need more stones than are supplied by the wall itself. This is especially true if the old wall has been long neglected, since stones tend to bury themselves over the years. Nearby field stones may have come from the wall and can often be recovered with the use of a pick and spade, crowbar and if necessary a winch.

b Fillings are likely to be in very short supply, but avoid breaking up face stones if possible since these also are limited. As you clean out the damaged area, place the fillings and face stones together beside the wall so that the available fillings may easily be found when needed.

c Don't scrape off moss and other vegetation from old stones except as needed for a good fit. Don't worry if you need to place the stones differently than before, since you are trying to build the strongest structure possible, not recreate the details of the old wall.

d New stone brought in to repair an existing wall should be the same type as the rest of the wall. This makes for the easiest working and usually for the strongest repair. It also looks better, as does old, weathered stone as compared to newly quarried stone. As a Devon waller said, new trimmed blocks in an old wall are just 'cream on pilchards'.

e If you want to 'age' a repair which stands out unattractively, slosh the repaired section with 'manure tea' to boost the growth of lichens and mosses over the fresh stone.

Gapping

Gapping, ie the simple repair of existing breaches in the wall, is straightforward unless the gap has formed under a mortared coping. But it is only a little faster than building the equivalent amount of wall afresh. Follow this procedure:

1 Remove any loose or poorly fitting stones around the edges of the gap, unless this is likely to further disrupt the wall. Check the courses to either side. If they look a bit ropey, widen the gap by about 600mm (2') each way to reach undisturbed stonework.

Throw the stones just far enough from the wall to leave a path from which to work. Sort out stones roughly by size as you lay them out, but don't spend much time on this and keep the fillings in with the face stones. Always strip the wall from the top to avoid working under overhanging stones which may fall and hurt your hands. If the coping is mortared, it is safest and usually easiest to knock off the overhanging sections first with a sledgehammer before cleaning out the gap (see also point **5**, below).

2 Check that the uppermost remaining course is firmly bedded and that none of its stones is tipped inward or is acting like a wedge to disrupt other stones.

3 On small gaps the courses can be lined up by eye, without the use of guidelines. On longer gaps it is best to set lines at a convenient height (eg the height of the throughs if this is above the bottom of the gap) by pinning them to the undisturbed wall at either end of the gap. Move the lines up in intervals of about 300mm (1') to keep the new courses level with the old.

4 Rebuild the gap to fit the wall on either side, giving it the same batter, arrangement of throughs and coping, regardless of personal preference. Otherwise the repair looks out of place and may interlock poorly with the rest of the wall. Take care to make a good bond with the face stones and fillings on either side and be sure the joints are broken here as elsewhere.

5 If the existing coping is mortared and you don't want to knock it down (eg when it has trimmed topstones and suitable replacements are unavailable) build up under the coping with care. When you near the bottom of the coping, build up the far side first by placing the face stones through the wall from your side. Then mix up a rough mortar and push it against the backs of these stones to hold them. Add fillings and a little more mortar to make up for the unavoidably poor fit. Finally, push in the face stones on the near side so that they bed into the mortar.

Rebuilding

Rebuilding, ie taking the wall down to its footings before reconstruction, is the best answer to major gaps and to an existing wall in generally poor condition.

1 Strip down the old wall about a rood at a time, if you are working alone. This avoids the clutter of more extensive dismantling and preserves such shelter or barrier value as the old wall still has. It also shows you the line along which to rebuild and marks out the position of stiles, gates, cripple holes etc which you may want to retain. Another reason to rebuild in stages is that it's a boost to morale to see the contrast between the old wall and your own work.

Follow this sequence when stripping down the old wall:

(1) Clean off the turf around the base and throw it back out of the way. Use a spade and pick to reveal the foundations clearly.

(2) Remove the topstones and lay them about 1.2m (4') or more from the wall, being careful not to break them.

(3) Pull down face stones and fillings and place them about 0.6–1.2m (2–4') from the wall. Keep a good mix of fillings and face stones, but generally sort out the face stones by size: smallest farthest away, biggest near by. Unless you prefer to work only from one side, put them equally along both sides.

(4) When you come to the through stones, lift them carefully and set them against the topstones for reuse.

2 The old footings should normally be left in place, but check to make sure they are well filled, solidly bedded and on the true horizontal. Replace any round-backed footings with more rectangular ones if they are available.

Even where the footings need replacing, it is best to rebuild along the line of the old wall where the ground is already well compacted. New walls often settle several inches or even as much as a foot over the first two or three years and during this period they are at their weakest. Walls rebuilt on the old lines settle only an inch or two and so are less subject to initial disruption. If you rebuild in a different style with more batter you may have to widen the trench and supply bigger footings.

3 Check the existing wall heads. Often they are solid enough to leave standing.

4 Build the wall in the usual way. Where you are rebuilding the whole thing you can choose your own dimensions and style and should set up appropriate batter frames and guidelines to achieve this. Where you are rebuilding to the old dimensions, run guidelines from a standing section of the old wall to the new work and build towards the old wall.

Final Points

LEAVING THE DAY'S WORK

a Unless you have brought the unfinished wall to a head leave it roughly stepped at the end of the day's work. This way the next day's section can be firmly interlocked both along and through the wall.

b Move all usable face stones, throughs and topstones along the line to the next section to be built, or pile them up for collection and reuse elsewhere.

c Clear out of the way all stones which might interfere with farm machinery or access along tracks or roadways beside the wall. Small stones can be left in fields which are under permanent pasture.

d Shovel loose soil from the foundation trench out of the way or spread it over the adjacent field.

TESTS FOR FIRMNESS

Most wallers trust their own work and leave it alone to settle once it is up. In competitions the judging is mainly by eye, although judges are likely to give a tentative tug at any stone which looks loose. We have been told three more forceful ways of testing for firmness which, even if legendary, might be employed to good effect:

a Induce a sheepdog to walk along the top of the finished wall. This might not be very revealing in most cases, but we were given this advice specifically for testing Galloway single dykes (p18)!

b Run a wheelbarrow along the top. A really solid wall is supposed to be able to take you as well, pushing the barrow loaded.

c Run up to the wall and take a flying kick at it, with both feet, as high up as you can. Listen for the sound of shifting fillings – if you hear any, the wall has been poorly built and will settle badly. Several wallers have sworn to us that their employers (or the employers of fellow craftsmen, or masters of apprentices they knew) used to test the walls regularly in this way back in the rough old days.

Then there is the story, told by an old craftsman in Yorkshire, of the two men who wanted to get paid for a terrible piece of slap work they were building. When it was finally up, one looked at the other and said, 'I'll stop here and hold as well as I can while thou goes and draws for 't'.

7   Retaining Walls and Stone Hedges

Retaining walls are built to retain and stabilise terraces, road cuttings and embankments, river banks and other steep slopes to which soil slump or rock slides are likely to cause problems. Stone hedges are free-standing stone-faced earth banks used as farm boundaries and stock fences and are characteristic of the South West. The techniques used are similar in both, but stone hedges have particular design features or variations which are not found in most retaining walls. There are, as well, intermediate forms such as West Country retaining walls which are built to local stone hedge patterns and the stone-and-earth 'ditches' of Ireland (p21) and certain parts of Wales. So, while retaining walls and stone hedges are described under separate headings here, you will need to consult both sections before attempting to build some types of retaining walls.

Retaining Walls

GENERAL FEATURES

Most retaining walls are built to almost exactly the same design as free-standing walls. They are made up of horizontal courses of face stones, wedged and packed with smaller stone fillings, and have a straight batter which tapers from wide at the base to narrow at the top.

The diagram below shows the two main variations within this 'standard' form (herringbone and other patterns are discussed under 'Stone Hedges', p91). Yorkshire wallers usually build a normal two-faced wall, although the hidden inner face is left rougher and with a steeper batter than the outer face and throughs and large face stones are placed so that they project into the cavity between the wall and the bank. Scottish dykers build a one-sided affair, using various sizes of fillings which bind not only with the outer face stones but with the earth bank behind.

Both methods ensure that the wall sits solidly on its own footings and both seem to work equally well. Perhaps the Yorkshire style is best where there are plenty of face stones and small fillings, or where the wall projects above the bank so that its top is free standing, while the Scottish type is most suitable where many of the fillings are large and irregular and so bind well with the earth bank.

In either case the batter of the outside face is the same as for a free-standing wall of the same type of stone. The base width depends on the batter and wall height, but in general it can be a bit thinner than for an equivalent free-standing wall because to some extent it is supported by the bank behind it. For a 900mm (3') high wall, a base width of 0.45m (1'6") is generally adequate. However, where a high wall is subject to vibration or the bank is unstable, as at a roadside or on a slope of scree or wet clay, the wall should be built a little wider than normal, eg 600mm (2') for a 900mm (3') high wall or 0.9–1.2m (3–4') for a 1.5–1.8m (5–6') high wall.

PROCEDURAL POINTS

The procedure for building a dry stone retaining wall is essentially the same as for a free-standing wall (p63). The following points show how to adapt normal walling techniques to retaining walls.

a Prepare the bank by cutting it back and digging it out to a vertical face the height of the proposed wall. Cut it back at least 150mm (6") deeper than the proposed base of the wall, to give you room to work when placing the stones.

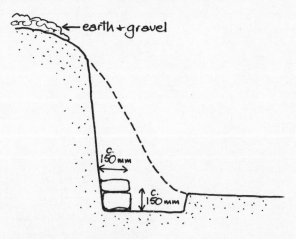

b Dig a foundation trench for the footings down to firm subsoil or bedrock. About 150mm (6") is usually deep enough.

c Build both ends of the wall first, if these mark

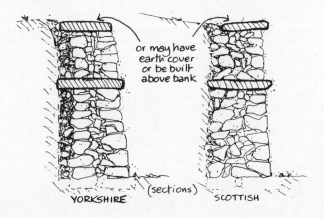

YORKSHIRE   (sections)   SCOTTISH

or may have earth cover or be built above bank

definite heads. Choose large stones for the ends – they should have a flat bed and two good faces if possible.

d If the wall merges with the bank at either end, you can build it up along the whole section as convenient. Be sure to key the ends into the bank at their sides as well as at the back.

e Build up in horizontal courses with the biggest stones at the bottom. The stones should be level or tipped slightly down and out and firmly wedged as necessary. Although it is usually impractical to set up batter frames, it helps to run a guideline between the wall ends and to move this up in roughly 300mm (1') stages.

f In the Yorkshire style, build up both the inner and outer faces together, with fillings between, as in a free-standing wall. Don't worry if the inner face is irregular but be sure that the stones sit securely. Pack more fillings between the inner face and the bank. These tie the wall to the bank and ensure good drainage. Keep the level of the fillings as high as the face stones.

In the Scottish style, place and wedge as necessary each face stone and pack behind it with fillings to give a solid single-faced structure. Whichever style you use, place the stones with their long edges running into the bank for strength.

A certain amount of earth always slips down from the bank as you work. This is fine as long as you pack the earth down as you proceed and do not use it in place of stone fillings.

g Place throughs at the same level and spacing as for a free-standing wall of equal height. Their outer face should be flush with or sticking out no more than 25–50mm (1–2") from the wall while their backs should project well into the cavity between the wall and the bank. Dig out the bank as necessary to take the ends of the throughs, rather than breaking them off short. Do this for other long stones too. The more face stones which project into the bank the better, as long as they are well seated.

h If you have plenty of big stones, use some of the most awkwardly-shaped ones as fillings

rather than breaking them up. In the Scottish style, a proportion of big fillings is important to strengthen the wall while small fillings are necessary to wedge up face stones. If you try a face stone and it doesn't fit, use it to pack the wall cavity.

i If the top of the wall is at or below the top of the bank, finish the wall flat. In Scotland a cover band is placed at this point, while in Yorkshire the wall is left uncoped if the aim is to let earth and plants cover the top, or is given a flat coping if it is at the bank top. In a few districts a layer of turf is cut out from the adjacent field and packed down flat along the wall top in place of a normal coping.

j If the top of the wall projects above the bank top, build the projecting part as a two-faced, free-standing wall even if you have not done this below. Top it with whatever type of coping you prefer (p73).

k Finish the work by shovelling the remaining pebbles and earth from the top of the bank behind the top of the wall to help knit the two together and use up the spoil. If there is still earth remaining, spread it over the top of the bank.

PROBLEM SITUATIONS

Slopes

a Start the wall at the downhill end as with a free-standing wall. Make sure this end is provided with a really solid head. On a steep slope, the bottom end stone must be massive and absolutely stable to support the weight of material above. When in doubt, concrete the end to keep it from shifting.

b Where the wall is built to retain scree or other loose material on a steep slope, several adaptations are necessary. The diagram at the top of the next page illustrates a method which has been used successfully by the BTCV at Cwm Idwal in Snowdonia and at other sites where there may not be a level base from which to start and where the aim is to blend the stonework in with the existing hillside as much as possible.

It is important to base the wall on bedrock. This may mean starting it considerably farther down the slope than planned, at least in places, and possibly building up and concreting a level platform using progressively larger stones until the real footings can be placed. Stones should be placed tilting down at the inside edges rather than being placed level or slightly tipped to the outside as is normal, to help trap debris which

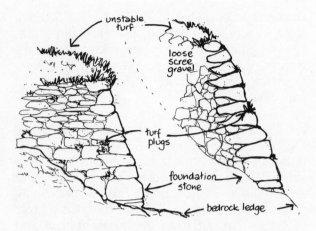

sifts down over the wall. Turf should be plugged into the wall during construction, where possible, to promote a quicker vegetation growth over the wall and help stabilise it. However, the weight-bearing surfaces of the stones should be left free of earth during construction to make them as stable as possible.

c When winning stones from a hillside for use in the wall, take them from uphill to make it easier to shift them and to keep from destabilising the slope below the wall. Where high rainfall and runoff are likely to cause erosion problems, fill in the holes left by the removal of big stones with small stones when possible.

d Where the base of the wall is a path or is in soft soil or peat, it is worth digging in the foundation stones to their entire depth to provide a solid base for the wall.

e Where runoff is likely to affect the wall, you can dig a cut-off drain a foot or so above it along its line. Make the trench 300–600mm (1–2′) deep, depending on the depth of the soil, and about as wide at the top. If possible, fill the ditch with small stones to help keep it from clogging with earth and vegetation.

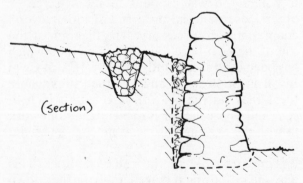

(section)

f Where the bank is inherently unstable, eg clay or sand which tends to slump when wet, ordinary retaining walls must be built extra wide for strength. In this situation it may be easier to use gabions instead. These are wire baskets filled with stones which are built up in rows like giant blocks. They are flexible and porous and

so allow some settling of earth and drainage of water, yet are extremely stable due to their great weight. Commercially-made gabions are produced by River and Sea Gabions (London) Ltd, 2 Swallow Place, London W1R 8SQ, who have descriptive literature available on request. Gabions can also be home made from chain link fencing or galvanised wire. Details are given in another publication in this series, 'Waterways and Wetlands' (BTCV, 1976).

Traffic and vibration

a Where the wall supports a footpath or track, it is worth using large flat topstones even where these would not otherwise be required. If too small stones are used they may be shaken loose, kicked or pushed off the wall.

b Where the wall retains a bank which takes motor vehicles, extra strength is required depending on the amount and type of traffic. There should be a verge at least 500mm (20″) wide between the road and the top of the wall. The coping may need to be mortared.

c On a high wall supporting a roadway, several rows of throughs are necessary and it is best to construct the wall in tiers, inset about 300mm (1′) above each row of throughs. The sketch below shows a magnificent example, built about

200 years ago, of this sort of construction: a 4.5m (15′) high wall built of Coal Measures stone in Cawthorne, South Yorkshire (OS grid ref: SE258089). Other throughs are used in addition to the stones topping the tiers, and each extends 0.9–1.5m (3–5′) into the bank. The wall is 1.8m (6′) wide at the base, while the upper part is free standing and has the normal dimensions for a wall in this locale: 600mm (2′) wide at road level and 450mm (1′ 6″) wide at the top. It is topped with a mortared coping of trimmed half-round upright stones.

Buttresses may also be used to support a high wall, and the same wall as described above has a row of buttresses along one side, placed about 3.6m (12′) apart. The top of each buttress is about 1.8m (6′) above ground level while its foundations are about equally far into the ground. The sketch shows how the courses progress from nearly horizontal at ground level to steeply tilted at the top, to resist the weight of the main wall. Great care has been taken to fit the end of the buttress to the side of the wall.

Stone Hedges

GENERAL FEATURES

The standard stone hedge design specified for roadside work by the County of Cornwall is shown below. Farm hedges are frequently higher than this, 1.8m (6′) and possibly much more where they border a track worn below field level. Whatever the size, they illustrate the general principle that the width of the hedge at its base should equal its height.

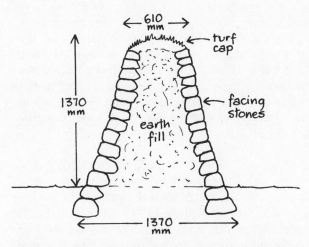

There are a number of ways to face an earth bank, some of which have been illustrated in the chapter, 'Walls in the Landscape'. Ignoring local or individual preferences, the main factors which determine the style are:

a Type of available stone. Granite, sandstone, elvan (whinstone) and irregular clearance or river-washed stones are most suited to building in roughly level courses. Slate is best used upright or, if fragmented, in the herringbone ('Jack and Jill' or 'Darby and Joan') pattern. In the Cornish specifications shown above, the top two rows, if granite, may either be finished (trimmed) or random (rough). If the top two rows are slate they are built in herringbone to use up the small pieces split from the 'raisers' or face stones during construction. Herringbone also provides a good rooting medium for plants growing along the hedge's crown or 'comb'.

b Cost. The cheapest stone is that which is cleared from the fields, but for larger jobs quarried stone is often necessary. Quarried slate, which is much cheaper than granite, is used increasingly even in granite areas despite the dislike of local craftsmen. One way to save stone is to stop at the 0.9–1.2m (3–4′) level and finish off the top of the hedge with turf. This is often done with granite hedges. Turfs are often used on the south- and west-facing slopes where the sun promotes quick growth of vegetation to help bind the hedge face, while stones may be used on northern slopes or under trees where turf tends to dry out or may have difficulty in taking root. Methods of cutting and constructing turf-faced banks are covered in another handbook in this series, *Hedging* (BTCV, 1975).

CONSTRUCTION PROCEDURE

To build a new stone hedge, follow this procedure:

1 Lay out the line of the proposed hedge by pinning two guidelines parallel to each other and at the correct width. If the dimensions are not specified, make the width equal to the proposed height, which should be at least 1.7m (5′6″) if it is to shelter cattle. Note that stone hedges are built to begin and end at gates rather than wall heads. This requires that the alignment be tapered to meet the gate posts (see page 101 for details).

2 'Nick out' (point **4**, p65) along both lines. Next, 'splay' (cut out) the turf first along all of one side of the trench and then along the other. Cut it about 25–75mm (1–3″) deep and lift it carefully to the side so that it can be used to finish the hedge. Only cut out the length which is to be built that day: 4.5–7.3m (5–8 yards) for a skilled pair of workers.

3 Dig down to a firm subsoil, usually about 150–225mm (6–9″). Dig out one side, then the other, leaving the floor of the trench sloping slightly down towards the centre to provide a firm footing of inward-sloping stones. Shovel the earth into piles at the sides to use when building the bank.

4 Set out stones and earth for the day's work, if this has not already been done. The quantities required are given on page 56.

5 Erect a batter frame or 'pattern' just beyond the end of the section (put a frame at each end if starting a new section which does not connect with any others). Or you can use a frame which you hold up against the side of the hedge from time to time. Designs are shown on page 49. Make sure the frame is vertical and level across the base. The self-supporting type of pattern has the advantage of allowing you to use guidelines, which should be strung at 300mm (1′) above ground level, tied to the pattern and pegged into the finished bank at the other end of the section (or tied to the other pattern). Make sure the lines are taut.

6 Use the largest available stones in the foundations. In Cornwall these are known as 'coins' or 'grounders' and are often completely or half buried below ground level. Start at the left end and work to the right, if you are right-handed. Hold each stone with the left hand and tamp it in place with the back of the hammer or a short stick so that it sits firmly. Pack behind the stones with earth as necessary to keep them steady. Lay one side of the bottom course, then cross over the trench to lay the other side (pairs of workers should work from opposite sides at the same time).

As in most dry walling, stones are placed long edge into the wall for strength, although 'shiners' (stones running along the wall) may be used occasionally if they have a good batter and are well tied in by other stones along their tops. In Cornwall the stones are placed with the smaller of the two short edges outward, while in Devon the opposite is the case. Craftsmen in each county claim their method is strongest.

In either case, the stones are placed so that they tilt slightly down and into the wall, which is opposite to the usual method in dry walling. This allows water to run into the bank and promotes a better growth of plants between the stones to help anchor them in place.

The degree of tilt depends on the batter. In Cornwall the batter may be either straight or concave, while in Devon a concave batter is always used. With a concave batter the hedge, as it settles, remains slightly concave or straightens out. With a straight batter the hedge may belly out and become weak as it settles.

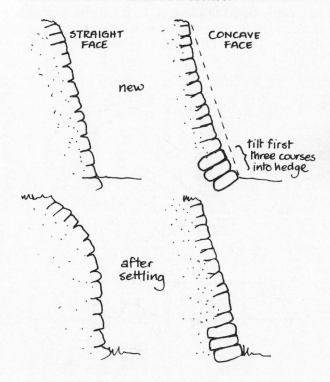

A concave batter is also supposed to create less wind turbulence and thereby improve the hedge's shelter value. To achieve the correct curve for a concave batter, the first three courses are tilted strongly down into the hedge while succeeding courses are brought gradually up so that the top layers have their faces nearly perpendicular, as shown in the diagram which follows. The batter frame should show this exactly. A rule of thumb is to have about 75mm (3″) of batter in the first 300mm (1′) of hedge height and to decrease this progressively to perpendicular at the top.

7 After the first course is placed along both

sides, shovel earth into the centre and pack it firmly. The best way to tamp, while the hedge is low enough, is with your heel, but you can also use a stick or the hammer. Tamp towards the centre so as not to dislodge the stones. Then use the stick or hammer to finish consolidating around the stones. Bring the earth packing slightly above the level of the course so that the next course is adequately supported.

Some Cornish hedgers pack a layer of earth on top of the stones to help bed in the next course, although their general rule is that 'stones hold the earth, and not vice-versa'. In Devon the stones are left bare on top so that the next course beds onto stone and not earth. In the Devon method, stone wedges or 'chips' may be placed between or behind the stones to hold them steady (Devonshire 'chip and block' construction is explained further below). Cornish hedgers frown on this since they feel that the bank may become unstable if the wedges shift when the hedge settles. The best technique seems to be to use wedges from behind, to steady the face stones when required, but to avoid using them in front in the same way that pinnings are generally to be avoided in dry stone walls (p71). Whatever the method, it is best to avoid more dirt than is necessary in front of the face.

8 'Pitch' (place) the next row of face stones ('raisers' or 'pitchers') as you did the first, setting them in slightly to conform to the batter and breaking the joints as in a normal dry wall. After steadying them, pack behind with well-tamped earth as before.

Changes of direction in hedges are usually accommodated by curved sections, which are built in the same way as straight. But if a sharp angle necessitates a corner, build this up first before adding the course to either side. Use stones with two good faces for the corner, if you have them.

In Cornwall, the emphasis when building horizontal courses is on a neat block-masonry appearance, especially when using trimmed stone. Unfortunately, the more regular the stone the more poorly it binds, and trimmed granite hedges especially are likely to collapse outward or inward as the bank settles. Where the stone is naturally irregular, a stronger method and one that is preferred in Devon is to build in the 'chip and block' or rough rubble style, where large 'blocks' and small 'chips' are used together. Even in chip and block construction an effort is made to use the biggest stones near the bottom, but little trimming is done except to knock off awkward projecting

noses or inside corners which would otherwise keep the stones from tightening as they settle.

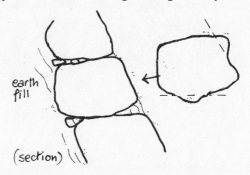

Throughout the South West, hedges are often faced in courses of vertically placed stones where the stones are fairly small or long and thin. Don't use large blocks for this – the result is then weaker than a horizontally coursed wall. When building in vertical courses it is most important to break the horizontal joints as shown below.

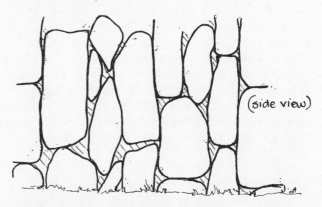

When building with vertical stones, it is usually necessary to trim off rounded ends so that the next stones above will sit securely, although when using very fissile material you can usually tap down the upper stones between two lower ones without any shaping. With vertical courses, some hedgers recommend putting a turf layer about 25mm (1″) thick on each course, tamping it down well between the stones. This makes a bed for the next course and insures a quick growth of grass over the hedge to help bind it.

With the herringbone style there is no way to break the joints between courses. In this method horizontal layers are often placed between every two diagonal courses to give a good bed for those above. (See diagram on page 94.)

9 Continue to pitch and pack the courses, bringing up the batter according to the frame. If you are using a standing frame, raise the guidelines 300mm (1′) at a time for accurate construction.

10 There are various ways to finish off the hedge. In the County of Cornwall specifications, the stonework is brought to within 450mm (1′6″)

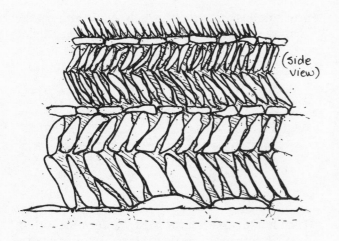

(side view)

of the proposed top height, above which are placed two rows of small stones known as 'toppers' or 'codgers'. These may be placed in the usual way or in the herringbone pattern, as discussed under point **a**, page 91. A row of turf is then placed above the stonework on both sides to keep rain from washing the earth out from the top or 'comb'. The bank must be brought up to its final height, well packed and given a rounded profile before the turf is put on. Use the topsoil and turf set aside for this purpose when you cut the foundation trench. A single or double staggered row of young hawthorn, beech or other hedge shrubs can be planted on top. Details are given in *Hedging*, (BTCV, 1975).

In certain exposed parts of the Lizard Peninsula a 'thatch' of three rows of turf is placed over the top stones to finish off the hedge (Rule, 1974). One row on each side is placed earth down, then a row on the back of it is placed earth upwards. More earth is packed on and a final double row is placed which overlaps the other rows by about two thirds their width. Finally an earth cover is put on to finish. This method promotes quick binding of the turf.

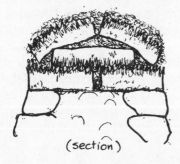

(section)

Archie Radmore near Plymouth, Devon, usually finishes his hedges with an upright or a buck-and-doe coping, projecting above the top of the bank. Or he simply finishes off with about 100mm (4″) of turf, placed grass side up, above the normal stonework. The latter is probably the most-used method throughout the South West.

11 When leaving an unfinished hedge overnight, make sure that its end slopes gradually enough so that it won't slump even if it rains.

Protection, Maintenance and Repair

South Western hedges of both turf and stone used to be left half built to settle, and even now are considered 'tender' until new vegetation starts to grow on them. During this period cattle can easily paw the stones loose or tear them down by climbing the banks, so cattle should be kept off the fields for several months or else a temporary fence should be erected about a yard back of the bank foot. Cattle should be kept off other retaining walls in the same way.

Once the bank is firmly bound by growing vegetation, livestock present little problem unless a stone or two is loosened in some other way. Rabbits and rats cause the most trouble since sections of stone facing may slump inward after they have burrowed extensively. If trees are planted along the top they may become lopsided over the years and tend to break down one side of the bank, usually the one away from the prevailing wind. Trees and to a lesser extent brambles and briars which root in the steep sides of a tall bank tend to loosen and dislodge stones. Whenever a break occurs, sheep and cattle are sure to investigate and accelerate the erosion.

Despite these problems, dry stone retaining walls and stone hedges need to be checked only occasionally once they have settled and knit together. As with free-standing walls, the quicker any break is made good the less likely it is to spread, whether or not livestock are present to further the damage. The following points apply to routine maintenance and repair:

a The wall or bank should be checked every few months, or more often if cattle are in the field, for obvious signs of a break.

b Once a year a close check should be made for dislodged stones. At this time also, unwanted trees or shrubs growing from the sides should be cut back or dug out. If the bank has a live hedge on top of it, you can renew the soil and keep the plants vigorous by shovelling earth which has slumped to the base of the bank up among the hedge plants. Be sure not to disturb the stonework when doing this.

c To tear down a section of retaining wall or stone hedge for repair, start by clearing the turf and debris from the base with a spade. Then lever up the top course of stones to loosen the

94

turf above them. This makes the top course easier to pull out. Throw the stones along a line behind your work area. Cut off the overhanging turf with a spade or mattock and place it on top of the bank. Continue to pull out loose stonework to either side until you reach undisturbed material, and extend the gap downward until you reach a course which seems to be firmly and correctly placed. Don't tamp down the earth packing, but throw as much of the soil up onto the bank as you can. Remaining soil should be shovelled back out of the way.

In most cases you only need to cut down and rebuild one side of a stone hedge. Where both faces are damaged but the centre is firm, repair one side at a time to keep from weakening the bank more than necessary. If the centre needs repair, pull down and clean out the hedge right through and build it back up from both sides at once.

Build up a gap exactly as you would a new retaining wall or stone hedge. For short sections guidelines are unnecessary, but for sections over a few yards long it helps to stretch a line across the gap and pin it to the wall at either side. Leave it clear of the wall face by about 6mm ($\frac{1}{4}''$) to give you room to build. Move the line up 300mm (1') at a time. As when repairing a free-standing wall, you may need more stone than is provided by the gap itself especially where some of the old face stones have settled inward and disappeared into the earth fill.

8 Wall 'Furniture' and Special Applications

This chapter covers the design and construction of wall openings such as smoots, stiles and gates, combinations of walls and fences and unusual applications such as bee boles and shooting butts. The sections on stiles and gates deal only with those designs which are most closely associated with stone walls. Other designs, more general to all types of fences, are included in other handbooks in this series, 'Footpaths' (1983) and 'Fencing' (1986).

Whatever the item of wall 'furniture', remember that it is much easier to build something into a wall as the wall is being built than to add it later. Unless an existing wall is already in the process of reconstruction it is seldom worth ripping down a section to add an opening or built-in stile. It is important to think ahead when erecting a new wall to decide where such items will be required. And when rebuilding a long stretch of old wall, note whatever furniture it contains and replace it as before, unless you are sure it no longer serves a useful purpose.

Smoots and Cripple Holes

For a general description of smoots and cripple holes see page 11.

Small smoots may be built to:

a Allow and control the passage of rabbits and other small mammals through the wall.

b Allow runoff and flood water to drain through the wall.

c Bridge tree roots which might otherwise damage the wall (p84).

It is not always easy to determine why an existing smoot has been built, and local usage may be confusing since in some areas all small openings may be called by only one name whatever their purpose. The site may give clues, though. Walls built up and down a slope have little need for cross drainage so any openings are probably just for animals. The holes in walls built across slopes may be used by animals, but are often most important to keep flood runoff from disrupting the foundations, especially in areas such as the Lake District where high rainfall combined with steep gradients make runoff a problem. But in limestone country, subsoil drainage is so fast that water-drainage smoots are seldom necessary whatever the wall's orientation.

Whatever the purpose of different small smoots, all are usually about the same size, 150mm × 150mm (6″×6″) and are built in the same way:

a Dig the foundation trench and place the footings across the line of the smoot. The footings which form the base of the smoot itself should not come above ground level.

2 Build up the sides of the smoot as miniature wall heads (p77). This requires just one or two good stones on either side, but they are important to keep the fillings in place. Don't construct the smoot by simply omitting a few stones from the bottom course, since this exposes and weakens the wall's centre.

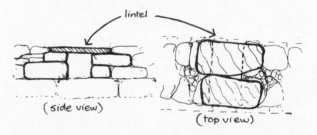

3 Top the smoot with lintel stones placed side by side, as shown above. Continue building in the normal way above the lintels.

In the Mendips, small smoots called 'pop holes' are often built in a zig-zag pattern (see page 9).

Large water smoots are built to allow the passage of streams or ditches through dry stone walls. The size of the available lintel stones determines the width of the watercourse that can be spanned. Usually two throughstones placed as in the diagram above are used to top the hole, but where the stones are too small, heavy iron bars or old axles or wooden rails or sleepers can be used instead, although the result is likely to be fairly short-lived. Sheet metal should not be used since it quickly rusts and bends. Sections of large-diameter reinforced concrete pipe can be used, making the smoot into a culvert. Sometimes wallers roof openings in ingenious ways: Margaret Brooks (1973, p104) reports one wall incorporating a dry stone arch and Rollinson (1972, p10) says that in the Lickle Valley in the Lake District there are a few gable-roofed holes.

Cripple holes, built to control the passage of sheep through the wall, are constructed the same way as large water smoots. Their dimensions are usually 450–610mm (1′6″–2′) wide by 610mm (2′) high. In Scotland, according to Prevost (1957, p99), these holes are often built narrower at the base than at the middle and top. Elsewhere they are generally rectangular. Sometimes two cripple holes are built side by side to speed the passage of sheep. An unusual version, shown on page 11, combines a cripple hole with an easily dismantled section of wall to produce a 'cow creep'. Cripple holes should be left blocked off with stone slabs when not in use.

Build large water smoots and cripple holes in the same way as small smoots, but remember the following points:

a Take extra care to build the sides smooth and straight and to find suitably strong lintel stones.

b There are two ways to floor a large opening. You can leave it in grass, which is quick and easy but may allow the sides of the hole to settle inward and the floor to become rutted if it is much used. Or you can continue the foundation trench through the smoot or cripple hole and floor it with large flat footings to ground level. This is more time-consuming but is usually worth the effort in the long run. As with lintels one sometimes sees unusual floors in smoots. Margaret Brooks (1973, p106) found one with a cobbled bottom near Skipton in North Yorkshire.

c Make sure that the foundations of a large water smoot extend to the bottom of the ditch or stream. Otherwise, fillings may be washed out of the wall and the smoot collapse. Build the smoot high enough so that the lintel remains clear of flood water levels and allows branches and other debris to pass, but build the sides as close to the water course as possible to minimise the required span of the lintel. These smoots require checking from time to time to make sure they have not become blocked, especially if bars or a gate have been fixed across to keep sheep from pushing through (p102).

Stiles

Stiles are designed to allow people to pass through or over walls but to keep livestock (except goats, which can manage any stile) at bay. Whatever the type, the stile must not encourage people to use the wall's coping as a handhold or a top step, since the whole point of the stile is to keep people from climbing the wall and knocking off topstones. Ladder-type and other wooden stiles, which are not dealt with here, must be designed without any strengtheners running into the wall since the vibration from these inevitably disrupts the

stonework. Built-in stiles are usually more effective than free-standing types and take less maintenance than wood or ready-made steel structures. There are two main sorts of built-ins: step stiles and through stiles, both described below.

STEP STILES

Step stiles, if well designed, allow the walker to cross the wall without changing his pace. The most common type uses especially long throughstones, built into the wall so that they stick out at right angles and form a diagonal series up one side of the wall and down the other. They are most often installed in areas where large flat flags are available, although sometimes flags are bought or brought into an area of less suitable material. Step stiles can use sections of railway sleepers or reinforced concrete posts rather than stones, but these decay in time and are usually less satisfactory than slabs. The diagram below shows a typical step stile built in Skiddaw Slate.

This stile has two steps either side, and above the top step is a sill and a gap for people to cross more easily. The top of the wall is brought to small heads on both sides of the gap. More typically, this type of stile has three steps on either side which brings the top step high enough to allow the coping to be carried across the top. In Hepple, Northumberland, on the B6341, there is even a six-step stile, but while ideal for pedestrians this also allows sheep an easy passage and is not designed for a stockproof wall. Very occasionally, a short wooden post is built upright into the top of the wall beside the stile, to provide a handhold, but unless it is cemented in place the post may weaken the coping.

Keep these points in mind when building this type of stile:

a Put in the first step at least 450mm (1′6″) above ground level, and the other steps spaced so that the top step is no more than 610mm (2′) below the top of the wall.

b Stepping stones should be 75–100mm (3–4″)

thick for strength and should stick out 300–375mm (12–15″) to provide a safe platform. If, as is usually the case, you must leave some steps shorter than others, grade the steps from biggest at the bottom to smallest at the top.

c The stepping stones must be securely anchored within the wall, otherwise they may prise it apart instead of strengthening it. The best stones project right through the wall, so that they form two steps at once. Only exceptional stones are long enough for this, especially low in the wall where they must be 1.5–1.7m (5′–5′6″) long to serve in this way. If a stone can't reach through, at least twice as much of its length must be buried in the wall as sticks out.

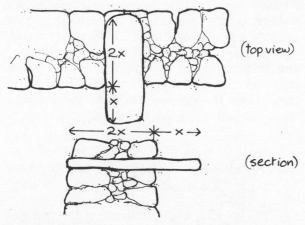

d Place and build up around the steps the same way as when placing throughstones (p72), but be especially careful to use large face stones at this point to spread the wall's weight as evenly as possible. Cross all joints and follow the other rules given on page 63. The stones must be absolutely immovable, whatever the weight put on them. To ensure this, Fields (1971, p51) recommends that the face stones directly above and anchoring the stepping stones should be twice as long as the exposed parts of the stepping stones.

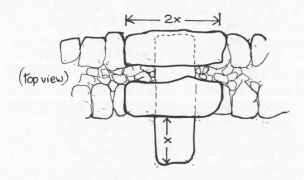

Cornish stone hedges usually have stiles of hewn granite. Rule (1974) describes these stiles as having three rungs or steps built into the bank rather than projecting out from it.

To build a South Western step stile:

1 Cut the foundation trench across the line of the stile in the same way as along the rest of the hedge.

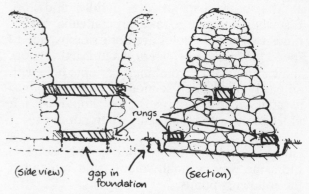

2 Build one side of the foundation up to but not across the line of the stile. Bring it close enough to the gap on both sides so that the first step can be placed with its end resting solidly on the foundation's facing stones.

3 Place the first step.

4 Cross to the other side of the hedge and repeat steps 2 and 3, placing the second step across from and on the same level as the first.

5 Lay stones between the ends of the steps so that the hedge's earth fill is protected by a stone facing all around.

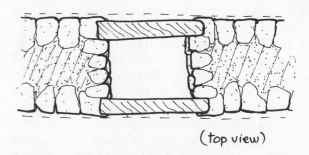

6 Build two or three rows of hedge on top of the foundation to secure the ends of the first two steps. Face the sides of the gap as well as the outside of the hedge with stone.

7 Place the third step 300–357mm (12–15″) above the first two and along the centre line of the hedge.

8 Finish building the hedge above the steps, giving the sides of the gap at least as much batter as the outside of the hedge. Continue facing the sides with stones up to a point at which the hedge can be finished off in one of the usual ways (p93).

Sometimes step stiles use a staircase-type design, although this is less stockproof, particularly against sheep, than the types shown above. The following sketch is of a stile in the wall of the churchyard at Morwenstow, Devon, which incorporates a vertical slate sill above the granite steps.

Retaining walls sometimes have stairs built through them, again where convenience for people is important and stockproof qualities are not. Fields (1971, p48) gives these rules for making stone stairs solid and durable:

a Choose slabs which are wide enough for footroom, long enough to tie into the faces of the wall on both sides and thick enough to bear the weight of a man carrying a load.

b Buttress each step from below with a foundation of smaller stones.

c Build the wall to a head at each side of the steps for strength.

d Dig in a slab at the top and another at the bottom of the wall so that their tops are at ground level. Each slab should be about 500mm (1'8") wide and long enough to reach at least 150mm (6") beyond the stair gap on either side.

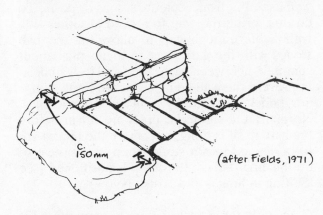

(after Fields, 1971)

THROUGH STILES

Through stiles are almost as common as step stiles and are particularly suited to areas where long gritstone or slate slabs are scarce. The main problem in their design is to make a passage which is wide enough for people but too narrow or difficult for lambs.

To build the usual type of through stile, also known as a 'squeezer':

1 Build the wall to 450mm (1'6") above ground level. The stone which is to form the flat base of the stile should be a throughstone if possible.

2 Continue the wall to the top, leaving a gap of about 250mm (10") or just enough for people to walk through sideways on. Build the sides of this gap as wall heads. (Although a small lamb could squeeze through this opening, it probably wouldn't be able to jump onto the sill.)

(side view)

To assist the passage of well-padded pedestrians, or those with bulky packs on their backs, you can build the top half of one wall head with an inset to make it somewhat wider at the top, as shown in the drawing above. Another way to achieve the same effect is to taper the gap so that it is narrow at the bottom and comfortably wide at the top.

Webster and White (1973, pp6–7) describe several variants of the squeezer stile. In one, the base of the stile is laid between 225mm (9") and 300mm (12") above ground level and the stile is built only 175mm (7") wide up to about the 760mm (2'6") level to prevent lambs getting through. From there the stile is tapered out to 300mm (12") at the 910mm (3') level. In another version, trimmed stone slabs are set into the wall in the design shown below.

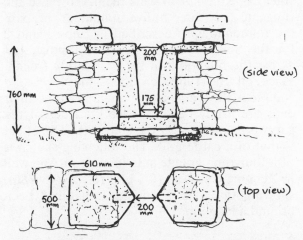

(side view)

(top view)

Where long stone stoops are available, these can be incorporated into the stile to protect the wall heads and give people something to grasp.

Do not bother to build the foundations and bottom of the wall across the line of the stile, if you plan to use stoops. Instead, dig the stoops into the ground so they are solid, with their inside edges about 250mm (10″) apart. Wedge a large stone between them at the bottom to act as a sill. Then build the wall to a head on either side of the stoops. They can be the same or, as shown below, of differing heights with their inside edges even closer (about 175mm (7″)), to make them proof against lambs yet make them easier for people to pass.

Another use of a large stone slab in a through stile is shown in the example below from Great Haseley, Oxfordshire. This design is not particularly easy for people, however.

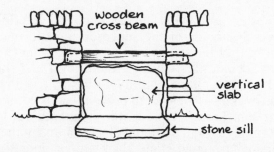

Cornish hedges often have through or 'rung' stiles, as Rule (1974) calls them. To place the rungs, usually three to five in number, prepare the foundations as described in steps 1 and 2 for the South Western step stile, above, but across the full width of the foundation trench. Place all the rungs on the same level and complete the bank above them so that their ends are firmly bedded. Face the sides of the gap with stones as for the step stile. The effect is that of a cattle grid. The following sketch is of a four-rung granite stile in an Iron Age wall in Zennor, Cornwall (OS grid ref: SW456386), showing that this is one idea that has been around a long time.

Similar stiles are found on the Isles of Scilly, where they often have five rungs, the middle one of which is about 300mm (12″) high so that it sticks up as a sill. The other rungs should be about 150mm (6″) high, and all are about 100–150mm (4–6″) wide. Their spacing depends on the number of rungs: 150mm (6″) apart for a five-rung stile and somewhat farther apart where fewer rungs are used. The stile opening can be made to any convenient width and is determined largely by the length of rungs available. One disadvantage of this sort of stile is that it has to be cleaned out from time to time to keep the gaps between the rungs from filling up with debris and vegetation.

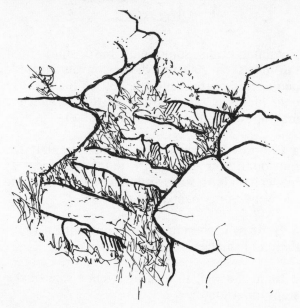

Gates

DESIGN AND METHODS OF HANGING

It is always best to hang a gate not from the wall itself but from separate stoops or posts. To do this, bring the wall to a head at either side with a big enough gap to allow for the two stoops with the gate fixed to them, plus about 50mm (2″) between each stoop and its wall head to prevent the wall being disturbed if the stoops are knocked about by vehicles or machines. Normally the stoops or posts are set in before the gate itself is hung, but where the hinges are to be leaded into a stone stoop it is easiest to do this first, before the stoop is positioned (see 'Setting in hinges and posts', below).

Gate ends for vehicle access are usually built about 3m (10′) apart, but check the access requirements first and the dimensions of ready-made gates if these are used. Often old gate openings were built too narrow for today's needs and one sees them now, the gate rotted and the gap walled up around the stoops. Traditionally, the stoops were of stone: hewn granite, mica schist, slate, gritstone, rhyolite columns or any other stone which does not split or crumble too readily. Metal, reinforced concrete or wooden posts can be used instead. In every case, it is most important that the stoops be dug in so that they are absolutely solid, at least one third of their length in the ground. In most cases this will mean a hole at least 760mm (2′6″) and preferably up to 1.2m (4′) deep. Dig out each post hole a little bigger around than the stoop, set the stoop in and hold it upright while you pack and tamp the earth a few inches at a time. The bottom foot of earth must be especially well tamped if the stoop is to stay secure.

An unusual method of setting a wrought iron gate post, described by an Aberdeenshire waller, is shown below. The bottom of the bent rod is leaded into a hole drilled in the foundation stone and the rod is held upright and firm by the weight of the wall built above its bend.

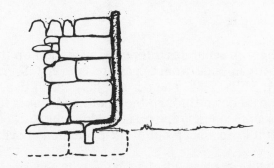

A disadvantage of this method is that any severe stress on the post, such as being struck by a vehicle, will tend to disrupt the wall head.

Small gates can be hung directly from wall ends, although this is not as good as hanging from a stoop. The wall is built up to a head and at the proper height the bottom and top hinges, which are of steel with long flat shafts, are set into position. The head is then completed above the hinges. Alternatively, the hinges can be leaded or cemented into holes drilled in the stones. In either case, it is most important that the gate ends be solidly built and that the bottom hinge be fixed to or above a large carefully trimmed boulder set above the footings.

In many parts of Ireland, gates are hung not from stoops nor from the wall itself but from massive cylindrical pillars built next to the wall ends. To build a pillar, a temporary wooden post is driven in and a string is swung from this to mark the approximate radius. After the pillar is built around the post it is removed and a mushroom-shaped cap is added on top. Often the finished pillar is plastered and painted over. Although iron eye-hinges are now usually used, most Irish gates were originally hung from perforated stone hinges at the top and rotated on spud-stones at the heel in the primitive 'harr-hanging' method described below (Evans, 1957, p102).

South Western turf and stone hedges require a carefully designed gate end to allow for the extra width and batter of the earth bank. Although the hedge can be brought to a square end like an enormous wall head, this wastes material and requires a good supply of rectangular stones with two or three good faces to form the corners. Usually the hedge is tapered to the gate end as shown.

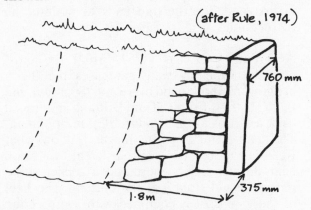

(after Rule, 1974)

The gate post of hewn granite is set 375mm (15″) inside the base line of the hedge and is backed by a 900mm (3′) high head of flat stones so that it is not forced out of line as the earth in the hedge settles. The hedge's batter is progressively reduced from a point 1.8m (6′) from the post, and the base made correspondingly narrower, until at the post itself the hedge is nearly vertical. The same concave frame or pattern which is used to judge the normal batter is used to guide the reduction in base width from the usual 1.5m (5′) or so to 760mm (2′6″) at the post.

The simplest traditional gate is the loose-rail type. This is ineffective against sheep and is easily displaced by cattle, so it has mainly been replaced by swinging gates, but one often comes across tell-tale stoops drilled with a set of three or four holes which once took loose-rail gate poles. Often the holes are round, but an impro-

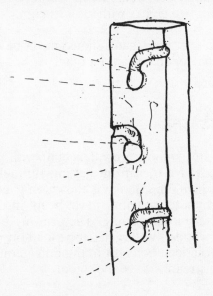

ved method uses square holes on one stoop, to take the trimmed butts of the rails, and smaller round holes on the other stoop to take the thin ends. An even better design has the rails set out in deeply curving grooves which open in opposite directions to make it harder for cattle to nose the rails out of place.

To set the rails in position, place their butt ends in first and flex the thin ends to fit into the correct holes.

According to Evans (1957, p102) the most primitive type of swing gate uses the 'harr-hanging' method found in Ireland, Scotland, the Lake District, Cornwall and Brittany and traced back as far as 5th millenium BC Mesopotamia. The gate swings not on hinges but on what Raistrick (1966, p24) calls a 'creak' or hook near the top of the post and a socket stone (Evans' 'spud stone') at the bottom. The heel of the gate post is equipped with a projecting iron stirrup and peg or spud, which swivels in the stone socket as shown below.

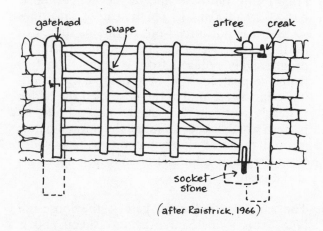

(after Raistrick, 1966)

Generally the gate is hung against the front of the stoops, as shown, and is balanced so that if left short of the fully open position it swings shut by itself. When gates are hung between rather than in front of the stoops they are usually hung from two creaks without a stirrup.

Note that for safety, gates should never be hung so that they open out onto a road.

WATERGATES

Large water smoots are often built with gates to prevent livestock from getting through. A simple if ingenious design is shown on page 12, where rhyolite columns have been installed across the smoot opening. The drawing below shows a wooden watergate suspended on short chains from iron bolts set in the lintel stone on the downstream side of the smoot.

The wall separates a forestry plantation on the upstream side from a pasture below (OS grid ref: SE081568). The design allows flood debris to pass down through the smoot and makes for easier cleaning if the opening does get blocked, yet it keeps sheep out of the plantation above.

Watergates can also be built between smoot heads if each head is provided with a hole at the appropriate level to take a pole. The gate can either be hung by chains from a fixed pole or fixed to the pole itself which swings freely in its holes.

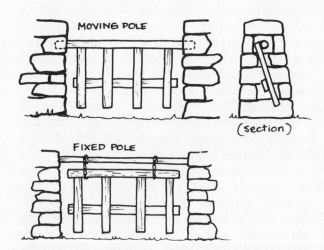

The gate opens both ways if built as shown, but for one-way opening you can build projecting stop-stones into the wall heads behind the gate to either side.

SETTING IN HINGES AND POSTS

Methods are similar for setting gate hinges (discussed above) and fence posts (discussed in the following section) into stone. In each case, a hole should be drilled deep enough to hold the hardware securely, ie somewhat more than the length of the hinge bolts or pins and about 100mm (4") deep for 900mm (3') fencing standards. Drill the hole as explained on page 59 and make it about 6mm ($\frac{1}{4}$") bigger in diameter than the item to be fixed. Enlarge the hole near its base so that the hardened metal or cement forms a plug which cannot be pulled out through the opening. When doing this you should also flare the top of the hole slightly, to about 12mm ($\frac{1}{2}$") bigger than the item to be fixed. This ensures that the fixative will flow in more easily.

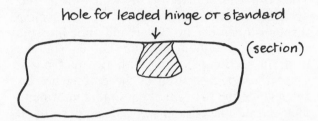

hole for leaded hinge or standard

(section)

The hinge or post can be secured using lead, rock sulphur or cement.

Lead and rock sulphur

The use of heated lead or rock sulphur is most appropriate where the hole is more or less vertical, for ease in pouring, and where it can be made relatively clean and absolutely dry. Even a trace of water causes lead to spit explosively and this can severely burn or blind you. Heated sulphur has less of a tendency to spit than lead, but even so it is important to wear goggles and gloves and to be extremely careful not to spill any hot metal. An advantage of lead is that you can use scraps (eg bits of old pipe) provided they are not too crusted with mineral deposits etc. Most of the impurities stay in the ladle if you pour gently and a small amount reaching the join should not cause problems.

Use the following method when fixing with either lead or sulphur:

1 Clean out the hole, using a bicycle pump to blow out debris or a piece of plasticine to which dust and rock fragments will stick.

2 Position the hinge bolt or fence post securely. For the post, it is best to wedge it in place with one or two small pieces of steel forced into the hole beside it.

3 Heat an adequate amount of metal in a crucible over a 'Calor' gas or other burner until it melts, and then pour it in using a long-handled ladle. For small jobs, you can melt the metal in the ladle directly. Pour the metal into the near side of the hole. This forces any debris in the hole up and out the far side and so directs any

spitting away from your face. Keep pouring in the metal until it fills the hole and is flush with the surface of the stone all round.

4 Pound the surface of the metal flat and fully firm all around the hinge or post using a lump hammer and a wedge with a flattened end.

Cement

Cement can be used to fix hinges or posts into rock in any situation but it is most appropriate where the hole is angled so that pouring is difficult, where the hole cannot be made clean and dry or where the necessary equipment for safely melting metal is unavailable. The disadvantage of a cement fixing is that it is less secure and long lasting than a metal one.

1 If possible, prepare the hole in advance and leave it filled with water to soak for several days before cementing in the hinge or post. This ensures that the cement sets properly. If the hole is too dry when the cement is poured, the stone absorbs water from the cement and causes it to become weak and crumbly. If you cannot drill the hole in advance, at least wet it thoroughly before cementing in the hardware.

2 Secure the hinge or post in position, using small wedges as necessary.

3 Mix up a thin mortar or grout of cement and water, using enough water to form a smooth creamy paste which pours readily into the hole.

4 Pour in the grout, making sure that it flows into all parts of the hole, and tamp it down. If the poured grout seems too watery, stir in a little dry cement to absorb the excess moisture.

To pour cement into an angled hole, follow the same method but form a small cup of putty or plasticine around the underside of the hole to help direct the cement into the hole and to contain any overflow.

Walls with Fences

Occasionally walls are built too low through poor workmanship or a mistaken effort to save time and money. Or the wall's purpose may have changed, eg from fencing cattle to sheep, requiring that it be made higher. The best solution in the long run is to remove the topstones and to add more courses as the opportunity arises and stones become available. Or, if the coping is of locked top construction and you have plenty of topstones available, simply add another coping above the first to bring the wall up about 300mm (1′). Meanwhile, you can make the wall stockproof by putting up a simple fence along its line, using 2.1m (7′) posts (light creosoted coppice poles or larch thinnings will do for the short term) placed about 4.6m (15′) apart, with two strands of barbed wire stapled to the posts above the wall. For greater stability in rocky terrain where the posts can only be driven in a few inches, set the posts alternately on opposite sides of the wall. A more secure solution, where the posts can only be driven in a short distance, is to wire the posts through the wall as shown below.

Pass each wire through the wall, around the post and back through the wall. Then twist the ends together and tighten them with a batten, bringing the post tight up against the wall. This is also a good way to extend a 1.5–1.8m (5–6′) wall the extra 300–600mm (1–2′) necessary for fencing deer. Always bring the stonework up to a uniform level before adding any wire fencing.

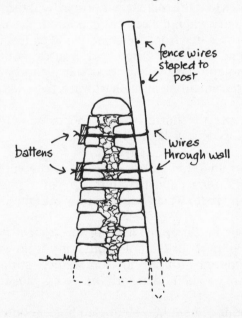

fence wires stapled to post

battens

wires through wall

To keep blackfaced sheep and other hill breeds from jumping a wall, which is especially a problem on steep slopes, Rainsford-Hannay (1972, p60) recommends driving 900mm (3′) long and 75mm (3″) minimum top diameter fence posts into the ground 450mm (1′6″) out from the wall's base. Drive the posts in every 4.6m (15′) with straining posts every 90 metres (100 yards) and at changes of direction. Strain and staple a single line of plain wire 100mm (4″) below the top of the posts. This is sufficient to keep the sheep from jumping. Rainsford-Hannay says that two workers can put up 0.8 kilometres ($\frac{1}{2}$ mile) of this sort of fencing in a day.

Where the ground is too rocky and hard to drive in fence posts, or where a fairly permanent solution to a too-low wall is required, it is best to set the fence in the top of the wall itself. This is expensive and troublesome but it serves the purpose well and is often seen along roadside and railway-cutting walls, especially in Scotland. There are several methods, all using 760–910mm (2′6″–3′) long flat steel standards drilled to take one or two strands of wire above the top of the wall, with the top strand about 450mm (1′6″) above the coping. The standards should be set with their broad face across the line of the wall, to take the wire straight through them.

The posts can be fixed in the wall with mortar or leaded into holes drilled in projecting throughstones or the coverband (not into the topstones). In either case, you should install the posts in sections starting with two end posts. Once these are secured at the correct height, run a guideline between them so that intermediates can be placed and wedged temporarily at the correct height before being fixed.

The diagram below shows how to set standards in the wall using mortar. This is quicker than leading-in when a new wall is built and is used more often these days than the drilled method.

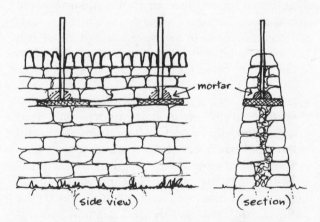

mortar

(side view)   (section)

The standards are wedged and mortared at the base, and the wall is built around them. You can fix the standards in mortar most securely if you cut and bend them to a T-shape at the base as shown.

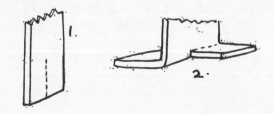

1.   2.

In slate districts one occasionally sees a variation of this approach, in which some of the slate topstones are taller than the others and are drilled to take the fence wires. It is important to position these projecting topstones securely and to place them somewhat closer together than metal fence posts.

Leaded-in standards can be set into the wall, as shown above, or into the coverband or projecting throughs behind the wall as shown below.

The leaded-in design is best when setting standards in an existing wall. If you are fencing sheep, set the standards on the side where the sheep are kept so that they can't jump onto the wall top and then over the fence. See 'Setting in hinges and posts', above, for the procedure when leading-in standards.

If, in repairing a fence with standards, you find that the wire is still good but that one or two standards are bent or broken, you can replace them without cutting the wire if you saw slits through the standards and slip them over the wire through these as shown.

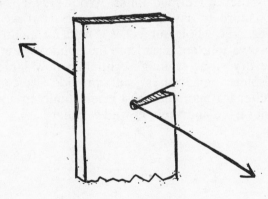

Other Applications

Dry stonework can be used for anything from limekilns to beehive huts, but the examples shown below are a few of the applications most often found today.

BOLES

The thick walls surrounding many old Irish farms often contain cavities of one sort or another, known as 'keeping-holes' in the south and 'boles' in Ulster (Evans, 1950, p101). Traditionally these were used as dog-kennels, duck-houses or simply storage places for large pots.

In the east of Ireland, and much more frequently

(after Evans, 1957)

in northern England, boles in garden walls were built specifically to house the old-fashioned type of straw bee skep. In these niches the hives survived the winter, helped out with a packing of straw in frosty weather. Today bee boles make good garden seats, out of the wind and well protected, especially if their tops are built not with the ordinary flat lintel but with an arch. This requires placing formwork in the correct shape, laying the arch stones on top and mortaring them. When the mortar has dried the form is removed. The rest of the wall can be built dry around and above the arch.

Interesting and unusual bee boles are sometimes found in unexpected locations. Lake District walls seem to be full of them, sometimes in pairs, sometimes even marching in a stepped series up the hillside. More on this facet of local history can be found in Wood (1973, p204). For more details, consult R M Duruz and E E Crane (1953), 'English Bee Boles', National Beekeeping Museum Pamphlet No. 1.

BUTTS

Dry stone shooting butts are drier and much longer lasting than ones made of turf and sod. The example below was built by the BTCV on a leaders' training course near Dunkeld, Perthshire (OS grid ref: NO982496).

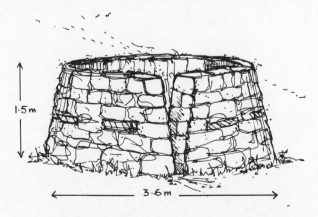

The opening or 'haik' tapers from 610mm (2') wide at the top to just 150mm (6") at the bottom. This keeps cattle and sheep from getting into the shelter. Inside is a stone seat (a projecting

105

slab placed sideways on) and a niche beside it for the user to put his coat and bag out of the way.

A similar design has been adapted by the Countryside Commission for Scotland to provide sheltered view indicators, an example of which can be seen at their Battleby Display Centre, Redgorton, Perthshire.

CAIRNS

Most cairns are just heaps of stones used to mark pathways in rocky terrain, but the example below shows that with care a cairn can be a long-lasting and handsome structure. It is built in dry stone with the inside packed with carefully placed angular fillings.

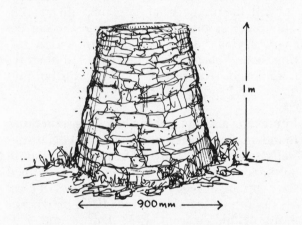

This cairn is designed for use as a view indicator, with a plaque set in mortar on the top, and was built by the Countryside Commission for Scotland for the Battleby Display Centre.

BRIDGE FOUNDATIONS

Dry stone piers can be built to support small and medium-sized bridges, but they must be made of very large boulders to prevent undermining by flowing water. The method is essentially the same as for wall heads (p77) but great care is required and often the stones must be trimmed to sit securely. Smaller stones can be used to fill wire gabions (p90) which can be piled up to achieve the same effect. Vehicular bridges are beyond the capabilities of most groups of volunteer workers, but footbridges are covered in detail in another handbook in this series, *Footpaths* (Agate, 1983).

SHEEP ENCLOSURES

Dry stone sheep enclosures are often encountered in upland areas and are built to many local patterns. They usually consist of a single chamber but some have interconnected 'rooms' which once were used for sorting out mixed flocks from several farms. In Derbyshire and South Yorkshire the enclosures are often circular; in Northumberland they are mostly square. In Scotland there are both circles and ovals. Similarly the local names for these features vary, for example in southeastern Scotland they are known as 'beilds' or 'stells' while in the Highland west they are termed 'fanks'. Wood (1973, p244) has more to say about enclosures, but as he adds, 'the whole subject is a field for amateur observation, not least from the point of view of the dry stone walling'. Although now largely obsolete, enclosures still provide welcome shelter for man and beast when stumbled upon miles from anywhere in wild weather.

Conservation and the Volunteer Worker

BTCV aims to promote the use of volunteers on conservation tasks. In addition to organising work projects it is able, through its affiliation and group schemes, to offer advice and help with insurance cover, tool purchase and practical technical training.

To ensure the success of any conservation task it is important that the requesting person or agency, the volunteer and the leader all understand their particular responsibilities and roles. All voluntary work should be undertaken in the spirit of the Universal Charter of Volunteer Service, drawn up by the UNESCO Coordinating Committee for International Voluntary Service. Three of its most important points are:

1 'The work to be done should be a real need in its proper context and be directly related to a broad framework of development.' In terms of conservation, this means that tasks should be undertaken as integral parts of site management plans, not as isolated exercises. Work should never be undertaken solely for the benefit of the volunteer. Necessary follow-up work after tasks should be planned beforehand to ensure that volunteer effort is not wasted.

2 'The task should be a suitable assignment for a volunteer.' Volunteers cannot successfully tackle all types of work and they should not be used where there is a risk of serious accident or injury, where a financial profit will be made from their labours, where the job is so large that their efforts will have little overall effect, where the skills required are beyond their capabilities so that a bad job results and they become dispirited, or where machines can do the same job more efficiently and for a lower cost.

3 'Voluntary service should not replace paid local labour.' It should complement such work, not supplant it. Employers should make sure in advance that the position of volunteers and paid workers is clear with respect to any relevant labour unions. Further advice may be found in 'Guidelines for the relationships between volunteers and paid non-professional workers', published by the Volunteer Centre, 29 Lower King's Road, Berkhamstead, Hertfordshire HP4 2AB.

Volunteers are rarely 'free labour'. Someone has to pay for transport, materials, tools, insurance, refreshments and any accommodation charges. Before each party makes a commitment to a project it should be clear who is to pay for what. While volunteers may willingly fund their own work, 'user bodies' should be prepared to contribute and should not assume that all volunteers, who are already giving their time and effort, will be able to meet other expenses out of their own pockets. Several grant-aiding bodies may help pay the cost of environmental and conservation projects, notably the Nature Conservancy Council, the World Wildlife Fund and the Countryside Commissions. Details may be found in 'A guide to grants by the Department of the Environment and associated bodies for which voluntary organisations may be eligible', available from the Department of the Environment, Room C15/11, 2 Marsham Street, London SW1P 3EB.

It is important that volunteer workers be covered by some sort of public liability insurance for any damage or injury they may cause to property or to the public. Cover up to £250,000 is recommended. Additional insurance to compensate the volunteer for injury to him- or herself or to other volunteers on task should also be considered.

The volunteer group organiser should visit the work site well before the task, to check that the project is suitable and that volunteers will not be exploited and to plan the best size of working party and the proper tools and equipment. Volunteers should be advised in advance on suitable clothing for the expected conditions. They should be physically fit and come prepared for work and they should genuinely want to volunteer – those 'press-ganged' into service are likely to work poorly, may do more harm than good and may be put off a good cause for life! Young volunteers need more supervision and are best suited to less strenuous jobs where achievements are clearly visible, and it is recommended that where they are involved the task should emphasise education. Note that the Agriculture (Avoidance of Accidents to Children) Regulations, 1958, legally restrict the riding on and driving of agricultural machines, vehicles or implements by children under 13 years.

Volunteer group organisers and 'user bodies' both should keep records of the work undertaken: the date of the project, jobs done, techniques used, number of volunteers and details of any notable events including accidents, unusual 'finds', publicity etc. Such information makes it easier to handle problems or queries which may arise after the task. It also provides a background on the task site for future visits, supplies practical data by which the site management plan can be evaluated and allows an assessment to be made of the volunteer effort.

Studies and Surveys

As yet, there has been no nationally standardised and co-ordinated study of dry stone walls which would give a national picture of walls or stone hedges that are of particular interest and which should be protected.

Such studies as have been undertaken are mainly specialist botanical or historical projects (see the Bibliography), which although valuable for their own speciality, do not cover all aspects of the walls' historical and wildlife value. However, the Cornish Biological Records Unit have been running a long-term survey to define the distribution of the various types of stone hedges, their features, management and wildlife value. Information is gathered by members of the public, using standardised survey cards. The survey card is reproduced overleaf. Further details can be obtained from the Cornish Biological Records Unit, Trevithick Building, Trevenson Road, Pool, Redruth, Cornwall TR15 3PL. Similar cards could be made up for any part of the country, using the wall types characteristic of the area.

For those interested in either the results of studies, or in initiating a project, probably the best contact is the County Biological Records Unit or Centre for the area with which you are concerned, who should know if any work has been undertaken. Many studies have been done of field systems and other archaeological features, including walls. The local or County Museum, County Archaeologist or archaeology department of the college or University for that area may be able to help. At the very local level, many villages and parishes have local history or archaeological societies amongst whose membership there is a fund of knowledge of their local landscape and its history.

CORNISH HEDGE SURVEY CARD

INSTITUTE OF CORNISH STUDIES: BIOLOGICAL RECORDS CENTRE

Hedgerow survey

Hedges occupy a greater acreage than our National Nature Reserves, and support a large proportion of our lowland wildlife. The purpose of this survey is to define the distribution of the various hedgerow types, their management and their wildlife potential. The need for this study is urgent as the agricultural trend towards larger fields is causing a loss of hedgerows at a rate of approximately 5,000 miles a year.

How to complete the card

1 Put a diagonal line through each appropriate compartment to indicate that the feature is present. If unknown, please insert a query (?).

2 This is essentially a preliminary survey, and the animals and plants on the card are indicator species to help in assessing the character and value of the site. Further details or records, or a note that they are available, would be welcomed.

3 Please return the completed cards to: **Biological Records Centre, Institute of Cornish Studies, Trevenson House, Pool, REDRUTH, Cornwall TR15 3RE.**

HEDGE TYPES: Please mark sketch that the hedge most closely resembles.

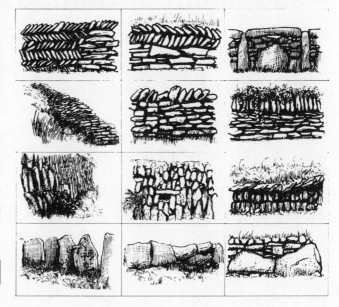

WALL INCLUSIONS	Trap holes	Bee bole	Deer leaps	Columbaria	Other
DITCH	Present	Absent			

NAME and ADDRESS of OWNER/TENANT (if known)				**PARISH**		
AGE of HEDGE (if known)				**GRID REF.**		
TYPE	Dry stone	Stone and earth	Earth	Planted		
POSITION	Estate boundary	Roadside	Between cultivated fields	Between uncultivated fields Moor/Wood/Other		
ASPECT	North	South	East	West		
HEIGHT	0–1.5m	1.5–2.5m	2.5m & over	Mature trees		
WIDTH	0–1.5m	1.5–2.5m	2.5m & over	Recently repaired		
MANAGEMENT	Hand clipped	Layered	Mechanically cut	Unmanaged		
CONDITION	Bank sound	Bank disintegrating	Tipping	Litter		

	FAUNA	Ants	Bank vole	Birds' nests	Lizards	Rabbits	Rats	Snails
In a 30m length	**WOODY SPECIES**	Ash	Beech	Birch	Blackthorn	Bramble	Broom	Cherry
		Elder	Elm	Gorse (Furze)	Hawthorn	Hazel	Holly	Hornbeam
		Oak	Poplar	Privet	Rose	Rowan	Sycamore	Willow
	HERBACEOUS SPECIES (please list)							

		DATE			

NAME of SURVEYOR .... ADDRESS ....

....

109

Associations, Competitions and Courses

The Dry Stone Walling Association

In 1938 the late Colonel F Rainsford-Hannay formed the Stewartry of Kircudbright Drystane Dyking Committee to further the knowledge of and enthusiasm for the walling craft. In 1968 the Committee founded a national organisation called the Dry Stone Walling Association. The DSWA, now a registered charity and based at the National Agricultural Centre in Kenilworth, Warwickshire, is a thriving organisation with a growing membership covering the whole of Great Britain, reflecting the upsurge of interest in walling over the last few years.

The DSWA offers four levels of membership, as follows. Open Membership is for all those interested in walling/dyking, whether or not they practice the craft. Junior Membership is for those under 16 years of age. Professional Membership is for working wallers/dykers, and Corporate Membership is for companies and associations interested in the craft and in supporting the Association. All members receive regular newsletters giving details of events, courses and other activities.

There are also currently 16 local branches of the DSWA, representing most of the traditional walling areas of Britain. The branches organise their own competitions, courses and other activities. A list of branches is available from the DSWA.

Competitions

Walling competitions, demonstrations and other events take place throughout the year, particularly at agricultural shows during the summer months. The DSWA gives details in its newsletters of all events of which it is notified, and the DSWA branches have details of local events. Another source of information is the 'National Calendar of Events' (price £2.50) produced each year by the Royal Agricultural Society of England, NAC, Kenilworth, CV8 2LZ, which lists all shows, open days and sales known to them.

The English National Walling Championships are held biennially in September in even-numbered years, and alternate with the Scottish championships run by the Stewartry branch of the DSWA at Gatehouse-of-Fleet. The 1988 English Championships were held near Settle, North Yorkshire and comprised 10 sections including those for Master Craftsmen, Professionals, Amateurs, Trainees and Beginners. Details of both Championships are available from the DSWA.

Training and Certification

Training courses on dry stone walling are run by the BTCV, and by the Branches of the DSWA. For further information contact the headquarters of the BTCV, and local Branches of the DSWA.

For those employed in agriculture or horticulture, courses in walling can be arranged through the regional network of the Agricultural Training Board. For further details contact your local county office or the Scottish office of the ATB.

The DSWA run a Traineeship, with the aim of increasing opportunities for people wanting to become professional wallers. Under the Traineeship scheme, which is supervised by the Agricultural Training Board, a limited number of grants per year are available to professional wallers taking on a trainee. Traineeships last for a maximum of two years, and for successful completion trainees are required to pass the Initial and Intermediate Certificate of the Craftsman Certification Scheme (see below). For further details contact the DSWA. The Rural Development Commission (formerly CoSIRA) is involved with the Traineeship in England, and offers advice and assistance to people starting rural businesses.

The Master Craftsman Scheme is a national certification scheme run by the DSWA, and is open to all individual members of the DSWA. There are three grades – Initial Grade, Intermediate Grade and Master Craftsman – and candidates are required to progress through the grades before being recognised as a Master Craftsman. The DSWA and its Branches will advise on, and where appropriate, organise training courses designed to assist candidates to obtain their required level of craftsmanship.

The Register of Professional Wallers, circulated regularly by the DSWA to possible employers and interested organisations, lists all Professional Members under the categories of Master Craftsmen, Intermediate Certificate holders, Initial Certificate holders, and Uncertificated Wallers. The 1988 register listed 44 Master Craftsmen spread throughout Britain, a number that indicates the strength of interest in maintaining and improving standards in the craft of walling.

The National Proficiency Tests Council include walling as part of a category of tests, the standard required being equivalent to the Initial Grade of the DSWA Craftsman Certification Scheme.

Relevant Organisations

Agricultural Training Board

Summit House, Glebe Way, West Wickham,
Kent BR4 0RF ☎ 01 777 9003
(Scottish Office) 13 Marshall Place, Perth
PH2 8AH ☎ 0738 31481

Association for the Protection of Rural Scotland

14a Napier Road, Edinburgh
EH10 5AY ☎ 031 229 1898

Botanical Society of the British Isles

c/o Dept. of Botany, British Museum,
Cromwell Road, London
SW7 5BD ☎ 01 589 6323 Ex. 8701

British Ecological Society

Burlington House, Piccadilly, London
W1V 0LQ ☎ 01 434 2641

British Herpetological Society

c/o Zoological Society of London, Regent's
Park, London NW1 4RY ☎ 01 722 3333

**BTCV (British Trust for Conservation
Volunteers)**

Head Office: BTCV, 36 St Mary's Street,
Wallingford, Oxon OX10 0EU ☎ 0491 39766

North Division Office: BTCV, Conservation
Training Centre, Balby Road, Doncaster,
South Yorkshire DN4 0RH ☎ 0302 859522

Area Office Yorkshire and North Midlands:
BTCV, Hollybush Farm, Broad Lane,
Kirkstall, Leeds, West Yorks
LS5 3BP ☎ 0532 742335

Area Office North West: BTCV, 24 Seymour
Grove, Old Trafford, Manchester
M16 02H ☎ 061 872 7640

Area Office North East: BTCV, Springwell
Conservation Centre, Springwell Road,
Gateshead, Tyne & Wear
NE9 7AD ☎ 091 482 0111

West Division Office: BTCV Conservation
Centre, Firsby Road, Quinton, Birmingham
B32 2QT ☎ 021 426 5588

Area Office South West: BTCV, The Old
Estate Yard, Newton St Loe, Bath, Avon
BA2 9BR ☎ 0225 872856

Area Office Wales: BTCV, Room 109,
Agriculture House, Old Kerry Road,
Newtown, Powys FY16 1BF ☎ 0686 628600

South East Division Office: BTCV Southwater
Country Park, Cripplegate Lane, Southwater,
West Sussex RH13 7UN ☎ 0403 730572

Area Office London: BTCV, The London
Ecology Centre, 80 York Way, London
N1 9AG ☎ 01 278 4293

Area Office East Anglia: BTCV, Animal
House, Bayfordbury Estate, Hertford,
Hertfordshire SG13 8LD ☎ 0992 583067

Northern Ireland: Conservation Volunteers,
The Pavilion, Cherryvale Playing Fields,
Ravenhill Road, Belfast
BT6 0BZ ☎ 0232 645169

British Trust for Ornithology

Beech Grove, Station Road, Tring,
Hertfordshire HP23 5NR ☎ 0442 823461

Civic Trust

17 Carlton House Terrace, London
SW1Y 5AW ☎ 01 930 0914

Community Service Volunteers

237 Pentonville Road, London
N1 9NJ ☎ 01 278 6601

Conservation Association of Botanical Societies

323 Norwood Road, London
SE24 9AQ ☎ 01 674 8044

Conservation Trust

George Palmer Site, Northumberland Avenue,
Reading RG2 7PW ☎ 0734 868242

Council for British Archaeology

112 Kennington Road, London
SE11 6RE ☎ 01 582 0494

Council for National Parks

45 Shelton Street, London
WC2H 9HJ ☎ 01 240 3603/4

Council for the Protection of Rural England

4 Hobart Place, London
SW1W 0HY ☎ 01 235 9481

Council for the Protection of Rural Wales

31 High Street, Welshpool, Powys
SY21 7JP ☎ 0938 2525

Country Landowners' Association

16 Belgrave Square, London
SW1X 8PQ ☎ 01 235 0511

Countryside Commission (England and Wales)

Headquarters: John Dower House, Crescent Place, Cheltenham, Glos
GL50 3RA ☎ 0242 521381

Countryside Commission for Scotland

Battleby, Redgorton, Perth
PH1 3EW ☎ 0738 27921

Dry Stone Walling Association

YFC Centre, National Agricultural Centre, Kenilworth, Warwickshire
CV8 2LG ☎ 021 378 0493

The Environment Council

80 York Way, London
WC2H 9HJ ☎ 01 278 4736/7

Farming and Wildlife Advisory Group

National Agricultural Centre, Kenilworth, Warwickshire CV8 2RX ☎ 0203 696699

Field Studies Council

Preston Montford, Montford Bridge, Shrewsbury SY4 1HW ☎ 0743 850674

Friends of the Earth

26–28 Underwood Street, London
N1 7JQ ☎ 01 490 1555

The Game Conservancy Trust

Burgate Manor, Fordingbridge, Hampshire
SP6 1EF ☎ 0425 52381

Institute of Terrestrial Ecology

Monkswood Experimental Station, Abbots Ripton, Huntingdon, Cambs
PE15 2LS ☎ 04873 381

Landscape Institute

12 Carlton House Terrace, London
SW1Y 5AH ☎ 01 839 4044

Mammal Society of the British Isles

Baltic Exchange Building, 21 Bury Street, London EC3A 5AU ☎ 01 283 1266

National Farmers' Union

Agriculture House, 25–31 Knightsbridge, London SW1X 7NJ ☎ 01 235 5077

National Farmers' Union of Scotland

17 Grosvenor Crescent, Edinburgh
EH12 5EN ☎ 031 337 4333

The National Trust

36 Queen Anne's Gate, London
SW1H 9AS ☎ 01 222 9251

National Trust for Scotland

5 Charlotte Square, Edinburgh
EH2 4DU ☎ 031 226 5922

Nature Conservancy Council (Great Britain headquarters and headquarters for England)

Northminster House, Peterborough
PE1 1UA ☎ 0733 40345

Nature Conservancy Council (headquarters for Scotland)

3 Cables Wynd, Leith, Edinburgh
EM6 6DT ☎ 031 554 9323

Nature Conservancy Council (headquarters for Wales)

Plas Penrhos, Ffordd Penrhos, Bangor, Gwynedd LL57 2LQ ☎ 0248 370444

The Open Spaces Society

25a Bell Street, Henley-on-Thames, Oxon
RG9 2BA ☎ 0491 573535

Ordnance Survey

Romsey Road, Maybush, Southampton
SO9 4DH ☎ 0703 792000

The Ramblers' Association

1/5 Wandsworth Road, London
SW8 2XX ☎ 01 582 6878

Royal Society for Nature Conservation

The Green, Nettleham, Lincoln
LN2 2NR ☎ 0522 752326

Royal Society for the Protection of Birds

The Lodge, Sandy, Beds
SG19 2DL ☎ 0767 80551

Rural Development Commission (formerly CoSIRA)

141 Castle Street, Salisbury, Wiltshire
SP1 3TP ☎ 0722 336255

Scottish Conservation Projects Trust

Balallan House, 24 Allan Park, Stirling
FK8 2QG ☎ 0786 79697

Scottish Landowners' Federation

18 Abercromby Place, Edinburgh
EH3 6TY ☎ 031 556 4466

Scottish Wildlife Trust

25 Johnstone Terrace, Edinburgh
EH1 2NH ☎ 031 226 4602

Stone Federation

82 New Cavendish Street, London
W1M 8AD ☎ 01 580 5588

Town and Country Planning Association

17 Carlton House Terrace, London
SW1Y 5AS ☎ 01 930 8903

Woodland Trust

Autumn Park, Dysart Road, Grantham, Lincs
NG31 6LL ☎ 0476 74297

Worldwide Fund for Nature

Panda House, Weyside Park, Godalming,
Surrey GU7 1XR ☎ 0483 426444

Bibliography

Written material on the craft, history and natural history of dry stone walling is very limited. Aside from one or two general works and regional booklets, there is a scattering of chapters and articles in countryside books and magazines, plus a few detailed but unpublished research theses. Those which have been useful in the compilation of this handbook are listed below along with some of the relevant background sources on geology, geography and rural land management.

Alexander, Bruce (ed) (1974) — *Crafts and Craftsmen* Croom Helm. Short sections on walling and masonry tools and history.

Archer, Peggy (1972) — *Cornish Stone Hedges* Western Morning News. 27 June 1972. The conflict over the removal of ancient hedges in West Penwith.

Beddall, J L (1950) — *Hedges for Farm and Garden* Faber and Faber. Brief but useful sections on South Western turf and stone hedges and dry stone walls.

Bennison, George M and Wright, Alan E (1969) — *The Geological History of the British Isles* Edward Arnold. Detailed reference text.

Blandford, Percy (1974) — *Country Craft Tools* David and Charles. Includes walling and masonry tools.

Brainerd, John (1973) — *Working with Nature: A Practical Guide* Oxford University Press. Brief section on walling and how to break and move stone.

Brooks, Margaret A (1973) — *Dry Stone Walls and Wall Building in West Yorkshire* Institute of Folk Life Studies, Dept of English, University of Leeds. Vols 1 (text) and 2 (photos). Unpublished dissertation on types and history of West Riding walls, terms and techniques and how craftsmen learn and use walling skills.

Butchart, N C (1976) — *Walls as Fences* Industrial Past. John Keavey, 17 Uplands, Skipton, N Yorks, Autumn 1976: 9–10. Walling history and construction briefly reviewed.

Chantree, Peter (1971) — *Dry Stone Dykes* Scottish Field. March 1971: 26–7. Brief description of uses, construction methods.

Council for the Protection of Rural England (1975) — *Landscape – The Need for a Public Voice* CPRE. Duplicated. Critique of 'New Agricultural Landscapes'.

Countryside Commission (1974) — *New Agricultural Landscapes* Countryside Commission. A strategy for balancing productivity with amenity and wildlife needs.

Crawford, O G S (1936) — *The Work of Giants* Antiquity. June 1936: 162–74. Ancient stone hedges in West Cornwall. Good photos.

Davey, Norman (1976) — *Building Stones of England and Wales* Bedford Square Press. List of quarries producing building stone.

Dry Stone Walling Association (1988) — *Building and Repairing Dry Stone Walls* Pamphlet outlining basic techniques, available from DSWA.

Evans, E Estyn (1957) — *Irish Folk Ways* Routledge and Kegan Paul. Chapter on stone and other 'ditches' and the traditional use of dry stone in buildings etc.

Fields, Curtis P (1971) *The Forgotten Art of Building a Stone Wall* Yankee, Dublin, New Hampshire, USA. Practical details on walling in mica schist and granite and on the safe handling and splitting of boulders.

Garner, Lawrence *Dry Stone Walls* Shire Publications Booklet covering the history of drystone walling. Available from DSWA.

Hawkes, Jacquetta (1951) *A Land* Cresset Press; Penguin (1959). The influence of geology on Britain's history and culture.

Her Majesty's Stationery Office (1976) *Institute of Geological Sciences* HMSO. Government Publications Sectional List 45: regional geologies etc available from the IGS, Exhibition Road, London SW7 2DE.

Hoskins, W G (1967) *Fieldwork in Local History* Faber and Faber. Short chapter on why and how to study the history of walls and hedges, with references.

Jenkins, J Geraint (1965) *Traditional Country Craftsmen* Routledge and Kegan Paul. Brief illustrated treatment of dry walling, slating and masonry, with references.

Marshall, A W (1960) *Dry Stone Walling* Farmer and Stock-breeder Supplement. Dec 1960: 14–15, 17. Brief illustrated practical article. Area not stated but appears to be Cotswolds.

McManners, M A (1961) *Dry Stone Walls* The Countryman. Autumn 1961: 545–8. Wildlife interest in a Yorkshire limestone wall.

Nature Conservancy Council (undated) *The Conservation of Limestone Pavement* NCC. Leaflet explaining the significance of these features and the threats to their future.

Ordnance Survey (1976) *Map Catalogue 1976* OS. Lists maps published for the Institute of Geological Sciences.

Prevost, W A J (1957) *The Dry Stone Dykes of Upper Annandale*, with Glossary Transactions of the Dumfriesshire and Galloway Natural History and Antiquarian Society. Third Series, 1957: 84–101. Walling traditions, methods and terminology in northern Dumfriesshire compared with Galloway and other districts.

Rainsford-Hannay, F (1972) *Dry Stone Walling* Stewartry of Kircudbright Drystane Dyking Committee, Cally Estate Office, Gatehouse-of-Fleet. First published by Faber and Faber (1957). Walling history and techniques, mainly Galloway but also other regional styles. Excellent photos. Available from DSWA.

Raistrick, Arthur (1966) *Pennine Walls* Dalesman Publishing Co, Clapham (via Lancaster). Illustrated booklet on the region's walling history, craftsmen and techniques. Out of print.

Rishbeth, J (1948) *The Flora of Cambridge Walls* Journal of Ecology. 36: 136–48. Floristic variations on mortared walls in the area.

Rollinson, William (1972) *Lakeland Walls* Dalesman Publishing Co, Clapham (via Lancaster). Companion booklet to Raistrick.

Emphasis on geology and history.

Rule, Ann Louise (1974) ***Hedge Building in Mid and West Cornwall*** Institute of Folk Life Studies, Dept of English, University of Leeds. Unpublished dissertation on stone hedge design, construction, tools and technology.

Segal, S (1969) ***Ecological Notes on Wall Vegetation*** Dr W Junk, 13 Van Stolkweg, The Hague, Netherlands. Highly technical. Extensive bibliography.

Shirlaw, D W Gilchrist (1966) ***An Agricultural Geography of Great Britain*** Pergamon Press. Regional soils, climate and farming patterns.

Stowe, E J (1948) ***Crafts of the Countryside*** Longmans, Green. Short illustrated chapter on dry walling.

Trueman, A E (1949) ***Geology and Scenery in England and Wales*** Penguin Pelican. The influence of bedrock on the landscape of each part of the country. Clearly written.

Webster, G and White, A J (1973) ***Management and Design Notes 4.*** Gates and Stiles. Recreation News Supplement. Countryside Commission. December 1973: 10. Designs and photos.

Wood, Eric S (1973) ***Field Guide to Archaeology*** Collins. Information on many countryside features.

Woodell, S R J and Rossiter, J (1959) ***The Flora of Durham Walls*** Proceedings of the Botanical Society of the British Isles. 3: 257–73. Similar study to Rishbeth.

Glossary

Batter The slope (taper) of a wall or hedge, expressed as an angle or as a ratio of horizontal to vertical dimensions.

Batter frame A wooden or metal frame used as a guide to the correct batter and to the heights of throughs, topstones etc when building a wall or hedge. Also known as a pattern (South West), template or wall gauge (Cotswolds) or walling or dyke frame (Scotland).

Bed Deposition layer in sedimentary rock. In walling, the flattish base of a stone or any plane along which it splits readily.

Bee bole A niche in a wall built to store straw bee skeps.

Breccia Rock composed of sharp-angled fragments cemented in a fine matrix.

Broch An Iron Age round tower built of dry stonework as a citadel against raiders. Found especially in the Orkneys and Shetlands.

Buck-and-doe A form of coping alternating large and small upright topstones. Also known as cock-and-hen (Cotswolds).

Chain A traditional unit of measurement, 22 yards (20m).

Chip and block A type of stone hedging in which small stones (chips) and large stones (blocks) are intermixed within each course (Devon).

Clearance wall A wall built largely from stones cleared from the surface of adjacent land. When the wall is made extra wide to accommodate the stones it is also known as an accretion wall or consumption dyke (Scotland).

Cleavage The structure by which certain metamorphic rocks, eg slate, split most readily, often at an angle to the original bedding plane.

Coping The line of stones along the top of the wall which protects the structure beneath. Also known as the cap, comb (Cotswolds and South West), cope or topping.

Course A layer of stones in the face of a wall or hedge.

Coverband A layer of throughstones placed on top of the double dyking to anchor it and form a base for the coping (Scotland).

Cripple hole A rectangular opening at the base of a wall built to permit the passage of sheep. Also known as a hogg hole, lonky or lunky hole, sheep run, sheep smoose, smout hole, thawl or thirl hole.

Crown The top of a bank or hedge. Also known as a comb (Devon).

Ditch A long narrow trench dug as a boundary, barrier or drain. In Ireland and parts of Wales, a bank or other raised barrier.

Double dyking The part of a normal dry stone wall which has two rows of face stones packed between with fillings. Also known as doubling (Galloway). Distinguished from single dyking in which only one thickness of stones is used with no fillings.

Dry stone wall A wall built without mortar. Also known as a drystane dyke (Scotland) or dry stone hedge (Cornwall).

Dyke A wall (Scotland). Also spelled dike.

Elvan See whinstone.

Face An exposed side of a wall, hedge or bank.

Face stone A stone whose outer surface forms part of the face of the wall.

Fence A structure serving as an enclosure, barrier or boundary, loosely used to include walls, hedges, banks, ditches and dykes.

Fillings Small, irregular stones placed between the two faces of a wall to pack the space between them. Also known as hearting (Scotland).

Fissile Rock characterised by a tendency to split readily along planes of bedding or cleavage.

Flag A thin-bedded sandstone which breaks up readily into flat slabs. Loosely used for a flat slab of any type.

Foliation The structure, similar to but less regular and perfect than cleavage, by which the minerals in rocks such as schist and gneiss are arranged in parallel planes due to metamorphism.

Footing A stone at the base of a wall, or the foundation of a wall in general. Also known as a found.

Freestone Stone which has no tendency to split in any particular direction.

Galloway hedge A combination dry stone wall and thorn hedge which is constructed along a hillside so that the hedge shrubs root through the wall and are protected by it from livestock on the uphill side.

Gap A breach in a wall due to defect or damage. (v) To fall, leaving a breach; to repair a breach.

Grit Any hard sandstone, especially one in which small pebbles are mixed with the sand to give a rough texture suitable for millstones. Also known as gritstone.

Head The smooth, vertical end of a wall or section of wall. Also known as a cheek (Scotland).

Hedge A line of closely planted shrubs or low-growing trees. In Devon, an earth-filled bank used as a barrier or boundary and faced with stones or turf. In Cornwall, any earth or stone barrier.

Herringbone A type of stone facing in which alternate courses of stones are angled in opposite directions.

Joint In walling, the crack between two adjacent stones in a course.

Lamination A structure of fine, closely spaced layering along the bedding planes in certain sedimentary rocks.

Lintel A stone slab or wood or metal beam placed over an opening to bridge it and support the structure above.

Locked top A type of coping in which the topstones are pinned into a solid unit using long thin wedge stones. Mainly Scotland.

March dyke A major enclosure wall running between estates (Scotland).

Masonry Stonework characterised by the use of cut and trimmed stone.

Oolite Rock, usually limestone, composed of small round calcareous grains.

Pein The striking surface of a hammer head.

Pinnings Small stones wedged into spaces in a wall face.

Quartzite Sandstone consisting mainly of quartz grains cemented into a hard continuous mass by silica.

Rag Any of several kinds of hard coarse rock, mainly limestones, which break irregularly. Also known as ragstone.

Retaining wall A wall built across the face of a bank or slope to keep the soil from slipping.

Rhyolite A volcanic rock similar in composition to granite and usually exhibiting flow lines.

Rood The traditional unit of wall measurement, 6 yards (5.5m) in granite districts in Scotland and 7 yards (6.4m) in limestone districts and through most of Yorkshire.

Rubble Rough, mainly untrimmed, walling stone; walls or copings characterised by such stone.

Runner A long face stone used in a wall head (Scotland).

Scarcement The in-set between the outer edge of the footings and the first course of face stones (Scotland).

Shooting butt A small, usually circular enclosure built to shelter grouse shooters.

Smoot A small rectangular opening in the base of a wall. Rabbit smoots (Scotland: pen hole; Mendips: pop hole) are designed to permit the passage of hares and rabbits. Water smoots (Scotland: double water pen) are designed to permit the passage of water.

Spar Any of various nonmetallic, lustrous and readily cleaved minerals, such as felspar.

Stile A set of steps over, or an opening through, a wall, hedge or other fence designed to allow passage to pedestrians but not livestock.

Stoop An upright monolith set into the ground against the wall head of a gate or stile. Also spelled stoup.

Subdivision wall A wall built to divide a major enclosure into smaller sections, often somewhat lower and less well constructed than the boundary wall.

Through A large stone placed across the width of a wall to tie the sides together. Also known as a throughstone or a throughband or tieband (Scotland).

Tie A throughstone used in a wall head (Scotland).

Topstone A stone used in a wall's coping. Also known as a cope stone, topper or topping.

Wedge A small stone placed under or behind a face stone to position it securely.

Whinstone Any hard dark-coloured rock such as greenstone, basalt, chert or quartzose sandstone. Also known as elvan or elvin (Cornwall).

Index

Aberdeenshire dykes — 20

Banks and hedges, compared to walls — 29
Batter — 69
Batter frames — 48, 66
Bedding, of stones — 53
Birds, nesting sites in walls — 36
Blonks — 18
Boles — 105
Bonders — 7, 9
Boots, working — 43
Boulders, as obstacles — 83
Breaking stone — 56
Bridge foundations — 106
Buttresses — 91
Butts — 105

Cairns — 106
Caithness flag fences — 20
Cashels — 22
Cattle creep — 11
Celtic field systems — 22
Cement, for fixing — 103
Central England, walling styles — 7
Clothing — 43
Cob walls — 8
Codgers — 94
Combers — 7
Competitions — 110
Concrete, use and abuse of — 61
Coping — 73
Coping, on slopes — 82
Corners — 79
Costs, of fencing — 33
Costs, of walling — 32
Cotswold walls — 7
Courses, of stone — 66
Courses, on slopes — 81
Coverband — 17
Cripple holes — 11, 96
Curves — 79
Cutting stone, tools for — 46

Damage to walls — 33
Danish fences — 22
Dating of walls — 26
Double dyke — 17
Double water pens — 18
Doubling stones — 18
Drilling stones, tools for — 46
Drills, for granite — 58
Dry Stone Walling Association — 110
Dunecht course dyke — 20

Elizabethan period — 23
Enclosure Acts — 24
Enclosure era walls — 62

Fauna of walls — 36
Fences, with walls — 103
Field size, for agricultural efficiency — 32
Fillings — 68
Firmness, tests for — 87
First aid kit — 44
Flora of walls — 34
Footings — 65
Foundations — 65
Future of walling craft — 36

Gabions — 90
Galloway dyke — 17
Galloway hedge — 19
Galway walls — 21
Gapping — 84
Gates — 100
Geological periods — 6
Gloves — 44
Gneisses — 54
Gneisses, splitting — 59
Goggles — 44
Grading of stone — 67
Grading of stone, on slopes — 81
Granite — 54
Granite, splitting — 58
Group work, organising — 50
Guidelines — 48, 66

Half dyke — 18
Hammers — 46
Handling stone — 41
Hedges, stone — 91
Height of wall, against stock — 61
Herringbone pattern walls — 16
Hinges, setting into stone — 101

Intakes — 24
Ireland, walling styles — 21
Isle of Man, walling styles — 19

Jack bits — 7
Joints — 67
Jumpers — 7

Key stones — 9
Kingswell West Dyke — 25

Lake District, walling styles — 12
Law, relating to walls — 38
Lead, for fixing — 103
Lichens — 27
Limestone pavements — 9
Limestones — 53
Lining out — 65
Loss of walls and banks — 29
Lunky holes — 18